Agricultural Policies and World Markets

Agricultural Policies and World Markets

Alex F. McCalla
University of California, Davis

Timothy E. Josling
Food Research Institute, Stanford University

MACMILLAN PUBLISHING COMPANY
NEW YORK

Collier Macmillan Publishers
LONDON

Copyright © 1985 by Macmillan Publishing Company
A Division of Macmillan, Inc.

Macmillan Publishing Company
866 Third Avenue, New York, NY 10022

Collier Macmillan Canada, Inc.

Printed in the United States of America

printing number
1 2 3 4 5 6 7 8 9 10

Library of Congress Cataloging in Publication Data

McCalla, Alex F., 1937–
  Agricultural policies and world markets.

  Includes index.
    1. Agriculture—Economic aspects.   2. Agriculture
and state.   3. International economic relations.
I. Josling, Timothy Edward.   II. Title.
HD1415.M37   1985   338.1'8   85-8782
ISBN 0-02-949840-6

Contents

Foreword

There is probably no other single sector of the economy which is the object of both so much policy intervention and so much economic analysis as agriculture. Crowds of agricultural policy makers and administrators pounce upon agriculture and appear to take no rest before they have regulated every imaginable activity. At the same time hosts of agricultural economists apply all conceivable analytical tools in order to find out everything about what is going on in the farming industry, on input and output markets, and in agricultural policy. Yet, in spite of all these efforts we are still far from a state of affairs in which governments are happy with the results of their policies and economists feel that they can understand most issues.

This is particularly true when it comes to international trade. World markets for agricultural products are so distorted by all sorts of trade interventions that it appears sometimes doubtful whether they deserve to be called "markets." Agricultural policy makers all over the world have contributed to this situation, but few of them would claim that what we have is what they wanted to achieve. Agricultural economists, on the other hand, have never been tired of investigating developments in the world food economy. Yet there are still many blank spots on the map of our knowledge about international agricultural trade.

There are manifold reasons why agricultural policies are less successful than policy makers would hope for, and why economists have not yet managed to understand and explain all the issues which have fascinated them for so long. Many of these reasons fall into different categories, being of a political nature on the one hand and having to do with analytical problems on the other hand. But there is one basic difficulty which intrigues policy makers and analysts at the same time. This is the complexity of issues we are faced with when we deal with agricultural markets and trade. Looked at from outside, the agricultural and food economy may appear to be a small and homogeneous sector, but once we start to dig into some of the details we enter into a microcosm of complex relationships.

One of these complexities originates from the fact that there are manifold linkages between individual agricultural products. Many farm commodities compete for the same productive resources. Others are joint outputs of the same production process. Still others are inputs into the production of higher-valued agricultural products. On the consumption side, too, there are substitution possibilities and complementarities. Changing market conditions for one commodity, be it through policy intervention or due to economic factors, can have significant influences on other agricultural products. It is therefore the rule, not the exception, that policies which are targeted at one commodity market have side effects on other markets. Policy makers often overlook these side effects, and are surprised to find later that their policies lead to undesired outcomes. And analysts find it often difficult to analyze simultaneously the totality of effects of a seemingly simple intervention. Take, as an example, the recent introduction of quotas on milk deliveries in the European Community and the resulting cutback of milk production. It is likely that it will have an effect on the size of the beef surplus in the European Community and hence on international beef trade. However, nobody can definitely say whether beef production will increase or decrease in the European Community, since beef can be a substitute for milk production (because of competition for the same resources) or a joint product of milk (because calves of dairy cows can be fattened).

Another dimension of the complexity of issues is the close interdependence between countries at the international level. Times have passed in which agricultural trade played only a marginal role. World markets for agricultural commodities have grown much more rapidly than world agricultural production. According to GATT figures* agricultural trade has grown twice as fast as world production of agricultural commodities over the last two decades. This means that countries have become increasingly interdependent in agriculture. It also means that agricultural policies in different parts of the world have become increasingly interdependent. Another consequence is that macroeconomic influences on agricultural and food markets have intensified since monetary disturbances have now a stronger lever via agricultural trade. Again an example may illustrate this point. It relates to the links between U.S. and European Community grain policies

*GATT, *International Trade 1982/83*, Geneva, 1983, app. Table A1.

and the way in which they are conditioned by monetary developments. The recent rise in the value of the dollar has brought international wheat prices, which usually have been below prices in the European Community by a margin of 30 to 45 percent, very close to the domestic level in the European Community. This has helped the European Community save on export subsidies and may thereby reduce the financial pressure for a reform of the Common Agricultural Policy. Developments would have been different if the United States had adjusted its loan rate downwards, since the U.S. loan rate effectively puts a floor under world market prices. Hence the European Community's grain policy is, in a decisive phase for the future of the Common Agricultural Policy, directly dependent on U.S. policies and macroeconomic developments.

Complex relationships are an important feature of agricultural policy and its economic analysis. But they are often overlooked. Too often actual policies and economic analyses are based on a simplistic single-commodity, single-country approach. It is a great merit of this book by McCalla and Josling that it helps to overcome this deficiency. Starting from the simple partial approach it gradually climbs up the ladder of complexity, step by step. First the multicommodity dimension is included, and then the multicountry dimension is explored. By extending the approach to multiple goals and multiple instruments another dimension of complexity is added which is extremely relevant in actual policy making. Patiently the authors take us through all these steps. And at the end we realize that we have learned a great deal. It *is* possible to deal appropriately with the complex issues involved in agricultural policy analysis in an interdependent world. This book bears ample evidence of it.

Much as I liked to read the whole of this book, what attracted, if not excited, me most are the chapters in which McCalla and Josling apply their analytical approaches to practical cases. In these chapters the complex nature of agricultural trade issues becomes fully clear. At the same time the usefulness of an elaborate approach is aptly demonstrated. And finally some original empirical findings emerge. Practitioners of agricultural policy should find these chapters particularly useful. If they become convinced, by working through these case studies, that economic analysis has much to offer for solving complex agricultural policy problems, and if students of agricultural policy make use of this book in preparing themselves for a more effective dialogue with policy makers, McCalla's and Josling's efforts would be exploited in the best possible way.

Stefan Tangermann
Institute of Agricultural Economics
University of Göttingen
Federal Republic of Germany

Preface

This book deals with the complex question of the analysis of agricultural policies in an interdependent world. Virtually all governments intervene in their domestic agricultural sectors. The results of these interventions reverberate through international markets and impact on other countries' policy choice. The focus is deliberately analytical, using verbal and graphical analysis, to derive the impacts of alternative policy choices. It is a book designed to assist the economic policy analyst with understanding policy choice in the modern world of domestic agricultural policies linked through world commodity markets. It is, therefore, not a book that provides detailed institutional and historical information about particular country policy.

The book is explicitly directed at professionals and students working in the broad area of food and agricultural policy. This group hopefully includes academic economists interested in policy and trade, policy analysts in national governments and international organizations, policy analysts with private sector firms and associations, and graduate and senior undergraduate students.

All that is necessary to use the analytical techniques contained in the book is a solid grounding in intermediate microeconomic theory and a general understanding of the basic concepts of comparative advantage. Thus, we believe it would be useful as a textbook in advanced undergraduate and graduate courses in agricultural trade and trade policy analysis. It should also be of considerable relevance to courses in open economy agricultural policy.

The book was jointly conceived while the first author was on sabbatical at Stanford in 1982. No less than 13 jointly written outlines preceded actual writing. The book as now written bears little resemblance to any of those outlines and is better for it. In terms of the three parts of the book, Part One was a true joint effort with each of us sharing in the writing and review of these chapters. Part Two was originally drafted by McCalla and Part Three by Josling. However, all parts of the book were carefully cross reviewed by the other author. We believe it is a joint effort in which we both must share in criticisms and accolades (if any).

A work of this magnitude cannot be completed without the help of many people. There were indeed many colleagues who contributed at various stages. Two, Scott Pearson and John Antle, deserve special recognition. There are, however, four people to whom we owe very special thanks. Stefan Tangermann reviewed all chapters with great care. The manuscript in our judgment was much improved by his perceptive and always useful comments. We used most of them so the debt is large. Sarah Greene was always helpful, encouraging, and, in particular, understanding as we fell behind original deadlines. She never seemed to lose faith in us even when we were discouraged. Judy DeStefano typed nearly every word of all the drafts. She was not only a very efficient word processor person, who worked with both speed and accuracy, but much more. She took a continuing interest in the structure and organization of the operation and she helped keep the first author organized despite his inclinations to be otherwise. Finally, JoAnn Huffman deserves special thanks for drawing all the diagrams in record time, often from messy beginnings.

In addition, we would be remiss without thanking also the staffs at both institutions who helped in many ways, particularly Janice Aboytes and her steno pool at Davis.

Finally, to our colleagues and families who tolerated our sometimes less than sunny disposition during the long process, we owe a final and very special "thank you."

Alex F. McCalla
Davis, California

Timothy E. Josling
Stanford, California

Introduction

I OBJECTIVES AND PURPOSES OF THE BOOK

The complexity of food and agricultural policy analysis has increased significantly in the 1970s and 1980s. World markets for agricultural commodities grew rapidly in the 1970s. Many countries became increasingly dependent on world markets. During the 1970s and early 1980s, markets also became more volatile and unstable. Wide price swings in the post-1972 period are in sharp contrast with the relatively stable second half of the 1950s and the 1960s. This volatility came because the world shifted from a position of chronic oversupply to one of apparent shortages followed by a return to surplus conditions.

The end of the Bretton-Woods agreement for fixed currency values signaled a movement towards floating exchange rates during the 1970s which varied widely, reflecting different levels of inflation. World commodity markets seem linked to international capital markets and, in fact, appear to be even more volatile. As national governments, particularly the United States, tried to deal with severe bouts of inflation, interest rates rose and a global recession emerged which characterized the early 1980s.

Thus, the conduct of food and agricultural policy could no longer be pursued on a purely national basis focusing only on sectoral variables. Food and agricultural policies are now not only closely linked with national economies, but national economies are closely linked through world

1

markets. Thus, reality requires a more comprehensive approach to policy analysis. The book attempts to make a start in that direction.

Specifically, the objectives of the work are (1) to describe analytically and conceptually the reality of an interdependent world; (2) to identify major policy issues facing countries in the new environment; (3) to suggest analytical approaches to more comprehensive policy analysis tailored to recognize whether countries are large or small, exporter, or importer; and (4) to recognize that certain international issues transcend national boundaries and require "international" policy initiatives.

II THE POLICY SPECTRUM

Every sovereign state has policies relating to food and agriculture. These run the gamut from policies on resource development, agricultural production and prices, stocks and food distribution to income and asset equity policies. Each nation has a unique constellation of policies depending on the combination of means selected and on the differing policy weights given to various objectives. This outcome is often called "domestic" food and agricultural policy. In one sense, it is domestic in that predominantly national goals are being addressed. But too frequently the adjective domestic carries with it the implication that international factors can be ignored, either by the policy maker or by the policy analyst. Given that few, if any, countries can successfully pursue autarkic or isolationist policies, the small amount of attention given to the international dimensions of domestic policy, both in economic analysis and in actual policy formulation, is a major deficiency. Moreover, even autarkic policies can have significant international implications.

This book presents an analysis of national agricultural and food policies with emphasis on their interdependence through world markets. The study of interdependence adds an additional dimension to policy analysis. For example, the *size* of the country relative to world markets makes a significant difference to national policy options: It adds constraints and it also may add opportunities.

Large countries influence world markets whether they are behaving *passively*, i.e., accepting international market reactions without attempting to exploit them, or whether they are *actively* attempting to manipulate policy variables to influence world markets to their advantage. A "small" country, defined in terms of the size of national production and/or consumption relative to the world, may proceed with policy choice as if its internal actions will not influence world prices. However, it still must be cognizant of the fact that other nations are sufficiently "large" that their actions do influence prices and trade flows. In addition to size, the openness of national policy, in terms of the degree to which changes in international prices are transmitted to the national economy, is also critical in analyzing policy choice in an interdependent world.

This international dimension would be worth studying in the case of nations acting unilaterally, but there is also a set of policies which are best thought of as international. To analyze these we can postulate some global policy objectives which can be reached only by collective international action. But subsets of the global family can also cooperate or collude to better accomplish national or international objectives. Though this is a form of international policy, it is subglobal in the sense that it involves groups of nations acting in concert only to better accomplish national or international goals.

It is this range of policies from the national to the international that this book addresses. Table I-1 presents a depiction of this policy spectrum or continuum. It is intended both as a device for conceptualizing policy and as a means for defining more precisely the scope of the book. Policy can either be directed primarily at national or international objectives. This distinction is important for analysis in that it determines the way in which one assesses gains and losses arising from policy. Evaluation of policy benefits is familiar at the national level. In Chapter 9, the topic of evaluation of international benefits is taken up with a view to defining more precisely the analytical problems involved in the study of collective policies. The decision space provides another element in the continuum. One can distinguish among those taken unilaterally, those taken in small groups (plurilateral), and those taken in a multilateral framework.

The instrument space, the range and type of instruments used in policies, also varies from the purely domestic, through the national (i.e.,

Table I-1   The Nature of the Policy Continuum

Objective Space	National objectives				International objectives	
Decision Space	Unilateral decisions			Plurilateral decisions	Multilateral decisions	
Instrument Space	Domestic instruments	National instruments		Coordinated national instruments		Global instruments
Country Size	Any size	Small	Large	Usually large	Any size	
Policy Attitude	Autarkic	Passive		Active	Collective	
Policy Type	1,2	3	4	5	6	7	8

including trade policy instruments), and the coordinated national to the use of global instrumentalities for policies. Such global policy instruments are relatively rare, but have a place in the discussion of the attainment of global goals. The size of a country is a useful variable in the classification of policies, both because it influences the scope of using international markets for domestic ends and because it is linked with the need for policy actions to be taken into account by other countries.

A variable related to size but adding a further dimension is the policy attitude towards interdependence. In cases where no trade opportunities exist, autarky is a fact of life; such a situation is rare. In practice, countries may behave in an autarkic way even when trade is possible. More often, countries behave passively towards world markets, accepting their position in the market and not attempting to make use of it for policy ends even if they have the potential. On the other hand, there is a group of policies which actively seeks to use market power, either individually or collectively. International objectives require a collective attitude to policy—at the least, a willingness to modify national actions—sometimes actively manipulating trade conditions and sometimes reacting more passively to world markets. These five variables can be combined to give eight reasonably distinct policy situations. These are numbered in Table I-1 and described in Table I-2.

Table I-2 Typology of Policies Along the Continuum

Type	Policy description
1	Domestic policies on factor or commodity markets with minimal trade implications
2	Policies in deliberately autarkic countries
3	Agricultural policies of small countries which are small in terms of the market for a particular commodity
4	Policies of large countries where the country passively accepts its influence on the market but does not try to use this influence
5	Policies of large countries seeking to use their market power in meeting national objectives
6	Plurilateral policies by groups of countries using their collective market position to further national objectives
7	Multilateral policies decided collectively using coordination of national policy instruments to obtain agreed aims
8	Policies decided collectively but using instruments at a global level rather than relying upon coordination of national instruments

Food and agricultural policies take several forms. They may be commodity specific, in terms of producer support prices for rice or consumer prices for bread. This is the most frequent way that countries attempt to accomplish sector goals. Therefore, analysis requires cognizance of the direct impacts on the targeted commodity but it also requires analysis of indirect intercommodity and macro effects. Policies also may be generic in that they impact on the total sector. Examples would include a nonspecific credit subsidy, a change in the land tax, or a change in the exchange rate. Policies may also be targeted at specific groups in society, e.g., low income consumers, small farmers, or rural residents in general. Each of these policy types impacts on agricultural production, consumer demand, export availability and import demand, and, therefore, given any openness of the economy, world markets. Those impacts will be greater if the country is large. But the cumulative effects of small country policy will also influence world markets. The nature of the policy chosen is clearly influenced by whether the country is an exporter or an importer of the commodity or commodities in question. In practice, most countries are both importers and exporters, further complicating the analysis.

III THE STRUCTURE OF THE BOOK

The chapters that follow are grouped into three parts. Part One presents a characterization of the reality of an interdependent world. Part Two looks at national policy decisions in an interdependent world. Part Three looks at international decisions and collective goals. The thrust of each part is presented by way of a fuller introduction to the book.

A Part One: Interdependence in World Agriculture

The first part of the book contains a brief description of the state of world agriculture, an examination of the issues which transcend national boundaries, and an elaboration of the process of policy interdependence.

Global issues in food and agriculture bring immediately to mind the interrelated problems of world hunger, population growth, developing country food production, and the stability and security of food supplies through trade. The ability of the production system to meet growing world demand is in turn conditioned by the economic environment in the rural sector and by the nature of the systems of domestic and international marketing through which agricultural products pass on their way to the consumer. Governments intervene to influence each stage of the process, from production through marketing and international trade to final consumption. At each level issues can be identified, both those having to do with the underlying economic activity and those that relate to the adequacy of policy measures themselves. No perfectly satisfying classification of such issues is possible in an interconnected process. Issues discussed include the following:

1   Food balance issues, including the rate of growth of production, the adequacy of consumption levels, and the problem of distribution
2   Development issues, including the place of agriculture in the economy of developing countries, the role of agricultural trade in development, and the level of investment in agriculture
3   Farm income issues, including incentives to produce, protection against competition, and the problems of structural adjustment in developed countries
4   Stability issues, including the problems associated with short-term fluctuation of output often but not always caused by weather and the absorption of that variability within the system

Chapter 1 looks into such issues by way of reviewing the history of the past 15 to 20 years. Chapter 2 explores the nature of policy interdependence from an analytical viewpoint. If countries wish to take advantage of trade as a means of lowering food costs, then their economic environment necessarily reflects the actions of other countries. Typically, countries will accept the benefits, within the limitations of other domestic objectives, but try to avoid the consequences of "openness." The strains that this imposes on the system are a major reason for studying the international dimensions of agricultural policy. In addition, economic linkages among commodity markets and commodity policies give rise to a further form of interdependence. This is discussed in Chapter 3, where a two-commodity system is analyzed. Commodity linkages have become more important in recent years as the sector which produces food, animal feed, and industrial goods has become more sophisticated.

Chapter 4 concludes Part One by giving three examples to illustrate interdependence in practice. The influence of the Soviet Union on the wheat market, the development of the European mixed feed industry, and the impact of changing currency values on Mexican and Egyptian trade each demonstrate the importance of taking an international view of policy. The examples are not intended as complete analyses of these problems but more as an illustration of the general approach taken in the analytical chapters that precede them.

B   Part Two: National Policy Decisions in an Interdependent World

In Part Two our attention shifts to national policy problems and policy analysis. Unless a country is completely autarkic, these issues must be looked at in the context of interdependent world markets. How then should policy makers and analysts integrate world markets into their policy calculus? The answer depends on a number of considerations. First, it depends on the national role that the agricultural and food sector plays in the domestic economy and in foreign trade. Second, it depends on goals of the nation regarding growth, equity, degree of self-sufficiency, and the well-being of producers and consumers. Third, it depends on the political and economic philosophy of the nation in terms of willingness to intervene. Fourth, the answer also depends, in part, on the size of the country relative to world commodity markets in which it trades. If a country is small in the sense that its production and/or consumption is small relative to the world, it may be able to proceed with policy choice on the assumption that whatever actions it takes will not influence prices in relevant international markets nor will other participants react to that policy action. On the other hand, if a country is large relative to the total market, its policy actions will influence price and may well induce reactions from other countries, which means that it may choose to exercise international market power, unilaterally or collectively, to accomplish domestic objectives.

Thus, agricultural and food policy in any country is constrained by national objectives, resource endowments, and its historical and institutional evolution. The international interface may offer additional constraints but it also may offer additional opportunities. Thus, policy makers and analysts need to understand the ways in which the international environment influences and is influenced by domestic policy choice.

The analysis proceeds in sequential stages. First, objectives (goals), instruments, and constraints are discussed in general terms, as is the question of how one can measure the impact of policy change. These concepts are then used to look at the simplest case, namely small-country, single-commodity analysis. This is the gist of Chapter 5. Chapter 6 continues the single-commodity approach but explores the importance of being large. Largeness brings with it the possibility of the exercise of market power. Therefore, analysis must take into account impacts on world prices and how other countries might react. Chapter 7 introduces more reality by working through several conceptual problems of multigoal, multicommodity, multi-instrument policy choice. A series of cases in terms of specific generic policy instruments are explored. Chapter 8 completes Part Two with three "real world" illustrations of the applicability of simple policy models. These involve large-country unilateral policy action, illustrated by the case of the U.S. Payment-In-Kind (PIK) program, the case of Egypt and trade-offs between macroeconomic and agricultural sector objectives and collusive action in the international dairy market. The objective is to enrich the discussion with actual examples while demonstrating possible analytical approaches.

C   Part Three: International Policy Decisions and Collective Goals

The third part of the book addresses the task of analyzing policy actions from the viewpoint of international or collective goals. The problem is to strike the correct balance between the idealism of supranationality and the realism of a world of nation states. Countries go through the motions of discussing issues at an international level. If such discussions are a charade, having no bearing on actual decisions, then "international agricultural policy" is an empty box. Few would take such an extreme position. It is equally clear that policy as discussed, agreed upon, and implemented at the intergovernmental level is not a major preoccupation of most agricultural ministers or their colleagues in other branches of national administrations. Few would argue that it should be. International policy, in the sense of commonly agreed action to seek commonly formulated goals, is a secondary but not unimportant part of the agricultural policy spectrum. Part Three is intended to explore ways of analyzing the effectiveness of such policy actions.

In the preceding section of this chapter, there was a discussion of the policy continuum. In Table I-1 international objectives require multilateral decisions, however, the instrument space contains two options: international policy accomplished by the coordination of national instruments and international policy achieved through the use of global instruments. This offers a useful distinction among policy approaches which is taken up in Part Three. Another distinction is between the elements of policies which aim at equity or income redistribution and those which are oriented towards efficiency of resource use. Moreover, the source of funds for a policy is a further classificatory variable when looking at international policies. Those that are financed from national sources can be distinguished from those that involve international finance. To carry through three sets of classifying variables is organizationally complex. Luckily, there appears to be a considerable overlap among these three ways of viewing international programs. Those that aim at improving efficiency and stability commonly rely on the technique of coordinating individual country policies and do not involve large internationally controlled funds, while those that aim at redistribution and equity seem to involve both international funding and administration located outside direct domestic government control.

Specifically, Part Three proceeds as follows. Chapter 9 explores the nature of international goals, how these might be analyzed, and describes some of the institutional and decision-making characteristics of international policy. The issues of efficiency and stability are dealt with in Chapter 10, followed by discussion of the attempts to coordinate national actions in such areas as trade policy, commodity stocks, and bilateral food aid. The issues of equity and asset redistribution are treated in Chapter 11 and are followed by an examination of transfer programs involving development assistance, multilateral food aid, developing-country access to finance, and technology transfer. Some institutional initiatives fall under both headings. The Integrated Programme for Commodities, sponsored by the United Nations Conference on Trade and Development (UNCTAD), for instance, has elements of national-policy coordination for the stabilization of commodity markets and of international funding for the assistance of developing countries in international marketing. As the analytical issues of stabilization and development assistance are distinct, the treatment of two aspects of the Integrated Programme separately is an advantage.

Part Three concludes with an exploration of three actual policies concerned variously with questions of efficiency, stability, and equity (Chapter 12). The three chosen areas are (a) attempts to improve the efficiency and stability of international markets through multilateral trade negotiation via the mechanism of the General Agreement on Tariffs and Trade (GATT), (b) global transfers of food under food aid programs, and (c) the development of new technology targeted at developing countries and funded by developed countries through the family of international research centers funded by the Consultative Group on International Agricultural Research (GCIAR).

Part One

Interdependence in
World Agriculture

Chapter 1

Issues in World Agriculture

I INTRODUCTION

Policies respond to issues. Agricultural policies reflect the set of issues relating to the agricultural and food sectors of countries as perceived by those
groups with policy-making power. The issues arise from a dissatisfaction
with conditions in the farm and food sector such as low incomes, inadequate
consumption levels, and unstable prices. These issues are important in all
countries, though the balance among policy concerns will vary from country
to country. They are also issues of common concern to the international
community.

Although many of the issues in international agriculture are closely
related, it is useful to distinguish three broad categories. The first relates to
the development of the agricultural sector per se, its performance and its
relationship with the rest of the economy. The second category concerns
issues of food consumption, the adequacy of such consumption for proper
nutrition and the link between food supply and available incomes. The third
group of issues has to do with international trade and resource transfers, the
importance of trade to national food systems, and the role of transfers in the
search for an increase in productivity.

The discussion in this chapter focuses on these three issues in turn, dif-
ferentiating between those that are primarily of concern to low-income coun-

tries and those that characterize the agricultural problem in the developed nations. To understand these policy issues it is also necessary to review some basic facts about the performance of the agricultural sector. These facts include information on output growth and variability and factor use, and on the demand for the output of the sector, including the uses for the product, the location of demand, and the growth in the market. Trade patterns and trends are also essential information in understanding the context in which policy operates. This chapter is designed to give a brief overview of the sector at a global level and an introduction to the major policy isssues as background to the discussion of such policies in the remainder of the book.

II AGRICULTURAL PRODUCTION AND INVESTMENT ISSUES

A Global Production Trends

World agricultural output has grown at an average annual rate of about 2.2 percent over the past 15 years, with no clear-cut increase or decrease in this growth over the period (FAO, 1983a). The rate of growth in agriculture is about one-half of the overall growth rate of the world's economy. Aggregate production in developing countries has been increasing significantly faster than in developed countries over the period since 1967. Within developing regions, Africa has had a relatively low rate of growth of agricultural output; by contrast agricultural growth in Latin America and Asia has been about 70 percent higher than in Africa over the period since 1974. Among the developed countries, the centrally planned economies of Eastern Europe and the Soviet Union have managed output increases only one-quarter of that of the developed market economies of the west (see Table 1-1).

The trend of global production hides significant variations both from year to year and from region to region. Over the past decade, for instance, annual growth rates have varied between zero (in 1980) and 4.3 (in 1978), depending upon harvest conditions in major crop-growing areas. This short-term variability is important in terms of the security of food supplies, but can be contrasted with multiyear swings in output of many other industries. The world as a whole seems at present immune from serious agricultural recessionary slumps and expansionary booms.

The variability in output among countries is much greater than indicated by the aggregate figures. The distribution of growth rates among developing countries is particularly marked. Thirteen percent of those countries surveyed in a recent Food and Agricultural Organization (FAO) study (FAO, 1983b) experienced an absolute decline in agricultural output over the period 1967 to 1974, and a similar number (though not in all cases the same countries) showed a decline from 1974 to 1982 (see Table 1-2). Of these countries, about one-half were in Africa. On the other hand, 20 percent of developing countries posted increases of over 4 percent per year over the

Table 1-1 Growth Rates of Food Production (percent per annum)

	1967–1974	1974–1982	Total							
			1975	1976	1977	1978	1979	1980	1981	1982
World	2.2	2.2	3.1	2.0	2.5	4.3	0.9	0.0	3.1	2.5
Developing countries	2.8	3.2	5.4	3.0	2.7	4.7	1.7	2.4	3.9	2.4
Market economies	2.5	3.1	6.4	3.0	3.3	3.9	0.5	3.2	4.3	1.5
Africa	1.8	2.0	1.6	2.9	−1.8	3.6	1.7	3.4	1.8	3.7
Far East	2.7	3.4	10.7	0.5	7.2	4.3	−2.3	3.9	6.0	−0.2
Latin America	2.8	3.4	3.1	5.5	3.7	3.1	2.9	2.7	3.9	2.6
Near East	2.6	2.8	6.4	6.1	−2.0	4.3	3.1	1.9	3.1	1.9
Asian centrally plan. econ.	3.4	3.4	3.0	3.0	1.2	6.9	4.8	0.6	2.8	4.8
Developed countries	1.7	1.5	1.5	1.3	2.4	3.9	0.3	−1.8	2.5	2.5
Market economies	1.4	2.1	3.3	−0.4	4.0	1.8	3.4	−1.1	4.2	2.0
Centrally planned economies	2.3	0.5	−1.7	4.6	−0.4	7.9	−4.9	−3.2	−0.7	3.5

Source: FAO/UN, International Agricultural Adjustment: Fourth Progress Report, Rome, 1983.

Table 1-2 Distribution of Growth of Food Production Rates Among Developing Countries, 1967–1974 and 1974–1982*

Total food production (growth rates, percent)	1967–1974				1974–1982			
	No. of countries Total	%	Population 1970, total (million)	Average growth rate	No. of countries Total	%	Population 1980, total (million)	Average growth rate
Above 4	18	20	392	5.0	20	22	590	4.6
2–4	32	35	1,261	3.2	29	32	2,285	3.2
0–2	29	32	818	1.6	30	33	265	1.2
Negative	12	13	112	−1.6	12	13	78	−2.0

*Ninety countries included in the FAO study, "Agriculture: Toward 2000," plus China. These countries together account for 98.9 percent of the population of the developing countries.

Source: FAO/UN, International Agricultural Adjustment: Fourth Progress Report, Rome, 1983

period 1967 to 1974 and 22 percent achieved this growth rate during 1974 to 1982. Agriculture is thriving in some parts of the world and stagnating in others: policies both contribute to and reflect this performance variability.

As with any multiproduct sector, trends in aggregate output conceal many of the interesting developments within the sector. Agriculture produces a wide variety of commodities, each with its own characteristics in terms of supply, distribution, and consumption. The production of cereals is the most important and widespread economic activity in world agriculture. For example, in the crop year 1981 to 1982, some 460 million tons of wheat, 790 million tons of coarse grains, and 412 million tons of rice were produced (see Table 1-3). Two-thirds of the wheat and coarse grains were grown in developed countries, while most of the rice came from developing countries. Second only to the cereal sector in world agriculture is the livestock system, producing milk and milk products, meat, and such by-products as hides and skins. In 1981, for example, 472 million tons of milk were produced, together with 142 million tons of meat and 281 million hides. The most important milk products were cheese (12 million tons), butter (7 million tons), and milk powder (6 million tons). Of the meats, 55 million tons of pigmeat,

Table 1-3   World Production of Major Commodities, 1981, and Share of Production in Developed and Developing Countries

Commodity	1981 Production (mill. tons)	Developing share (%)	Developed share (%)
Sugar	99.5	57.8	42.2
Coffee (green)	5.8	(100)	—
Cocoa (raw)	1.7	(100)	—
Tea	1.9	87.4	12.6
Rice (paddy)	412.1	93.7	6.3
Wheat	460.4	34.8	65.2
Coarse grains	789.5	33.4	66.6
Cassava	125.6	(100)	—
Meat	142.3	37.1	62.9
Milk	471.7	23.5	76.5
Cotton	15.5	56.1	43.9
Jute	3.2	98.5	1.5
Hard fibers	0.5	(100)	—
Rubber	3.7	(100)	—
Citrus	53.1	53.9	46.1
Tobacco	5.7	60.7	39.3
Wine	314.6	13.2	86.8
Fats and oils	60.3	44.8	55.2

Source: FAO/UN, Commodity Review and Outlook, 1982–83, FAO Economic and Social Development Series, No. 25, Rome, 1983.

47 million tons of bovine meat, and 29 million tons of poultry meat were produced. Somewhat over three-quarters of the milk and nearly two-thirds of the meat was produced in developed countries.

If developed countries dominate the production of cereals (except rice), meat (except sheep and goats), and milk, the developing countries have their own specialties, in particular coffee, cocoa, tea, cassava, fibers, and rubber. In terms of volume, 126 million tons of cassava, 5.8 millions tons of coffee, 317 million tons of rubber, and 3.2 million tons of jute were the main products, followed by 1.9 million tons of tea and 1.7 million tons of cocoa. Of commodities produced in both developed and developing countries, sugar and fats and oils were the most important. Fifty-eight percent of sugar was grown in developing countries, and 45 percent of the fats and oils production came from those countries. Citrus, cotton, and tobacco also are widely produced in both developed and developing countries.

As with output growth, productivity in agriculture varies widely among countries. At the aggregate level, the growth of output of just over 2 percent per year has been accomplished with a small rise in the labor force, of about 1.1 percent per year. Thus, labor productivity has increased on average by just over 1 percent annually. The world's working population increases at a rate perhaps twice that of the agricultural labor force which results in a steady decline in the percentage of people employed in agriculture. New land for the agricultural labor force to work exists in some parts of the world—Latin America and Africa—but not to any degree in others—Asia, Europe, and North America. There appears to have been about a 0.6 percent increase in land area each year over the past 15 years in developing countries, and almost no increase in developed countries. Greater intensity of land use, in particular through irrigation and inorganic fertilizer use, has been more important as a method of increasing output. Some 30 percent of Asian agriculture is now on irrigated land, and developing-country fertilizer use has risen (from a low base) at over 10 percent per year since 1967.

Reliable estimates on labor productivity across countries are scarce, but what evidence there is shows a wide range in average product per worker. Yields of crops regularly differ among countries by factors of four or five. In addition to yield differences, techniques of production range from labor-intensive small holdings to large corporate farms with extensive capital equipment. The conditions of production of the same crop in different parts of the world (and, in some cases, different parts of the same country) vary so much as to make general statements on productivity of dubious value.

B Agriculture in Development

The agricultural production issue takes on different dimensions at different levels of development. In an economy dominated by the agricultural sector (as is typical for low-income countries) the performance of that sector is intimately linked with that of the economy as a whole. At the other extreme, mature industrial economies with agricultural sectors representing less than 5 percent of national income are not unduly influenced by agricultural performance. The issue of agricultural productivity is thus a vital matter for low-income countries: for the richer economies it is usually of concern primarily in the conduct of agricultural income policies.

Agricultural production issues in low-income countries commonly revolve around the questions of investment, producer price levels, and access to productive resources. To make the best use of national resource endowments, the available land area has to be allocated among farmers who in turn need access to capital to acquire machinery and to a flow of income to purchase other inputs from the nonfarm sector. The allocation of land through ownership and tenancy is a variable only over a long period of time or during periods of land reform. The price levels and investment decisions form the basis for annual or periodic policy choice.

It is reasonably clear, despite the absence of good, comparable data across countries, that agriculture in developing countries receives a share of investment considerably less than its share in employment and generally less than its contribution to Gross Domestic Product (GDP). Investment in agriculture in 19 major developing countries, over the second half of the 1970s, averaged only about 10 percent of total gross fixed capital investment (FAO, 1983b). By contrast, agriculture accounted for nearly one-quarter of GDP in these countries.

Two possible reasons can be adduced for this apparent lack of balance. First, required investment in agriculture per unit of additional output (the incremental capital-output ratio) may be smaller than in other sectors. This might be true if agricultural output could be expanded by labor-intensive technology, as some have argued. But the argument that labor-intensive technology is appropriate in labor-surplus countries presumably applies to other sectors besides agriculture. Thus, while agricultural expansion in developing countries may require less capital than similar expansion in developed countries, it is not clear that within a country agriculture is less capital intensive than other sectors of the economy. The second reason for a lower-than-proportionate use of investment funds by agriculture may simply reflect slower growth in that sector. If the nonagricultural sector is growing at 5 to 6 percent and the agricultural sector at 2 to 3 percent, then, even at the same capital intensity, less investment will be needed. It is generally true in developing countries that agriculture tends to grow more slowly than the economy as a whole (Krishna, 1982), suggesting that an agriculture that accounts for 25 percent of GDP might be expected to absorb 15 percent of investment funds.

Both these reasons have an element of circularity. If capital is not made available to the agricultural sector then growth will be slower and less capital intensive. Since in much of the developing world, and in centrally planned developed countries, agricultural investment is very much influenced by governments, the explanation for relatively low investment must lie in large part in government policy. If governments choose to limit or at least not to improve access to investment funds in the agricultural sector then the result will be slower growth and less adoption of capital-intensive technology in that sector. This has undoubtedly been the case in many developing countries.

Optimal investment patterns within a country are only likely to emerge if producers are rewarded for their investment by receiving a price for their output which corresponds to the value that society puts on that output. Short of coercion, there is no way of promoting production deemed unprofitable by the individual farmer. Governments can, as an alternative to reflecting the value of output in the market or procurement price, choose to subsidize inputs such as fertilizer or to grant access to capital at favorable rates. But the provision of realistic prices to give incentives to activities deemed desirable for expansion is in most cases the necessary step without which investment schemes rarely work. As a broad generalization, one can say that producer prices are lower in developing countries than in developed countries (Peterson, 1979), though the range of prices is impressive (see Table 1-4). Raising these prices would appear to be consistent with national development aims in most low-income countries. Problems arise to the extent that there are fiscal implications or unpalatable impacts upon consumers. Low farm prices often result from a more or less explicit tax on farmers, for instance, through low procurement prices paid by a state marketing board. These tax revenues or para-statal trading profits would have to be offset by tax increases or spending reductions elsewhere. And if consumer prices are subsidized, again either directly or by the trading losses of marketing institutions, then these prices would either rise or the cost of the subsidy would increase.

C Industrial Agriculture

These key issues for developing countries, which involve ongoing decisions on investment priorities and pricing policies, are a part of overall development strategy. This is less true for industrial countries. Not only is the agricultural sector in general smaller in relative terms in such economies, but the ability of that sector to compete for resources is usually greater. In economies which allow private capital markets, the farm sector has reasonable access to the pool of savings in the economy as a whole. Farmers generate most of their investment funds through accumulated profits on the sale of their produce. The price level set under government policies has a direct ef-

Table 1-4 Range of Developing-Country Farm Support Prices, 1975 and 1980, for Wheat and Rice, U.S.$ per Metric Ton

	Wheat*		Rice*	
	1975	1980	1975	1980
Developing countries				
Highest	276	461	504	878
Lowest	70	110	64	66
Median	145	199	156	203
Africa				
Highest	276	360	300	321
Lowest	121	193	80	107
Median	156.5	213	140	214
Latin America				
Highest	184	274	261	287
Lowest	70	155	128	136
Median	150	196	168	229
Asia				
Highest	210	461	504	878
Lowest	100	146	64	66
Median	127.5	160	143	168.5
Near East				
Highest	192	341	336	433
Lowest	119	110		
Median	151	154.5	—	—

*Nineteen developing countries for which data were available.
†Thirty-one developing countries for which data were available.
Source: FAO/UN, International Agricultural Adjustment: Fourth Progress Report, Rome, 1983.

fect not only on incomes but on investment and technical change. Hence, price policy in developed countries has come to be the main instrument by which the government stimulates or discourages production.

The primacy of price policy has in turn led to most of the important issues in developed-country agricultural production (Josling, 1974). The policy itself has become a part of the problem. Prices set at levels which appear to generate adequate incomes, comparable to those in the nonfarm sector, promote production often in excess of what can be profitably sold on the domestic and international market. Such excess capacity has to be financed if incomes are to be maintained. Taxing consumers to pay for the produce further reduces the size of the market; transfer payments from the treasury become visible expenditures vulnerable to political pressures when budget stringency is in order. Taxing consumers (and foreign producers) by restricting imports to expand the market for domestic production has the additional effect of irritating trading partners; the production issue becomes a trade problem. Similarly, taxpayer subventions to aid exports adds international objections to internal fiscal problems and threatens the stability of the trading system.

Perceived farm income problems are the main reason for this policy. They stem in the main from the dynamics of industrial agriculture. The farming sector adjusts to the process of industrialization and economic growth by a fundamental reorganization of production techniques away from heavy concentrations of labor on small plots of land towards a mix of less labor, more machinery, and more purchased inputs on larger land areas. Capital is needed and labor released. Farms are amalgamated and holdings consolidated. The urban sector benefits from the released labor supply, from the greater efficiency of production, and from the demand for farm inputs. If this process takes place rapidly, small farmers may be left behind (with inadequate resources to make a living) and migrants may feel forced off the farms by the pressure of relative price shifts. Governments typically behave ambivalently, on the one hand recognizing the adjustment process and assisting the amalgamation of farms and the movement of labor, and on the other by setting support prices at levels which act to keep many farmers in business. They encourage technology which releases labor and attempt at the same time to legislate for adequate returns to labor in rural pursuits. The resulting "farm problem" highlights the conflicting views about the policy response to the adjustment process.

Centrally planned economies face similar dilemmas which show up in different ways. Productivity growth in agriculture is relatively slow and the demand for food grows relatively rapidly because of still comparatively low levels of overall incomes. In this respect, many such countries are more similar to developing than to developed countries in that they tend to keep producer and consumer prices low. Operating more through production targets and the provision of inputs by the state than through private incentives, investment decisions and production techniques become an explicit act of policy. But the same issues of resource utilization within a modern agricultural sector exist even when public rather than private decisions determine the pace of adjustment. Without the ability of the sector to shift resources, through labor movement in response to wage incentives, public sector agriculture can easily get trapped in a low-productivity cycle. Excessive labor use and inadequate capitalization lead to stagnation and limit the ability of the sector to contribute to economic growth. Investment priorities switch to other sectors and the view of agriculture as a backward sector is reinforced. Though much of this book deals with price policies, and hence, concentrates on issues in mixed-economy rather than planned systems, the underlying problems exist under all types of economic regimes.

III FOOD CONSUMPTION ISSUES

A Global Food Consumption

The issue in international agriculture that draws the most public attention is undoubtedly that of hunger and the adequacy of food supplies to meet nutritional objectives. At a global level one can estimate the level and change in the availability of food supplies. World consumption of food necessarily follows the same trend as world production (assuming no change in the proportion of food lost in the distribution chain and no long-run change in the proportion of output kept as stocks). Thus, food consumption has risen at 2.2 percent, nearly one-half of 1 percent higher than population growth. With faster economic growth and higher income elasticities, it is likely that per-capita consumption has risen by somewhat more than 0.5 percent in developing countries. Aggregate supplies of food, converted into calories and divided by world population, would meet the standard measure of need used by the FAO and the World Health Organization (WHO). Even among developing countries, aggregate food supplies may meet these criteria (see Table 1-5). Nevertheless, hunger remains a critical issue for many coun-

Table 1-5 Developing Countries:* Calorie Supplies in Relation to Average Requirements

Region	No. of countries	Population, 1979	Calories per capita		Calories (percent of requirements)	
			1974–1976	1978–1980	1974–1976	1978–1980
Africa	37	360	2,174	2,184	93	94
Far East (including China)	16	2,208	2,144	2,270	94	100
Latin America	24	352	2,541	2,591	107	109
Near East	14	207	2,606	2,723	106	111
Total	91	3,127	2,326†	2,326†	96†	101†

*Ninety countries included in "Agriculture: Toward 2000" plus China, which together account for 98.9 percent of the population of all developing countries.
†Weighted average of included countries.
Source: FAO/UN, International Agricultural Adjustment: Fourth Report, Rome, 1983.

tries, and the (necessarily imprecise) estimates of those suffering from malnutrition vary from 400 million to 1 billion people.

B The Poverty/Hunger Problem

The most important food consumption issues relate to the low level of consumption endemic to low-income countries. Such low levels of consumption commonly go along with nutritional problems, exacerbated by acute food shortages during periods of inadequate supply. Available supplies may be adequate to meet normal nutritional requirements within a country, but the distribution of food within countries is never even. In the absence of extensive nonmarket distribution schemes, the distribution of food will follow that of income. In societies with unequal wealth, food consumption is likely to be a severe problem for those not in the mainstream of economic life.

Such problems show up in a number of ways. Chronic undernourishment, the intake of insufficient calories to maintain normal active life, is both a moral and an economic issue. Most governments, individually and collectively, recognize their responsibility to avoid such situations and know the benefits derived from better nutrition. Direct distribution of foods, or the provision of opportunities for such families to buy foods, form a important part of the consumption policies of low-income countries. Additionally, undernourishment is linked with disease and with physical and mental underdevelopment. Access to food by pregnant and nursing mothers and by children in the first 4 years of life is recognized as a crucial problem, requiring special attention. Such "vulnerable" groups are often targeted in national food policies through special programs. Acute shortages, occasioned by the interruption of normal supplies, raise different policy issues, as does the plight of populations uprooted from their normal place of habitation. Seasonal cycles of hunger are common in areas where food supplied are dependent upon local harvests.

The problems facing most developing countries with respect to food consumption revolve around the issues of income distribution, domestic marketing, sources of supply, and the level of consumer prices. Clearly, income distribution is more than an agricultural or food issue; however, it is equally obvious that in a country where one-third to two-thirds of the population are engaged in agriculture, the situation of that sector influences income distribution. Access to productive assets will determine whether rural families can provide for their own food needs or purchase those needs with earned income. Those with no land and uncertain employment are often at nutritional risk. The distribution system for farm products, including the price levels set on government procurements, determines the flow of marketable goods surplus to farm-family needs. Where this system is inadequate, other problems are made worse. Low incentives to farmers, common in developing countries, not only hinder the process of agricultural development and hold down farm incomes but also reduce the flow of goods to urban markets and encourage imports.

The government typically controls both domestic marketing channels and the flow of imports—either directly or by rationing foreign exchange. A key issue under such circumstances is the use of imports to supplement domestic output. By controlling the quantity imported and the price at which it is sold on the domestic market, both the demand facing domestic producers and the supply available to domestic consumers are determined. Food import policy, like investment policies for agriculture, is set as part of the general development strategy. Foreign exchange used for importing food reduces the amount available for capital expenditures and other imports necessary for industrial development. Overvalued exchange rates make such imports attractive and limit export earning activities, making necessary the rationing of foreign exchange. Concessional sales offer the recipient country an opportunity to take advantage of lower-priced imports of food, but can also lead to lower incentives for domestic produce if they have to compete with the lower-priced imports.

The price level at which consumers can buy food is clearly a crucial issue in meeting consumption problems in low-income countries. A low price to consumers is often dictated by the need to allow low-income families to purchase staples, and reinforced by urban interests either paying or receiving a money wage. Overvalued exchange rates again militate in favor of making the wage-good cheap to keep down costs. However, general policies of low prices entail either subventions from the treasury or low prices to farmers—both limiting domestic development. The international environment, through the level and variability of prices of foodstuffs, also has a major impact on these domestic food policy decisions.

C The Affluent Food Consumer

Pockets of poverty exist in generally affluent societies. Countries have policies to avoid incidence of malnutrition resulting from the lack of purchasing power of disadvantaged groups. However, the bulk of such policies are absorbed within the general social security system. Pensions, unemployment insurance, aid to single-parent families, and the like, all function as a means to avoid hunger and malnutrition. Industrial countries typically are concerned with other issues relating to food consumption, notably the price level for foods, the quality of foodstuffs, and the health problems of overconsumption. With the notable exception of the U.S. Food Stamp Program, developed countries have not generally oriented specific policies towards maintaining the level of food consumption by low-income groups.

The dominant food-consumption issue in developed countries tends to be that of food prices and their impact on inflation. Though food costs, typically accounting for only 15 to 20 percent of consumer expenditure, do not have the same influence on wage levels and industrial costs as in developing countries, at times of inflation they become of political concern. Ironically, the major problems in this area stem not from the nature of agricultural markets themselves so much as the influence of government policy on those markets. At times of high world prices, the governments of industrial countries may seek to protect consumers by means of subsidies on consumption or on imports or by taxes or embargoes on exports. But, in general, the development of agriculture leads over time to lower relative prices of the major foodstuffs which benefit consumers in terms of lower food costs. The price-support policies of developed countries in effect recapture these benefits and pass them back to the farm sector through higher prices than would otherwise have obtained. Low-priced imports are taxed at the border, rationed by quotas, or limited by government importing agencies. As a consequence, consumer interests seem to conflict with those of producers as each tries to reap the benefits of agricultural productivity.

Apart from this food-price issue, perhaps the major concern of consumer interests in developed countries revolves around the quality of foods. Governments, much more than in developing countries, become involved in grading, inspecting, and otherwise regulating the quality of goods offered to the consumer. In addition, through legislation on food additives and on chemicals used in food production, certain health standards are enforced, and through regulations on labeling and advertising, the consumer is provided with information upon which to make purchase decisions. Consumer education is also promised in many countries with the aim of improving nutritional standards: this includes information about problems of overconsumption which appear to accompany affluence.

In some countries, typically those with a low level of self-sufficiency in basic foods, the government additionally reflects concerns about the security of food supplies. Though this problem is of a different order of magnitude to that facing poorer countries, even affluent societies feel the need to guard against interruptions in overseas supply. This issue is seen as one where domestic producer and consumer interests overlap, apparently supporting increased domestic production and arguing against dependence on imports, and incidentally, providing a shifting target for economic analysis.

IV INTERNATIONAL TRADE ISSUES

A Agricultural Trade Flows

Agricultural trade can be classified loosely according to which of the three main regions of the world, i.e., West, South, and East, it comes from or goes to. Among the resulting nine types of trade flows six are of particular importance as is shown in Table 1-6. The most important of these flows is imports by industrial market economies of the agricultural products from other western industrial economies ("West-West" trade). The biggest items are animal feed ingredients, such as corn and soybeans, wheat, livestock products, and processed and semiprocessed foodstuffs, including fruit and vegetable preparations. Of these products, trade in animal feeds and in processed foods has been growing steadily, while livestock products and wheat are less dynamic markets. The second largest flow is imports by developing countries of the agricultural products from the western industrial nations ("West-South" trade). Wheat has historically been a major traded item, but feed grains and raw materials (such as cotton, hides, and skins) for processing and re-export are growing rapidly. Livestock imports into some regions (e.g., the Middle East) have also grown rapidly. Trade in agricultural inputs (seeds, fertilizer, breeding stock) are also an important part of this flow.

A third category of trade is imports by centrally planned developed economies (CPE), mainly Eastern Europe and the USSR, from the western industrial democracies ("West-East" trade). The main items are animal feed ingredients, principally corn and soybeans, livestock products, and food grains (wheat). This trade has grown particularly fast during the 1970s. A fourth category of particular significance in global trade patterns is imports by the developed market economies of the produce of the developing world ("South-West" trade). To the traditional export items, the tropical beverages, sugar, agricultural raw materials, one must add livestock products and fruits and vegetables. Trade in tropical beverages has not been a major area

Table 1-6 Major Agricultural Trade Flows, 1970s

Exporter \ Importer	West	South	East
West	Animal feeds Livestock products Processed foods Oilseeds	Food grains Feed grains Raw materials	Feed grains Food grains Livestock products
South	Tropical beverages Raw materials Oilseeds, fruits, vegetables, and sugar	Tropical beverages Raw materials Livestock products	Tropical beverages Raw materials Sugar
East			Food grains

of growth; other agricultural exports have fared somewhat better in volume terms.

As is obvious from Table 1-6, there are several possible regional trade patterns which have not, for various reasons, developed. South-South trade is mainly in tropical products and raw materials, as is South-East trade. Some East-East trade occurs, in particular, in food grains from the U.S.S.R. to Eastern Europe, but virtually no East-West or East-South agricultural trade takes place. The reasons for this particular trade pattern may be in the underlying production capacity as related to consumption needs: Developed CPEs do not generate large quantities of agricultural products in excess of domestic requirements.

This breakdown of trade by broad regions illustrates the development of trade shares. With the growth of West-West, West-South, and West-East trade, the share of total exports from the West has increased. South-West trade has not grown enough to compensate. On the other hand, the share of total agricultural imports has grown in the East and South relative to the West—the share of the East, depending heavily on U.S.S.R. imports, is now greater than its share in exports, i.e., it has become a net importer of agricultural products.

Agricultural trade expanded rapidly in the 1970s. There has, however, been a profound change in the nature of agricultural trade over the past decade. This change started in the mid-1960s, with the United States' decision to become a commercial exporter by moving price supports closer to world market levels. It was reinforced by decisions in centrally planned economies to allow expression of pent-up consumer demand for more varied western-style diets. Newly industrialized countries followed with economic development which resulted in similar shifts in consumption towards meat, at least among the urban middle class. The food and feed industries in developed countries found that they could circumvent the food-grain bias in their farm support systems by substitution among ingredients. Concessional sales of wheat gave way to commercial sales, as bread replaced other staples in urban consumption patterns in Asia. Latin American countries moved away from the reliance on heavy export taxes, encouraging a resurgence of exports from a fundamentally strong agricultural region. These and many other developments helped make the 1970s a remarkable decade for agricultural trade.

All this took place in spite of the other main feature of the decade, the massive instability of commodity prices for both temperate and tropical products. It also survived the post-1973 eruptions in oil markets, in international monetary affairs, and in inflation. It weathered economic recession, the deterioration in international cooperation, and the rising tide of confrontation and militarism. It received little help from a general reduction in trade barriers, which stayed high in agricultural markets. Certain developing countries were able to penetrate developed-country manufactured goods markets and, hence, earn foreign exchange, but this was not a consequence of agricultural trade liberalization.

B Developing-Country Trade Issues

Developing countries participate in international agricultural trade both as exporters and as importers. For each country the balance of concerns will differ, but in general, their interests are in a secure and stable market for their export commodities, heavily oriented towards the output from tropical agriculture, and a ready supply of temperate-zone foodstuffs and animal feeds ingredients to supplement domestic production. Some of the concerns of developing countries over their export markets have been price stability, the role of multinational corporations, the location of processing, the competition for synthetics, the incidence of local taxes in developed countries, the long-term price trends, and, in some products, competition with local suppliers. These concerns have absorbed a large part of international discussions on agricultural trade issues over the years. Though often rooted in domestic production conditions, the solutions have been sought at the international level.

Of concern to developing countries as importers of foodstuffs have been issues such as price stability, assurance of supplies, ability to pay for imports, undue dependence upon a small group of exporters, and the price level at which supplies are obtained. These issues, too, have been at the center of international discussions surrounding food security and food aid. As more developing countries have relied on food imports for domestic needs, the interests of such countries have been more clearly defined. In particular, they are now seen as distinct from the interests of the much smaller group of developing countries that export temperate zone commodities.

The issue of price stability in agricultural markets was elevated in the policy agenda by the events of the early 1970s, when grain and oilseed prices rose sharply (see Table 1-7). For producers of sugar, coffee, cocoa, and tea such instability was a common occurrence. Significant variations in supply from year to year operating in markets where demand tends to be price inelastic have always given the market for tropical products a degree of price uncertainty. The phenomenon of investment cycles, with expansion when prices are high leading to overproduction and falling prices, has also been common. In temperate-zone markets, government policies share some of the blame along with variations in yield related to weather: The common tendency to stabilize domestic price levels at the expense of making international prices less stable showed up particularly in the early 1970s (see Chapter 2).

Many of the concerns of developing countries focus on the institutional

Table 1-7   Prices of Major Agricultural Products, 1974–1983, U.S.$ per ton

	Crop year ending in									
	1974	1975	1976	1977	1978	1979	1980	1981	1982	1983[i]
Wheat[a]	177	161	151	111	113	139	170	179	169	158
Maize[b]	116	132	116	108	96	103	115	142	118	110
Rice[c]	584	439	295	257	337	330	387	477	390	272
Coffee[d]	1,237	1,373	1,394	2,980	5,053	3,420	3,737	3,322	2,546	2,766
Cocoa[e]	1,131	1,560	1,245	2,045	3,788	3,402	3,292	2,603	2,075	1,741
Sugar[f]	208	654	449	254	179	172	210	639	372	185
Jute[g]	278	353	377	296	320	397	385	310	282	286
Tea[h]	1,060	1,394	1,390	1,509	2,713	2,184	2,161	2,232	2,053	1,938

[a]U.S. No. 1 Hard Winter (1974 = No. 2 Hard Winter)
[b]U.S. No. 2 Yellow
[c]Thai, 5 percent (1974, average of less than 12 months)
[d]ICO, 1976, daily price
[e]ICCO daily price
[f]ISA daily price
[g]BWD fob C.-Chalna
[h]London, all tea
[i]Estimates
Source: FAO/UN, Commodity Review and Outlook, 1982–83, FAO, Economic and Social Development Series, No. 25, Rome, 1983.

arrangements for trade and on the processing activity which provides the major market for tropical goods. For historical as well as contemporary economic reasons, the location of processing is generally close to the market for the final product. Much of the production of raw materials for this processing industry was under the control of firms located in developed countries. The extensive nationalization of production which followed political independence for many tropical countries relieved some of the problems of the control over domestic agriculture but shifted the issue to one of trade relationships. Attempts to locate the processing in the producing country have faced the problem of protection of processing activities by way of tariff rates which increase with the degree of processing in the importing countries. Attempts to raise raw material prices have led to the search for synthetic alternatives to natural products, or the substitution of other agricultural raw materials. Economic control of trade by large firms has also been seen as a problem for exporters in developing countries. Additionally, the tax treatment of the final product has been, in some cases, seen as a policy which limits the market for tropical produce.

In a few cases, the tropical export competes directly with locally grown produce. Cane sugar competes with beet sugar, and tropical oil products compete with vegetable oil produced from temperate zone plants. Beef exports from some developing countries encounter competition from protected domestic beef production in industrialized countries. Tropical fruit also has to share a market with temperate climate fruit. In these cases, exporter concerns are with market access and commonly come up against the desire of the importing country to create or maintain income opportunities for domestic producers.

A final issue of importance to developing-country exporters is that of long-term price relationships for tropical goods, though concern with preventing the collapse of price in the short run is difficult to disentangle from the aim of firmer prices over a longer period. There has been a tendency to view the long-run price trend as a political matter to be resolved in the context of North-South transfers of resources. In such discussions, the more economic issues of the slow growth in demand and the often aggressive competition among developing-country suppliers often are ignored. The limits of political action to influence the terms of trade for tropical products, and the economic consequences of trying such an approach, are discussed in Chapter 11.

The issue of assurance of supplies arises particularly in times of market shortage. It is clearly linked with that of price stability, in that most countries would be able to purchase whatever commodities they wish if they were prepared to pay a high enough price. Physical shortages occur infrequently, and have to do with logistical problems of transportation and marketing. A special case of shortage is the political decision to block or embargo particular trade flows. The best assurance against this would seem to be the flexibility of trade flow which allows a country a choice of suppliers. Large importers naturally fear the possibility of absolute or physical shortages, and have tended to favor long-term supply agreements as a way of reducing if not eliminating the risk of nonavailability of imports. The smaller importers have not, in general, seen any advantage in such bilaterals. Supply assurance concerns extend to the input markets in many cases. The inability to purchase fertilizer, seed, or crop chemicals may be a real or apparent problem in some market situations.

If physical shortages are rare, economic shortages—the bidding up of the price to ration available supplies—are more common. Price instability may have its own costs to the importing country, making it difficult to budget and plan a food strategy. But high prices on world markets, in particular, if domestic production is low, can lead to severe problems of payments imbalance. Mechanisms have been devised to allow easier access to foreign exchange in such periods, through the International Monetary Fund (IMF) lending facilities. This, in effect, means that countries can look at import financing over a period of years, knowing that variations in the cereal import bill will not unduly influence spending on other imported products.

Import dependence as an issue is more difficult to define. At one level it relates to the feeling of vulnerability induced by knowing that one's domestic production alone is not able to feed the population in times of crisis. As such, it is similar to the concern over the assurance of supplies. If a country wishes to reduce its import dependency it can promote domestic production—at a cost. The cost is the premium for reducing risk, and will vary by country. Insofar as domestic production is based on imported inputs, the risk may only be shifted to other markets rather than reduced. At another level, the import dependence problem is one of possible hegemony, with a loss of freedom associated with reliance on overseas suppliers. This is often linked with foreign-policy considerations, but can also be tied in with the economic control over the economy. Once again, political and economic independence can be purchased at a price by stimulating higher-cost domestic output.

Long-term price trends in agricultural produce imported into developing countries are of crucial significance in any attempt to plan agricultural and food strategies. Unfortunately, as with export products, no objective criteria exist for separating long-run from short-run developments in these markets other than the test of time. Are grain surpluses the result of chronic over-capacity or of fortunate weather? Will technical progress in temperate-zone agriculture continue to put a downward pressure on real prices, or will constraints of land use, shifting weather patterns and environmental concerns, together with reductions in price incentives and the exhaustion of the present stock of yield-improving techniques, lead to higher prices in the future? Will latent demand be translated into market purchasing power in developing countries? And, will developing-country agriculture respond to economic incentives enough to limit the growth of world markets arising from demand pressures? Answers to such questions determine the long-run price trends, and in turn determine the options for domestic agricultural strategy in developing countries.

C Developed-Country Trade Issues

Just as developing countries have both importing and exporting interests in world trade, so developed countries view world markets both as a source of supply and a buyer of domestic goods. The complexity of trade policy issues reflects this ambivalence. As exporters, countries are concerned with market access, the orderly disposal of surpluses, and the general stability of prices. As importers, these same countries are interested in supply assurance and price stability. The orderly working of world markets provides a backdrop against which domestic policies can be developed. By contrast, disorderly world market conditions encourage isolation of domestic markets and pricing policies which are formulated on largely internal grounds (Johnson, 1973).

The concerns for market access, or trade liberalization, revolve around the degree to which foreign and domestic producers can compete for the domestic market in importaing countries. There is a natural tendency to use import controls as a mechanism for giving an increased share of the market to domestic producers. The cost is hidden in higher consumer prices and the justification is often reinforced by arguments about the need to contain foreign exchange outflow, the uncertainty of foreign supplies and prices, and the undesirability of being "dependent" upon imports. Exporters counter these arguments by pointing to the economic advantage of buying from the cheapest source and the contribution to reliability that could be expected from general liberalization and the mutuality of the dependence among trading nations.

Agricultural trade has not, in general, been subject to the same process of mutual trade barrier dismantlement that has characterized the industrial sector in the last 30 years. In large part, this has been the result of reluctance on the part of countries to subject their import-competing sectors to the same disciplines they expect of others in sectors where they export. Thus, through a succession of exceptions, waivers, and derogations, domestic price policies have come to totally dominate trade considerations. Access is limited to that amount that can be sold without jeopardy to these domestic programs. Unlike most industrial activities, where capital, and to a lesser extent labor, moves to take advantage of new trading opportunities, investment in agriculture responds only indirectly to world market prices and is geared to profit signals generated by domestic price policy. Only when domestic policy is modified to allow greater access does adjustment take place. Exporters wait upon this process and spend their waiting time developing submarkets in deregulated products or exploiting unintentioned gaps in the protective structure. The corn gluten–cassava example, developed in Chapter 4, clearly illustrates this process.

In periods of surplus, when domestic price support programs are threatened with excessive costs or required to adopt elaborate quantitative restrictions to avoid such costs, the search for foreign outlets for surpluses leads to further trade conflicts. Such exporter conflicts revolve around the use of subsidies to increase market share. With few markets granting ready access to such dumped surpluses, competition is channeled on those that remain open to such imports. Disputes center around the degree of subsidization, the "normal" market share, and the selling methods of various exporters. Often, the beneficiaries are the government-controlled import agencies who are in a postiion to pocket the subsidy of the successful bidder and still manage the domestic market in whatever way is desired. Food aid, to the developed-country policy maker, is itself tied in with the search for "needy" recipients willing to accept surplus products under general humanitarian guises. At such times of surplus, the range of prices between the insulated, high-cost import markets and the subsidized, low-price world markets can be extensive. By contrast, in times of shortage, the range of prices narrows considerably and world prices can rise above the levels obtaining in even high-cost importing countries.

Importing developed countries view these developments with a relative lack of concern, but the state of world markets helps to determine their domestic policies. The instability of prices tends to reinforce autarkic pressures, and occasional supply shortages appear to validate claims that consumer interests are served by high degrees of self-sufficiency. In general, importers tend to regard surplus problems as of interest to exporting countries, and incidentally benefit from higher receipts on import taxes or greater profits from state-trading operations. Similarly, importing countries often do not feel responsibility or concern for food-aid issues or matters of food security for developing countries. This implicit division of responsibility hides the real interaction between importer and exporter policies and serves to make worse the already difficult solutions to international trade problems.

Supply assurance and price stability issues are more immediate in the area of tropical products and raw materials. Much of this concern is devoted to ensuring a steady flow of products to processing industries. Historical links with former colonies often determine the flow of raw materials and have led to preferential access arrangements designed to secure that flow. More recently, raw materials such as those needed by the animal feed industry have become important to many developed countries. Concern over the price and reliability of supply of those commodities has grown, though this has been mixed with the desire to restrict their flow to keep up demand for locally grown feedstuffs. In short, food security for developing countries, short of foreign exchange and concerned with basic nutritional goals, is replaced in developed countries by feed security as a necessity for the development of livestock industries and raw-material security to keep up employment in processing firms.

V CONCLUDING COMMENTS

The purpose of this chapter was to provide a global overview of food production, consumption, and agricultural trade trends. These major trends provided a general backdrop for the discussion of major policy issues in production, consumption, and trade with that discussion divided into discussions of developed and developing countries. This broad overview is not intended as a definitive quantitative analysis of major trends. Rather, the purpose was to provide the reader with an overview of trends and issues as a prelude to the analysis which follows in subsequent chapters in which the book begins to delve analytically into policy analysis in a world-market context. The diversity and complexity of issues in agricultural trade has been illustrated. There exists a wide variety of objectives and measures of agricultural trade policies in different countries. Each country frames its policy with its specific needs in mind. But countries also operate in a common environment of world trade and monetary conditions. How individual countries react to the issues that face them is an important aspect of national policy. How countries collectively tackle such issues is the focus of international policy. Both topics are discussed in succeeding chapters, following the analysis of interdependence and the transmission of policy impacts through trade flows.

REFERENCES

FAO/UN. 1983a. *Commodity Review and Outlook 1982/83*, FAO, Rome.

FAO/UN. 1983b. "International Agricultural Adjustment: Fourth Progress Report," FAO Conference Document, Rome.

Johnson, D. G. 1973 *World Agriculture in Disarray*, Fontana, London.

Josling, T. 1974. "Agricultural Policies in Developed Countries: A Review," *J. Agr. Econ.*, **25**:229–263.

Krishna, R. 1982. "Some Aspects of Agricultural Growth, Price Policy and Equity in Developing Countries," *Food Res. Inst. Studies*, **18**:219–260.

Peterson, W. 1979. "International Farm Prices and the Social Cost of Cheap Food Policies," *Amer. J. Ag. Econ.*, **61**:12–21.

Timmer, C. P., Falcon, W. P., and Pearson, S. R. 1983. *Food Policy Analysis*, Johns Hopkins University Press, Baltimore.

ADDITIONAL READINGS

Johnson, D. (ed.) 1980. *The Politics of Food: Producing and Distributing the World's Food Supply*, Chicago Council on Foreign Relations, Chicago.

Johnston, B. F. 1977. "Food, Health and Population in Development," *J. Econ. Lit.*, **15**:879–907.

Mellor, J. W. 1978. "Food Price Policy and Income Distribution in Low Income Countries," *Econ. Dev. Cult. Chng.*, **27**:1–26.

Schultz, Theodore W. (ed.) 1978. *Distortions of Agricultural Incentives*, Indiana University Press, Bloomington.

Sinha, Radha (ed.) 1977. *The World Food Problem: Consensus and Conflict*, Pergamon Press, New York.

Sorenson, V. 1975. *International Trade Policy: Agriculture and Development*, Michigan State University Press, East Lansing.

Timmer, C. P. 1980. "Food Prices and Food Policy Analysis in LDCs," *Food Policy*, **5**:188–199.

Chapter 2

Policy Linkages Through Trade

I INTRODUCTION

The previous chapter has presented a brief picture of world agriculture from an international perspective. Decisions on policy are taken generally at a national level, but nations are connected internationally by trade. This both constrains and enlarges the scope for national action. In this chapter we begin to develop an analytical framework for looking at intercountry interdependence. The focus is on trade relations where world prices are the links between nations. Thus, an analysis of price transmission between international and national markets is of crucial importance. We begin looking at international markets by constructing a simple model using excess supply and demand functions for a single-commodity, two-country world. The model is static and assumes initially no government intervention. The next step is to introduce policy intervention at the national level, looking at some examples of single-commodity policy intervention, and to illustrate the impact on world markets. We then introduce storage policies as a further element in policy interaction through world markets. The question of cross-commodity linkages is deferred to Chapter 3.

II SINGLE-COMMODITY LINKAGES

A Graphical Analysis of Trade Linkage

The analysis of international markets can conveniently begin with the standard concepts of national supply and demand functions for two countries for a particular commodity. These are shown in Figure 2-1. Assume that Country A is a low-price producer, perhaps because of favorable resource endowments leading to low costs or because domestic demand relative to supply potential is small. In the absence of trade, domestic price would be P_A. For prices above P_A, producers in Country A would produce more than domestic consumers would buy. Thus, we can trace an *excess supply function (E_s)* for Country A, the supply function of exports onto the world market. It should be noted that at prices below P_A, Country A would be an importer; if we confine ourselves to prices above that level, we can ignore this part of the function.

Suppose that Country B has higher costs or large domestic demand relative to production potential. This country is also represented in Figure 2-1 where S_B and D_B are Country B's domestic supply and demand functions for the commodity. In the absence of trade, price would be P_B, which by construction and assumption is above P_A in Country A. For prices below P_B, consumers in Country B would demand more than producers would produce. As price fell, this difference would grow, thus tracing out an *excess demand function (E_d)*. This is the demand function for imports from the world market. Again, for completeness, it should be noted that for prices above P_B Country B would be an exporter. Now let there be trade between Countries A and B, for simplicity assuming zero transportation costs. Equi-

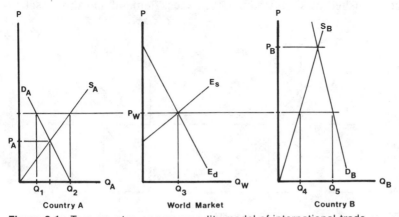

Figure 2-1 Two-country, one-commodity model of international trade.

librium in the international market occurs where $E_s = E_d$, yielding a world price of P_w. Country A exports $(Q_2 - Q_1)$ which is equal to Q_3, the volume traded in world markets, and is equal to $(Q_5 - Q_4)$, Country B's volume of imports.

With this basic model, it is straightforward to explore the most basic form of international interdependence. Suppose Country B (an importer) had bad weather in a given year, thus shifting S_B to S_B' in Figure 2-2. This shifts the world demand (E_d) to the right, resulting in an increase in world price to P_w' and an increase in the volume of trade to Q_8. Prices rise in Country A, reducing domestic consumption, increasing production, and therefore, expanding exports to $(Q_7 - Q_6)$. Thus, an internal event in one country is transmitted to another country through changes in prices in the international market.

It should be clear that the slopes of the excess supply and demand functions depend on the slopes of the domestic supply and demand functions. The slope of the excess functions are equal to the sum of the (absolute values of the) slopes of the domestic supply and demand functions. Therefore, at any given price, the elasticities of the excess functions are a weighted sum of the elasticities of the parent functions. If domestic supply in the exporting country is perfectly inelastic, the slope of the excess supply function is equal to the absolute value of the slope of the domestic demand function. Similarly, if domestic demand in the importing country is perfectly inelastic, then the slope of the new excess demand function is equal to the negative of the slope of domestic supply function. Conversely, the greater the slopes of the domestic supply and demand functions, the greater the slope of the excess functions.

As the world is not made up of a single exporter and a single importer, it is necessary in most situations to use a model of multilateral trading. This can be accomplished by simply adding the excess demand and supply sched-

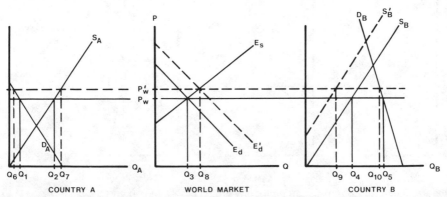

Figure 2-2 Transmission of supply shocks in single-commodity model.

ules of additional exporters and importers. The addition of more countries increases the slope of the world export supply and import demand functions relative to the slope of individual country functions. Thus, it is likely that even if there exist highly price-unresponsive functions in individual countries, the responsiveness of the aggregate excess functions will be quite high in a market with many trading countries.

B Trade Elasticities

It will be useful later on to have at hand the equations that lie behind these graphs. To develop these, we can, as in most economic models, start with an identity, add some behavioral equations, establish an equilibrium position where ex ante behavior is consistent with the ex post identity, and then express the set of equations in the form of relationships among variables. First, we need the identities. In the absence of any carry-over between years, we know that

$$S_w \equiv D_w \qquad (2\text{-}1)$$

where S_w is total world supply and D_w is total world demand. For any one country, in an open system, supply and demand can differ by the amount traded:

$$S_A + M_A \equiv D_A + X_A \qquad (2\text{-}2)$$

where M_A is imports into Country A and X_A is exports from that country. The left-hand side of the identity is total availability and the right-hand side is total disappearance of the commodity. These identities will always hold ex post (subject to measurement errors): The same relationships can be thought of as ex ante equilibrium or market clearing conditions. For the countries trading with each other:

$$S_A - D_A \equiv X_A - M_A \equiv M_B - X_B \equiv D_B - S_B \qquad (2\text{-}3)$$

Let Country A be a net exporter and Country B a net importer. Then for convenience we can define X_A and M_B as net exports and imports, respectively, and simplify the identities to

$$S_A - D_A \equiv X_A \equiv M_B \equiv D_B - S_B \qquad (2\text{-}4)$$

Again, this represents the ex ante market clearing equilibrium.

We can add the behavioral functions by assuming that (as in the diagrams) all prices are the same throughout the system:

$$S_A = S_A (P, \ldots) \qquad\qquad\qquad\qquad\qquad (2\text{-}5)$$
$$D_A = D_A (P, \ldots) \qquad\qquad\qquad\qquad\qquad (2\text{-}6)$$
$$S_B = S_B (P, \ldots) \qquad\qquad\qquad\qquad\qquad (2\text{-}7)$$
$$D_B = D_B (P, \ldots) \qquad\qquad\qquad\qquad\qquad (2\text{-}8)$$

where nonprice arguments are omitted for convenience. Therefore, we can write X_A and M_B as a function of price:

$$X_A = X_A (P, \ldots) = S_A (P, \ldots) - D_A (P, \ldots) \qquad\qquad (2\text{-}9)$$
$$M_b = M_B (P, \ldots) = D_B (P, \ldots) - S_B (P, \ldots) \qquad\qquad (2\text{-}10)$$

Since price changes are needed to restore the system to balance after any disturbance, we need to establish the sensitivity of quantities to price changed (i.e., the slopes of the lines in the diagrams).

$$\frac{dX_A}{dP} = \frac{dS_A}{dP} - \frac{dD_A}{dP} \qquad\qquad\qquad\qquad (2\text{-}11)$$

$$\frac{dM_B}{dP} = \frac{dD_B}{dP} - \frac{dS_B}{dP} \qquad\qquad\qquad\qquad (2\text{-}12)$$

It is common to translate these price sensitivities into elasticities, in part because this frees the expressions from dependence upon the units chosen. Thus,

$$E_{X_A,P} = \frac{dX_A}{dP} \cdot \frac{P}{X_A} \qquad\qquad\qquad\qquad (2\text{-}13)$$

$$E_{M_B,P} = \frac{dM_B}{dP} \cdot \frac{P}{M_B} \qquad\qquad\qquad\qquad (2\text{-}14)$$

where $E_{X_A,P}$ is the elasticity of X_A with respect to P, etc.

This can then be written in terms of the domestic elasticities of supply and demand with respect to price:

$$E_{X_A,P} = \left(\frac{dS_A}{dP} \cdot \frac{P}{X_A} \cdot \frac{S_A}{S_A} \right) - \left(\frac{dD_A}{dP} \cdot \frac{P}{X_A} \cdot \frac{D_A}{D_A} \right) \qquad (2\text{-}15)$$

$$= E_{S_A,P} \cdot \left(\frac{S_A}{X_A} \right) - E_{D_A,P} \cdot \left(\frac{D_A}{X_A} \right)$$

$$E_{M_B,P} = \left(\frac{dD_B}{dP} \cdot \frac{P}{M_B} \cdot \frac{D_B}{D_B} \right) - \left(\frac{dS_B}{dP} \cdot \frac{P}{M_B} \cdot \frac{S_B}{S_B} \right) \qquad (2\text{-}16)$$

$$= E_{D_B,P} \cdot \left(\frac{D_B}{M_B} \right) - E_{S_B,P} \cdot \left(\frac{S_B}{M_B} \right)$$

where the terms (S_A/S_A), etc., are introduced without changing the values of the right-hand terms in order to arrive at the weighted elasticity. The terms (S_A/X_A), etc., are the weights that must be applied to the domestic supply and demand elasticities to get to the elasticity of trade with respect to price.

III IMPACTS OF DOMESTIC POLICY ON INTERNATIONAL MARKETS

The analysis to date has assumed no government intervention in the domestic food and agricultural sector. Governments intervene in the food and agricultural sector for a variety of reasons including price and income enhancement for producers, subsidization of consumer prices, implicit and explicit taxation of the sector, transfers of income and many others. These interventions, whether by exporters or importers, by definition alter that country's interface with world markets and therefore alter conditions in world markets as seen by other countries. Two impacts can be distinguished: the effect on the world price level and the consequence for world price stability. The impact on price levels depends upon ther relationship between domestic and international prices. The implication for stability arises from the extent to which the domestic price is fixed by policy or is allowed to react to the changes in the world price level. In this section we add the instruments of intervention to our simple model of commodity and country linkages.

A Per-Unit Subsidies and Taxes

First consider the imposition by the importing countries of a per-unit tariff on imports. As shown in Figure 2-3, the imposition by Country B of a tariff equal to t essentially shifts their excess demand downward by the amount of

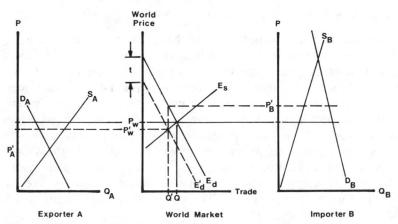

Figure 2-3 Impact of tariff on domestic and world market prices.

the tariff to E'_d. World price, and hence, the price in the exporting country falls to P'_A; price in the importing country rises to P'_B (they differ by t) and the volume of trade falls to Q' from Q. The result would be the same in terms of domestic prices and quantities (but not of government revenues) if Country A applied an export tax equal to t (analytically one would shift the excess supply function upwards by t). The world price, however, would rise in this case, to the level in the importing country. Intervention reduces trade, with a tariff decreasing world prices and an export tax increasing them. The tariff raises prices in the importing country by making imported products more expensive: It represents a combined producer subsidy and consumer tax. The export tax represents a producer tax combined with a consumer subsidy in the exporting country.

Import subsidies and export subsidies have just the opposite effects to trade taxes. In the diagram (Figure 2-3) these policies would shift the import demand curve upward or the export supply curve downward, leading to an increase in total trade. An import subsidy raises the world price, benefiting the exporter, and an export subsidy would lower the world prices to the advantage of the importer. The same analysis can be applied to domestic taxes and subsidies applied on the internal market, rather than at the border. The horizontal shift in the trade curves in Figure 2-3 will, under these conditions, merely be the quantity effect of the domestic tax/subsidy measure. All other results follow by analogy.

Policies of this nature, which shift the trade curves by a fixed amount per unit, do not alter the stability of market prices (in terms of absolute price variations). The slope of the excess demand and supply curves is preserved. Consequently, any exogenous shift in supply (for instance) in the market will have the same price change effect as with free trade. Per-unit protection shifts world price but does not alter its variance.

B Fixed Domestic Prices

Per-unit taxes and subsidies do not cover all the types of policies used in agricultural markets; governments are much more inventive in their kinds of intervention. One other type of intervention is particularly important. Countries often take direct, rather than indirect, action to regulate internal prices. Governments can fix producer or consumer prices directly, or they achieve similar ends by controlling trade prices at the border. These fixed prices could have a *producer bias,* i.e., producer prices above world prices, a *consumer bias,* i.e., consumer prices below world prices, or both. A brief taxonomy is presented in Table 2-1 which shows for importers and exporters what these various options might be. The examples of policies given in the bottom line are only illustrations. There are other instruments which could lead to the same results. The following sections attempt to shed light on the impacts of such fixed-price policies on world commodity markets.

Table 2-1 Taxonomy of Government Policies with Respect to Producer and Consumer Prices

Level of domestic price	Importers								Exporters			
	1	2	3	4	5	6	7	8	9	10	11	12
High (above W_p)	$\bar{P}_p\,\bar{P}_c$	$\bar{P}_p$	$\bar{P}_p$					$\bar{P}_p\,\bar{P}_c$	$\bar{P}_p$	$\bar{P}_p$		
World price	P_c	P_c		P_p		$P_p\,P_c$	$P_p\,P_c$		P_c		P_p	
Low (below W_p)	$\bar{P}_c$		$\bar{P}_c$	$\bar{P}_c$	$\bar{P}_p\,\bar{P}_c$					$\bar{P}_c$	$\bar{P}_c$	$\bar{P}_c\,\bar{P}_p$
Examples of policies	Variable import levies	Deficiency payments	State marketing	Variable consumer subsidies	Variable import subsidies	Free trade	Free trade	Variable export subsidies	Deficiency payment	State marketing	Variable consumer subsidies	Variable export taxes

P_p = producer price-variable; $\bar{P}_p$ = producer price-fixed or minimum
P_c = consumer price-variable; $\bar{P}_c$ = consumer price-fixed or maximum

43

The main difference between a tariff on the one hand and fixed domestic
or trade prices on the other is that the latter have the effect of changing the
slope of the excess supply function with respect to world market prices
(Johnson, 1975; Jones and Thompson, 1978; Josling, 1981). This is shown
in Figure 2-4. If the country fixed the price to producers at $\bar{P}_p$ (and allows
consumers to buy at world prices), the domestic supply function S'_A becomes
vertical relative to world prices. Thus, the excess supply function rotates to
E'_s. In other words, intervention has decreased the slope of the excess supply function (i.e., made it more inelastic). If, instead, the exporting country
guaranteed $\bar{P}_p$ as a *minimum* producer price, the domestic supply function
would follow S'_A below that price and S_A above it; the excess supply function
would also be kinked at the intervention price. If the government also made
consumers pay the fixed price $\bar{P}_p$ then domestic demand relative to world
prices would be D'_A. The combination of fixed producer and consumer price
would yield a perfectly inelastic excess supply function E''_s. This result
follows directly from the fact that the domestic price intervention *isolates*
domestic prices from world prices: Available export supply is strictly a function of domestic price and not at all of world prices. There are many other
possible combinations of fixed and guaranteed producer and consumer
prices that an exporter could use but these should be sufficient to illustrate
the point.

Consider now an importer which fixes producer prices at $\bar{P}_p$, as shown
in Figure 2-5. Domestic supply relative to world prices is perfectly inelastic
and is shown as S'_B. This rotates the importer's import demand function to
E'_d, assuming that consumers can continue to buy at world prices. With a
minimum guaranteed producer price, the domestic supply curve and the import demand curve would be kinked at that minimum price, following the

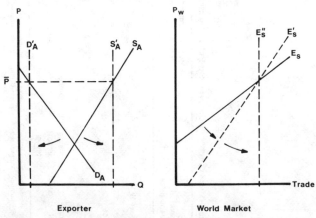

Figure 2-4 Impact on excess supply of exporter fixed-price policies.

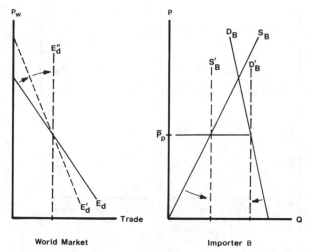

Figure 2-5 Impact on excess demand of importer fixed-price policies.

normal curves above that minimum price. If, in addition, the importing country made consumers pay the fixed price $\bar{P}_p$, the domestic demand would rotate to D'_B and excess demand would be E''_d which is perfectly inelastic with respect to world price.

Figure 2-6 illustrates the range of possibilities, with producer and consumer prices being either variable (i.e., market determined), or fixed (by policy) for both exporters and importers. In each case, domestic price intervention alters the shape of excess supply and demand functions. In all cases, it makes some part of the function steeper and in the extreme cases of fixed producer and consumer prices, makes the functions perfectly inelastic. Intervention creates the possibility of complex trade responses to world market price changes because of the "kinks" introduced into the functions.

Using these results we can see the impacts of such policy intervention on world markets. Suppose there is one exporter and one importer of wheat and that each pursues a policy of guaranteeing producers a fixed price of $\bar{P}_p$ above the free-trade price P^*_w. In the case of both the exporter and the importer, it is assumed that consumers buy at the world price. This case is shown in Figure 2-7. The result of intervention is to rotate and make the excess supply and demand functions more inelastic. The world price is lowered, as with the per-unit tariff policies discussed above, but now an additional impact of the policy is apparent. The steeper trade curves will add to market instability. Any shock to this market will result in larger absolute price changes. Unlike the fixed tariffs, taxes, and subsidies, fixed domestic price policies increase the variance of world market prices as well as altering

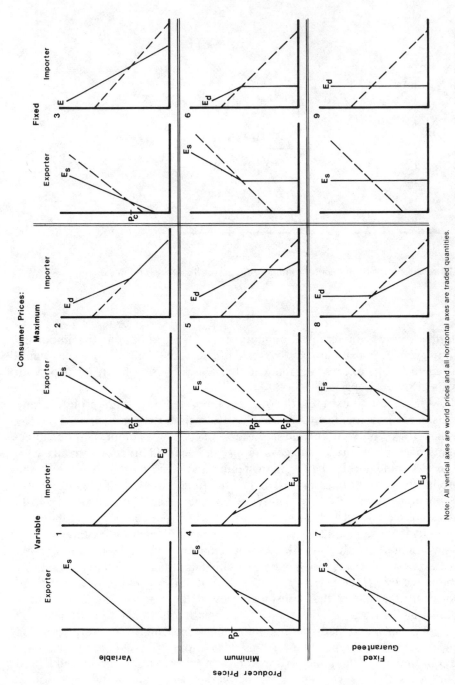

Note: All vertical axes are world prices and all horizontal axes are traded quantities.

Figure 2-6 Impacts of consumer and producer price policies on excess supply and excess demand.

46

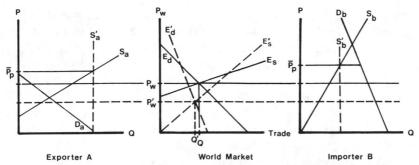

Figure 2-7 World market impacts of guaranteed producer prices.

the mean. Traded quantity can either increase or decrease, depending upon the relative slopes of the trade functions.

If countries were to fix the price to consumers as well as to producers, net excess supply and demand functions would become perfectly inelastic with respect to world price. In the two-country case, this would result in market failure with either no equilibrium or an infinity of solutions if, by chance, the trade functions coincided (Josling, 1977). This extreme patho- logical case of market failure would be improbable with more than two coun- tries participating in the market, as it is unlikely that all countries would fix both producer and consumer prices.

The transmission of supply shocks (and also demand shocks) through- out the trading system depends upon the slopes of the import demand and export supply curves: They in effect summarize the domestic adjustments to the supply shock. The central problem created by the tendency of countries to fix domestic prices, for producers, consumers or both, lies in the fact that such policies (by intention) lessen domestic quantity adjustments. Thus, a greater price change on world markets is necessary to clear the market fol- lowing any given supply (or demand) shock. This extra price instability rep- resents an externality relative to the national decision to stabilize price: The instability falls on other parts of the market outside the immediate concern of the policy maker.

C Importing and Exporting Instability

One can usefully distinguish two different situations with respect to the ex- ternality involved in domestic price stabilization. One would be where the supply shock (or demand shock) is within the "stabilized" country, and the other where such a shock is in other parts of the world system. If the shock is internal, one can talk of exporting or transmitting instability to the rest of the world if the world market is made more unstable as a result of that country's policy (active destabilization). If the shock is external, then the stabilized country could be said to be avoiding the import of instability by means of its domestic policy (passive destabilization). Analytically, the two cases are similar; politically they may carry very different connotations.

It may be worthwhile to formalize these concepts with the aid of the diagrams already used in this chapter. Figure 2-8 reproduces Figure 2-2 which illustrated the transmission of a supply shortfall in the importing country, and adds a similar situation where the supply shock is in the exporting country. The distribution of the adjustment to the supply change can be clearly seen in the world market segments of the diagrams. The supply shock in Country B shifts the import demand curve out by the full amount of the disturbance (E_d to E_d' in Figure 2-8a), but at that price level there is excess

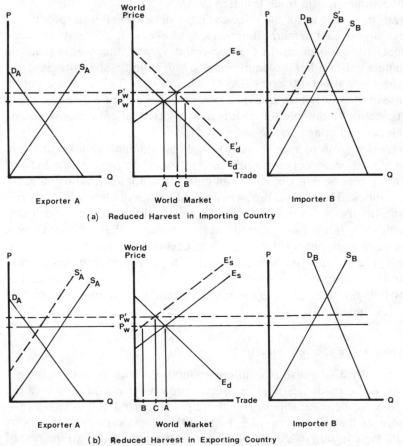

Figure 2-8 Distribution of the effects of supply shocks among countries.

demand. The price rises (in the world market and in both countries) to dampen the demand and stimulate supply. The new equilibrium quantity traded is at C. The movement from A to C can thus be decomposed into

A → B   Supply shock in importing country
B → C   Reduced import demand due to price increase
A → C   Increased export supply due to price increase

Hence, we can refer to the quantity AC as being the amount of the instability "exported," whereas BC was internalized on the domestic market. This occurs not through any policy intervention, but as a reflection of the size of the country in relation to the market.

The case of a supply shock in the exporter market can be handled in the same way. The reduction in domestic supply in Country A shifts back the world export supply curve by the amount (A → B). Quantity BC is released from the exporter's domestic market (the extra exports stimulated by the price increase), and quantity A → C is transmitted to world markets and "imported" by the importing country (as the only other actor in world markets in this example). In both importer and exporter shocks, we can define the proportion of the domestic supply shift that is passed onto world markets to be AC/AB while the proportion that is absorbed on the domestic market of the disturbing country is BC/AB.

It should now be clear what the effect is of domestic price-fixing policies. Figure 2-9a shows the importer supply shock in the presence of a fixed domestic price in the exporting country. The price rise in the world market elicits no export supply response because it is not allowed to impinge upon the exporters domestic sector. Thus, none of the adjustments is transmitted from the importing country. In this example, the importer must make all the adjustments to the shortfall, choking off the higher demand by increases in price. If, however, it is the importing country that has the fixed price policy—as in the Figure 2-9b—then all of the instability is transmitted. No adjustment takes place in the importing country. The price rises in the exporting country to meet the increased level of imports.

Figure 2-9c and d illustrates the case of exporter-generated instability. In Figure 2-9c, the importer has fixed domestic prices and hence imports none of the instability emanating from the exporter. In Figure 2.9d, the exporter has the fixed-price policy and hence exports all the instability onto world markets. Fixed-price policies, by transmitting all domestic instability in production, impose all the burdens on world markets and hence on other countries. Whereas at times this effect may be beneficial to world markets, as when one country's output is negatively correlated with that of the rest of the world, for any given output disturbance the result will be to destabilize world prices.

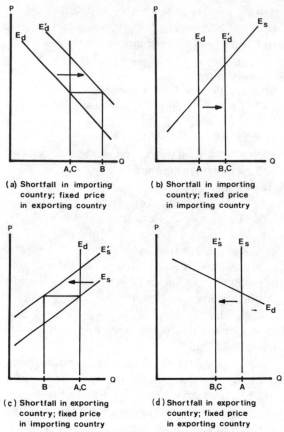

Figure 2-9 Price-fixing policies and their effects on the distribution of supply shocks.

D Price Transmission

This analysis has concentrated on quantity adjustments. It is useful sometimes to express the same relationships in terms of price adjustments. In Figure 2-8, in the absence of policy interventions, the change in price in each
country corresponded to the change in the world price:

$$\Delta P_A = \Delta P_w = \Delta P_B$$

The transmission of prices from world markets to domestic markets was
unhampered. However, in Figure 2-9 this is clearly not the case. In Figure
2-9a and d the world price determines prices in the importing but not in the
exporting country; in Figure 2-9b and c it is the exporting country which adjusts to world price changes while the importer isolates domestic producers

and consumers from that impact. A "pure" fixed-price policy in a country leads to a zero price-transmission elasticity (Bredahl, Meyers, and Collins, 1979) of domestic price with respect to world price, which can be written as:

$$E_{P_d, P_w} = 0$$

whereas a free market policy (or an *ad valorem* tariff) leads to an elasticity of unity:

$$E_{P_d, P_w} = 1$$

These price-transmission elasticities are now widely used in empirical models of trade to link domestic prices with those on world markets.

E Stocks and Stability

So far, our analysis has assumed that markets clear in one time period without any storage from one period to another. Stocks play an important part in the process of distributing instability and reducing the impact of supply (and demand) shocks in an open system. To incorporate stocks we need only to modify the identities used above for examining the trade equilibrium. Instead of Equations (2-1) and (2-4)

$$S_w \equiv D_w$$

for the world, and

$$S_A - D_A \equiv X_A \equiv M_B \equiv D_B - S_B$$

for countries A and B, we now need to add two more variables:

CI   For stocks "carried-in" from previous periods
CO   For stocks "carried-out" to the next period

Thus, the identities become

$$S_w + CI_w = D_w + CO_w \tag{2-17}$$
$$S_A + CI_A - D_A - CO_A \equiv X_A \equiv M_B \equiv D_B + CO_B - S_B - CI_B \tag{2-18}$$

Collecting the terms CI and CO together by identifying $C = CO - CI$ as the increase in stocks, we have

$$S_w \equiv D_w + C_w \tag{2-19}$$
$$S_A - D_A - C_A \equiv X_A \equiv M_B \equiv D_B - S_B + C_B \tag{2-20}$$

If C is positive, there will be a build-up of stocks. It will then appear as additional current demand and have the same sign as demand in the equations. Unlike D, C can be negative although CO cannot be less than zero. The carry-out function CO will, in general, depend upon price. If, for convenience, we ignore other potential arguments in the function, we can write

$$CO = CO(P, \dots) \tag{2-21}$$

and hence, since CI is exogenous, we have

$$C = CO(P, \dots) - CI = C(P, \dots) \tag{2-22}$$

Carry-out will, like current demand, generally be negatively related to current price. The lower the price, the more likely one can sell later at a profit; the higher the current price the less likely it is that future prices will be high enough to give a capital gain on the stocks. Equations (2-9) and (2-10) now read

$$X_A = X_A(P, \dots) = S_A(P, \dots) - D_A(P, \dots) - C_A(P, \dots) \tag{2-23}$$
$$M_B = M_B(P, \dots) = D_B(P, \dots) - S_B(P, \dots) + C_B(P, \dots) \tag{2-24}$$

Corresponding changes in Equations (2-11) and (2-12) lead to the stock-inclusive definitions of the trade elasticities:

$$E_{X_A,P} = E_{S_A,P}\left(\frac{S_A}{X_A}\right) - E_{D_A,P}\left(\frac{D_A}{X_A}\right) - E_{C_A,P}\left(\frac{C_A}{X_A}\right) \tag{2-25}$$

$$E_{M_B,P} = E_{M_B,P}\left(\frac{D_B}{M_B}\right) - E_{S_B,P}\left(\frac{S_B}{M_B}\right) + D_{C_B,P}\left(\frac{C_B}{M_B}\right) \tag{2-26}$$

Reverting to the diagrammatic representation of these relationships, we can conveniently add the carry-in, CI, to the current supply and the carry-out to current demand in the domestic diagrams and draw the excess demand and supply curves as being the difference between these stock-adjusted functions. The slope of the CO function in the exporting country adds to the slope of X_A, and that of the CO function in the importing country increases the slope of M_B. This additional price responsiveness of trade volumes gives the expected increase in stability to the system in the presence of stocks. This is illustrated in Figure 2-10, where the "nonstock" trade curves, $X_A = S_A - D_A$ and $M_B = D_B - S_B$ are less price responsive than the stock-inclusive curves, $X_A = S_A - D_A - C_A$ and $M_B = D_B - S_B + C_B$.

It is also straightforward to incorporate stocks into the analysis of the exportation or importation of instability. If the carry-out function responds to world prices, then an exporting or an importing country will normally build

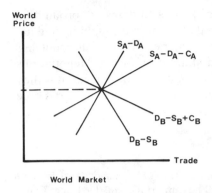

World
Price

S_A-D_A

$S_A-D_A-C_A$

$D_B-S_B+C_B$

D_B-S_B

Trade

World Market

Figure 2-10 Impact of stocks on excess demand and supply curves.

up stocks in times of adequate world supplies, and release them in times of scarcity, even if no response is forthcoming from domestic production or consumption. Unfortunately for world price stability, private stockholders usually will respond to domestic price signals rather than those on the international market. Government stocks are more likely to be world-price sensitive in these circumstances, effectively placing the government in the role of speculator but having the advantage of helping to dampen world price movements. One could, for instance, devise an "active" stocks policy which exactly offsets the negative effect on price stability of domestic fixed-price policies. More commonly, stocks policies react to domestic production fluctuations. Thus, the export of instability may well be less than in the absence of stocks. Again, the private stockholder will have little incentive to vary stocks with domestic production if prices are fixed or supported within narrow bands. The government may well engage in price-stabilizing speculative behavior by increasing stocks at times of adequate domestic supply, though this may not be "good" speculation if, at the same time, aggregate world supply is down.

IV SUMMARY

This analysis has focused on intercountry linkages through a single-commodity market. More complex links are discussed in the next chapter, taking into account the substitutability among products. The key conclusion from the analysis is that domestic policies distort the free-trade excess demand and supply curves, which in turn determine the level and behavior of the market-clearing world price. This is significant for all countries. Small countries, in the sense of their limited size in relation to world trade for a particular commodity, have to be aware of the impact that other countries' policies have on world market conditions. For larger countries, the shape of the trade curves facing them offer the possibilities of actively using policy to enhance domestic objectives. The responsiveness of stocks to domestic production variations and to world prices is an additional element in the stability and nature of the market. At an international level, the net effect of all countries' policies shows up in terms of the level and stability of prices. Negotiations on trade liberalization and price stability must take this into account if they are to be meaningful. These international aspects are taken up in Part Three of this book.

REFERENCES

Bredahl, M. E., Meyers, W. H., and Collins, K. J. 1979. "The Elasticity of Foreign Demand for U.S. Agricultural Products: The Importance of the Price Transmission Elasticity," *Amer. J. Agr. Econ.,* **61**:58–63.

Johnson, D. G. 1975. "World Agriculture, Commodity Policy, and Price Variability, *Amer. J. Agr. Econ.,* **57**:823–828.

Jones, B. F., and Thompson, R. L. 1978. "Interrelationships of Domestic Agricultural Policies and Trade Policies, in *Speaking of Trade: Its Effect on Agriculture,* Special Report No. 72, Agricultural Extension Service, University of Minnesota, pp. 37–58.

Josling, T. 1977. "Government Price Policies and the Structure of International Trade,"*J. Agr. Econ.,* **28**:261-277.

———. 1981. "Domestic Agricultural Price Policies and their Interaction Through Trade," in A. F. McCalla and T. E. Josling, (eds.) *Imperfect Markets in Agricultural Trade,* Allanheld, Osmun, Montclair, N.J., pp. 49–68.

ADDITIONAL READINGS

Corden, W. M. 1971. *The Theory of Protection,* Clarendon Press, Oxford.

McCalla, A. F., and Learn, E. 1967. "Non-Equilibrium Fixed Price Schemes in Agricultural Trade," *Ag. Econ. Res.,* **19**:111–116.

Shei, S-Y, and Thompson, R. L. 1977. "The Impact of Trade Restrictions on Price Stability in the World Wheat Market," *Amer. J. Agr. Econ.,* **59**:628–638.

Chapter 3

Linkages Through Commodities and Policies

I INTRODUCTION

The single-commodity analysis of the previous chapter is valuable as a first step in developing a policy analysis framework. In this chapter we develop the analytical framework to look at intercommodity interdependence, using a two-commodity model to illustrate cross-commodity linkages within and between countries. Simple graphic analysis can handle the two-commodity case and provide useful insights. Generalization beyond two commodities is conceptually possible but we stop short of such a complete formal model.

The next step is to introduce policy intervention at the national level. In the two-commodity cases we have to consider both commodity-specific and sectorwide policies. The final section looks at the impacts of macro policies and their linkages to agriculture both within and between countries. In all cases our analysis is essentially a large-country situation as we are working explicitly with sloping excess supply and demand functions. In later chapters, we directly address the small-country case, but here it is most useful to proceed directly to large-country analysis.

II MULTICOMMODITY LINKAGES

No country produces and consumes only one commodity. Therefore, policy analysis must attempt to take into account relevant intercommodity linkages and interdependencies. In the real multicommodity world, these linkages abound. Thus, policy options are in general constrained by basic biological and physical relationships among commodities. Agricultural production of different commodities competes for scarce resources (land, water, labor, and capital). Consumers seek to maximize satisfaction within a budget constraint by selecting optimal bundles of commodities. The marketing chain between producers and consumers deals in more than one commodity and also provides potential commodity linkages. It follows that the intercommodity linkages cause changes in one commodity to be transmitted *directly* through international markets for that commodity and *indirectly* through closely related commodity markets. The first task, then, is to identify these linkages more precisely. The analysis begins with a taxonomy. It then discusses some examples before turning to a simple model of trade interdependencies.

Most of the important commodity interdependencies can be placed in five categories:

Substitution relationships in production
Input-output relationships in production and processing
Complementary relationships
Substitution and complementary relationships in consumption
Closely related products in marketing and trade channels

Each of these relationships is discussed in turn, with respect to its implications for transmitting price influences among commodites.

A   Substitution in Production

This relationship is fundamental to agricultural supply analysis. Production is constrained by a fixed, or at least a constrained, resource base for agricultural production. The most obvious constraints are land and water, but labor and the availability of inputs may also be limited. Increases in the production of one crop necessarily reduce the resources available to produce other commodities. Examples of such a trade-off are food grains versus feed grains, food versus industrial crops (such as, wheat versus cotton or tobacco), and field crops versus livestock forage. The degree of substitution in part reflects biological and physical possibilities, but it also has an economic component arising from the relative profitability of alternative production activities. Aggregate policy analysis in the multicommodity case, therefore, requires knowledge not only of direct supply elasticities but also of cross-elasticities of supply.

For exposition it is convenient to use a two-commodity, two-country model where one exporting country (Country A) produces both wheat and feed grains. Assume that the importer (Country B) produces wheat but no feed grains. In this way, we can isolate the impact of production substitution since it occurs only in Country A. Ignore, for the present, any substitution which might exist on the consumption side. We can use the trade model introduced in Chapter 2 to illustrate the cross-commodity linkages. For simplicity, one can omit the domestic market diagrams and concentrate on the impact on trade and world prices. Assume no government intervention in either market, and the existence of competitive conditions throughout.

Such a model is depicted in Figure 3-1. Assume initially that the two markets are in simultaneous equilibrium at price P_w in the wheat market and P_f in the feed grain market. The analysis begins by perturbing one market. Suppose because of a rust infestation, Country B's wheat production contracts, i.e., shifts its supply to the left. This results in a shift outward of Country B's excess demand function to E_{dw} (step ① in Figure 3-1). The result will be to increase the world prices for wheat. Wheat exports expand to meet this increased demand. In the corn market, the rise in wheat prices causes corn supply in Country A to decrease. This in turn causes excess supply to shift to E'_{sf} and world corn prices to rise (step ②). The rise in corn price reduces Country A's wheat supply resulting in a shift to the left in the excess supply function to E'_{sw} (step ③). World wheat prices rise. The process continues until new equilibrium prices are reached, shown as P^n_w and P^n_f in Figure 3-1. In time, Country B's production could return to normal, thus setting off the reverse process.

The diagrams presented in Figure 3-1 show that, following the initial disturbance, prices settle down to new equilibrium levels of wheat and feed grain prices where both prices are higher than the original equilibrium—an intuitively reasonable result. But how do we know whether these sequential price adjustments converge to a new stable ratio of wheat to feed grain

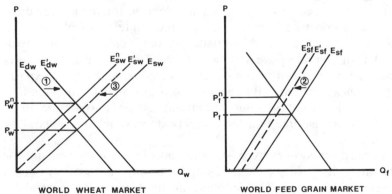

WORLD WHEAT MARKET   WORLD FEED GRAIN MARKET

Figure 3-1 Links through substitution in production: world wheat and feed grain markets.

prices? It can be shown that they will converge if the adjustment coefficients (slopes of demand and supply functions) in the primary market are greater in total than the coefficients of the cross relationships. A change in price in the wheat market causes, in this model, adjustments in the quantity supplied and demanded in both the exporting and importing countries for both commodities. If the magnitudes of the direct adjustments exceed the impact of the cross product, the system will converge to a new static equilibrium.

We have used this simple example to illustrate one set of realtionships, namely substitution in production between two commodities in one country. The process is the same, but more complicated, for the case of more than two countries, more than two commodities, and with substitution in all countries. This case could be worked through in a general equilibrium trade model. Chacholiades (1978, chaps. 3 and 6) discusses conditions for stable equilibrium in a two-country, two-commodity, two-input trade model. He also discusses generalization to m countries and n commodities. The interested reader is referred to his more formal mathematical formulation.

B   Input-Output Relationships in Production and Processing

A second set of interrelationships of obvious importance are those where one commodity is an input (intermediate good) into the production of another commodity. The most obvious example is livestock production where feed grains, oilseed meal, and grass are all inputs into the production of meat and dairy products. In developing countries, crop residues may serve as livestock feed or fuel. At the individual-farm level, these realtionships can be dealt with analytically as having fixed coefficients (Leontief), discrete choice variables (linear programming), or continuous relationships as in neoclassical production theory.

At the aggregate level we do not need to specify the specific form of the relationship. All we need to know is that the demand for the intermediate product is a derived demand from the final product. In terms of international markets we can illustrate the relationship in our two-commodity, two-country model. In Figure 3-2 we assume that the demand for feed grains is directly and positively linked to the demand for meat. Country A exports both commodities and Country B imports both. For simplicity, assume that feed grains and meat are not substitutes in production (or consumption) in either country. Further assume that the markets are in simultaneous equilibrium at P_m and P_f.

Now, perturb the system by postulating an expansion of demand for meat in Country B, perhaps as a result of economic recovery which increases per-capita income. The increase in the demand for meat shifts the import demand outward to E'_{dm} (step ①). Let us assume for simplicity that the current time period is sufficiently long to allow production adjust-

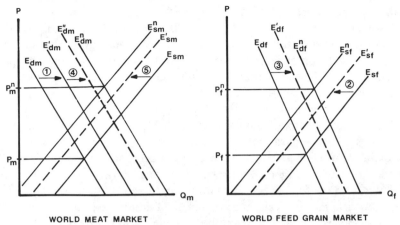

WORLD MEAT MARKET   WORLD FEED GRAIN MARKET

Figure 3-2 Input-output linkages: world meat and feed grain markets.

ment in both meat and feed grains. We also need to ignore the possibility of a negative short-run supply response to meat prices, even though such a response is often observed empirically. The shift in excess demand to E'_{dm} causes world meat prices to rise. Given the input-output relationship postulated in both countries the increase in world meat prices shifts the demand for feed grains outwards in both countries. This would shift the excess demand function of Country B to the right to E'_{df} (step ③). Both shifts reinforce the rise in world feed grain prices. In this case, the price change is large but quantities traded would change relatively little because demand expansion in both exporter and importer have offsetting effects. The higher feed price on world markets would increase meat production costs, expanding import demand (E''_{dm}, step ④) and contracting export supply (E''_{sm}, step ⑤) in the world meat markets. A new equilibrium would be established with higher prices for both meat and feed grains (P_m^n and P_f^n).

C Complementary Relationships in Production

Several kinds of complementary relationships in production can be identified, each of which has impacts on interdependencies in international markets. The first is when there are joint product relationships. Examples include the cases of wool and sheep meat, oilseed meal and vegetable oil from oilseeds, and, in many parts of the world, dairy products and meat from dual purpose animals. A second category is that of complements as inputs in producing a final product. Here the case of feed grains and oilseed meal in livestock production is probably the dominant one. Thus, the demand for corn and soybean meal are jointly derived demands from the demand for meat. A third category relates to intercrop relationships in farming systems, of which two types can be identified. The first includes sequential relationships such as multiyear crop rotations which alternate grain and other crops and multiple cropping, e.g., winter and summer crops, within a cropping year. The second case is that of simultaneous production of several crops in symbiotic intercropping relationships, such as is common in small-farm and subsistence agriculture in developing countries.

All these kinds of complementary relationships have implications to varying degrees where separate markets exist for the complementary products. The example of vegetable oilseed meal and vegetable oil can be used to illustrate the impacts of an exogenous shock in one market or another. In Figure 3-3 the markets for oilseed meal and vegetable oil are shown. Again simplifying our graphic analysis, we assume instantaneous adjustment for expositional purposes, recognizing that the lagged relationships may in practice apply. Assume that Country A is an exporter of both oilseed meal and oil and that Country B is an importer of both and that the only interconnection between the markets is that oilseed meal and oil are produced in fixed proportions from the original oilseed in the exporting country.

Assume that the increase in demand for meat postulated in the discussion of input-output relationships causes the derived demand for oilseed meal to shift to the right in Country B which shifts the demand for imports to the right to E'_{do} and causes world prices for oilseed meal to rise to P'_o. Given the assumption of fixed proportions in production, the increase in production of oilseed meal in Country A shifts the supply function of oil to the right. Country A's excess supply function shifts to the right to E'_{so}. This response causes world prices of oil to decline to P'_o. The magnitude of the price re-

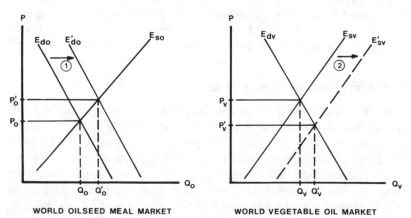

WORLD OILSEED MEAL MARKET   WORLD VEGETABLE OIL MARKET

Figure 3-3 Complementary relationships in production: world oilseed meal and oil markets.

sponse is determined by the fixed proportion ratio. Thus, the ratio of the old and new traded quantities must be the same, i.e., $Q_o/Q_s = Q_o'/Q_s'$. This simplified case is sufficient to illustrate the important implications for trade policy analysis. If complementary relationships exist between commodities for which there are separate international markets, then shocks which cause prices to increase (decrease) in one market will cause prices in the other market to move in the opposite direction.

D Substitution and Complementary Relationships in Consumption

All the discussion to date has been concerned with intercommodity relationships in production. However, most of these relationships also exist in consumption. Within the food group, poultry meat is to some degree a substitute for pork and pork is a substitute for beef. High fructose corn sweetener is a substitute for sugar. In many developing countries, corn has a substitution relationship with wheat and wheat for rice. Within the feed group, barley substitutes for corn. If wheat prices fall relative to feed grain prices, wheat can be used as a feed grain. There is extensive substitution among oilseed meals as well as among animal sources of protein. In the next chapter, we develop in detail the set of relationships of corn-soymeal feed mixes versus cassava-soymeal feed mixes in the European Community induced by policy price relationships. Here it may suffice to recognize that within the feed complex substitution, input-output and complementary relationships abound.

Detailed graphical analysis of these substitution relationships are not formally included because the analysis would proceed generally along the lines outlined in Figure 3-1 for substitution in production. The difference would be that an increase in prices of, say, beef resulting from a cold winter in an importing country would shift the demand for pork in the pork market to the right, resulting in rising world pork prices. As in the case of production, the same conclusion follows. Markets linked by substitution relationships in consumption cause prices in the two markets to move in the same direction. Issues of stability arise, but again, if the underlying supply and demand functions are well behaved and the magnitudes of the cross-demand coefficients are less than the sum of the slopes of the supply and demand functions, the market would converge to new stable equilibrium prices. Similarly, complementary relationships in consumption will cause international prices in the two markets to move in opposite directions.

On a more macro scale, rises in petroleum prices in the 1970s caused many nations to explore biological sources of energy. In the Unites States, the so-called "gasohol" program sought to use corn as a source of alcohol to blend with gasoline. Brazil pursued a similar program with sugar as the central commodity. Thus, if we identify the three basic demands for agricultural products as food, feed, and energy, the complexity of the levels of consumption substitution becomes clear. Consider, for example, three commodities —wheat, corn, and sugar—and three end uses—food, feed, and energy. Wheat is primarily a food grain but is used as feed if relative prices are attractive. Corn is predominantly a feed grain but is used as a food in many less-developed countries and is considered a possible energy source. Sugar is a food but has recently been used as an energy source particularly in Brazil. The web of relationships is illustrated in Table 3-1. This should clearly show that prices in these three markets should move in predictable relationships in the absence of any intervention. International markets are inextricably linked by substitution (and complementary) relationships among commodities. Therefore, policy analysis must take these relationships into account.

E   Closely Related Products in Marketing and Trade Channels

One final set of interrelationships deserves mention. The infrastructure that handles commodities in international markets is by no means unicommodity-oriented. International transportation systems (rail, truck, ship, and barge) handle a variety of commodities simultaneously. Thus, expansion in the trade of one, given capacity constraints, necessarily impacts on others. Similarly, processing firms often handle multiple commodities. International traders handle many commodities. For example, the large multinational grain trading houses simultaneously handle wheat, feed grains, and oilseeds among other things. International transportation handles similar commodities. Bulk carriers can and do haul all types of dry commodities. Refrigerated carriers can carry meat (processed or frozen), dairy products, fruits, and so on. These interrelationships represent an additional set of constraints on the functioning of international markets which move products on the long chain between the primary producer and the final consumer.

F   Multicommodity Linkages in Summary

The foregoing series of partial analyses of various kinds of commodity linkages were presented in sequential fashion to allow us to dissect and understand how international markets for pairs of commodities are interconnected and therefore how disturbances in one country in one commodity are transmitted through trade to other countries and to other commodities. But in the real world of international trade in most temperate zones, agricultural commodity markets are linked in various ways, involving substitution, complementary, and input-output relationships simultaneously in many countries for many commodities. The inclusion of more commodities and countries is

Table 3-1 Substitution in Consumption

	Food (direct consumption)	Feed (livestock production)	Energy uses
Wheat	X	x	
Corn	x	X	x
Sugar	X		x

X = dominant use; x = secondary use.

relatively straightforward, particularly in algebraic form. Graphics, however, become less useful. However, the information built up in the foregoing analysis should allow us to reason through more involved situations keeping in mind the following general propositions which result from the analysis just completed.

First, price variability in one market is linked by intercommodity relationships (cross elasticities of supply, cross elasticities of demand, and input-output coefficients) to price variations in other commodity markets. In general, happenings in one market will not destabilize other markets (i.e., lead to exploding price cycles) if the slope coefficients of adjustment in the first market are greater in magnitude than the cross-intercommodity relationships. This is an implicit generalization of a multicommodity cobweb.

Second, the magnitude of price movements in one market for a given disturbance depends on the slopes of all countries' supply and demand functions in that market and the magnitude of the cross terms. In general, the more inelastic domestic supply and demand functions are, the more inelastic world supply and demand functions will be. Therefore, price changes will be greater, relative to quantity adjustments.

Third, and offsetting to some extent point two, is the fact that the more countries that participate in a market the more elastic world supply and demand functions will be (as in the single-commodity case). Therefore, world markets should be more stable in terms of price fluctuations than isolated domestic markets.

Fourth, substitution and input-output relationships, whether in production, consumption or both, cause prices in the connected markets to move in the same direction. It is intuitively obvious that the greater the degree (magnitude) of substitution, the more stable both markets will be. Conversely, complementary relationships cause relative price differences between markets to widen.

Fifth, all markets are linked by the four sets of relationships discussed above. In fact, a completely general model should simultaneously take all of these relationships into account. This is not attempted here. Rather we conclude this section by presenting Table 3-2 which attempts to depict how

Table 3-2   World Commodity Market Linkages

	Rice	Feed grains	Oilseeds and oilseed meal	Livestock and meat	Dairy products	Sugar
Wheat	SC, mc	SP, SC, MC	MC, sp, cr	IO, sp, sc	io	sp
Rice	—	sc, mc	sc, mc	cr	io	sp
Feed grains	—	—	CR, SP, MC, sc	IO, sp, sc	IO, sc	SC, SP
Oilseeds and oilseed meal	—	—	—	IO, sp, sc	IO, SC, cr	SP
Livestock and meat	—	—	—	—	CR, sp, sc, MC	io, sp
Diary	—	—	—	—	—	io, cr

Linkages:	Strong	Weak
Substitutes in production	SP	sp
Substitutes in consumption	SC	sc
Input-output relationship	IO	io
Complements (relationships) in production	CR	cr
Closely related in marketing channels	MC	mc

the markets for the seven commodity groups in the analysis are linked by intercommodity relationships.

III   IMPACTS OF DOMESTIC POLICY ON WORLD MARKETS: THE MULTICOMMODITY CASE

Section II dealt with the problem of interdependence between commodity markets linked by substitution, complementary, and input-output relationships. In this section, the analysis is modified to take into account policy intervention by one or more countries. Policy intervention not only introduces discontinuities into economic relationships, but it also greatly increases the range of possible scenarios that could be considered. Therefore, we work through one case to get a flavor of the analytical approach, and leave the task of introducing policy interventions in other cases to the reader.

A   Substitution in Production and Policy Intervention

Suppose, as before, that there is substitution in production in the exporting country (Country A) between wheat and feed grains and there is one importer (Country B) who produces only wheat but imports feed grains as well. Two stages of the analysis of policy intervention are necessary: the first illustrating the effect of intervention on world price levels and the second exploring the implications for price stability. First, suppose a free market prevailed in both wheat and feed grains and simultaneous equilibrium existed with prices P_w and P_f in the wheat and feed grains markets, respectively (see Figure 3-4). Intervention by Country A to guarantee wheat producers a minimum price $\overline{PP}_w$ via a system of deficiency payments (therefore, allowing consumers to buy at world prices) would make Country A's supply function perfectly inelastic with respect to world prices below PP_w. Thus, the excess supply function $(E_{sw} - E'_{sw})$ is kinked at $\overline{PP}_w$. Two results would occur: Prices in the world wheat market would fall to P'_w (and volume would increase) and Country A's supply function of feed grains would shift to the left to S'_{fa} as some resources formerly involved in feed grain production shift to wheat. The result would be that world feed grain price would rise to P'_f. This would be the complete adjustment if there were no further shocks. To recapitulate, intervention in Country A's wheat market lowers world wheat prices (and expands trade) and increases world feed grain prices (and contracts trade).

Second, assume this new "after intervention" equilibrium, Country B experiences a bad wheat crop, shifting its domestic supply, thus increasing import demand to E'_{dw} (Figure 3-5) which causes world wheat prices to rise to P''_w. The magnitude of the price change is greater than it would have been in the absence of Country A's intervention. Thus, intervention increases world wheat market price variability. However, unless the shift in Country B's wheat supply is sufficient to raise world prices above $\overline{PP}_w$, the stochastic shock in Country B's wheat market has *no effect on prices in world feed grain markets* because Country A's producers have already adjusted production to take into account the support price of wheat. Therefore, the result of intervention and subsequent perturbations in this simple model causes world wheat and feed grain prices to move independently by isolating the world feed grain market from the world wheat market. Therefore, intervention in the wheat market has *stabilized* the feed grain market relative to shocks in the wheat market.

B General Results of Intervention

The preceding result, which seems to suggest that there are positive externalities to other markets of intervention in one market, becomes stronger if all countries intervene in the wheat market. Excess supply and demand functions become steeper, therefore, increasing instability. But there is, beyond the initial impact of raising feed grain prices, no impact on the feed grain market of shocks in the wheat market. If countries intervene in both markets, the total effect, as long as internal intervention prices are above world equilibrium prices, is to replace relative prices induced by intercom-

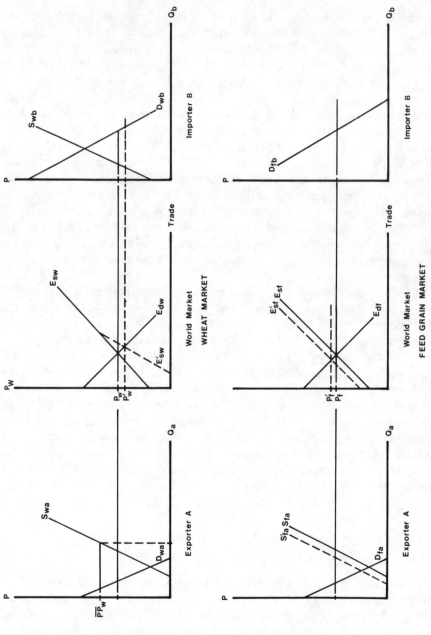

Figure 3-4 Effects of intervention in the domestic wheat market on the world feed grain market.

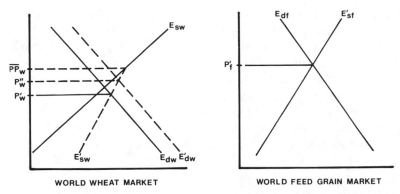

Figure 3-5 Implications of domestic intervention in wheat on transmission of supply shocks to feed grain markets.

modity interrelationships (substitution, complementarity, and input-output) with policy-determined relative prices. The result is to break these continuously changing relative price interconnections with policy-rigid or policy-fixed relative prices subject to policy choice. Therefore, complete intervention isolates domestic markets from world markets and isolates each world commodity market from other commodity markets. This interesting result has two implications. First, single-commodity analysis is not so far off base in a world of administratively set domestic prices. And second, the conclusion that domestic intervention in several commodities increases instability in each of those several commodity markets is in fact true in the total intervention case. It was not true in the case where there was intervention in only some of the markets.

The addition of more commodities and countries does not alter the basic results. Intervention in some markets increases price variability in those markets but tends to reduce it in those markets which do not have intervention. Intervention in all markets destabilizes all markets because all cross-market stabilizing influences are severed by policy-determined prices. Stated more formally, in a world of three-commodity markets linked by, say, substitution relationships, the following propositions are true in the case of an external shock in the first market: (1) If there is intervention in market one but not in markets two and three, market one will have greater price variability (less stable) but markets two and three will be more stable than in the absence of intervention in market one. (2) Intervention in markets one and two but not in market three means that a disturbance in market one destabilizes market one, has no effect on market two, and stabilizes market three relative to the free trade solution. Intervention in all three separates the markets, resulting in increased instability from shocks in that market but eliminates (reduces) instability in one market induced by happenings in another market. On reflection, this is an intuitively reasonable result. In the absence of intervention, the shock in one market is dissipated in all three markets. If intervention reduces intermarket linkages, more of the shock must be absorbed in the primary market and less in other markets. Completely isolating markets forces all of the adjustment into the primary market. Thus, it is not possible to say whether world markets of linked commodities with intervention are more or less vulnerable to exogenous shocks than in a free trade world. This result modifies the results in Chapter 2 (based on single-commodity analysis) that fixed-price intervention always destabilizes markets.

IV CROSS AND GENERIC POLICY LINKAGES

The result of the preceding analysis clearly shows that price intervention in a number of commodity markets essentially replaces market linkages (biological as well as economic) with administered linkages. For example, simultaneous setting of wheat and feed grain support prices in the United States or the European Community predetermines intercommodity and intermarket linkages by presetting relative commodity prices. This fundamentally alters the analytical approaches required to do comprehensive policy analysis. Instead of estimating, say, farmers' responses to continuously changing market prices where presumably future expectations can be rationally included, what is needed are reaction functions of farmers to discrete and often unpredicted policy-induced price changes. Internationally, it does little good for policy makers in one country to estimate supply responses in other countries on the traditional basis of estimating direct and cross elasticities of supply and demand, if policy discontinuities are not explicitly built in. In current jargon, this is called endogenizing government behavior (Abbott, 1979; Rausser et al., 1982) where policy analysis requires policy-maker reaction functions and estimates of their interaction in world markets. This kind of strategic approach may be more attainable by game-theoretic rather than traditional neoclassical approaches (Karp and McCalla, 1983). Suffice it to say that few countries pursue domestic intervention on a single-commodity basis. Rather administered prices for several commodities are set relative to each other in the political arena. These relative policy prices influence world markets in many ways which the framework of analysis developed in this chapter allows us to understand.

There are also a set of food and agricultural policies which are not commodity specific. These can be called generic policies. Examples would include credit policies, research and development policies, consumer subsidies such as food stamps, transportation policies, and input subsidy policies. To include these types of policy in the general framework of analysis of international linkages is relatively straightforward in a conceptual sense. To the extent that a generic policy does not discriminate among commodities, the impact on world markets of such a policy in a particular country would be to shift that country's aggregate supply function or the individual supply functions of all commodities. For example, suppose improved information was provided to all agricultural producers in a country which reduced risk and increased production efficiency. The result would be an increased supply at all prices for all commodities. In the cases of either exporters or importers, the impact on world markets would be to lower prices as net export supply expanded and net import demand contracted. Other participants in the world market would then receive lower prices for all commodities. Or stated conversely, a true generic policy should not alter relative prices within the agricultural sector. Rather, it would have its impact on general price levels.

However, some care would be needed to consider the reactions of the agricultural production sector to "generic" policies. It is unlikely, for example, that research expenditures will be necessarily distributed among commodities in a proportionate way. However, even if they were, it is more unlikely that productivity-increasing technology would be evenly distributed over time. Instead, if research and development resulted in a rapid increase in productivity for one commodity (e.g., hybrid corn), national cropping patterns would be altered which would alter relative prices and would impact on world markets in much the same way as would a specific commodity policy. The difference would be that this type of intervention would not tend to isolate domestic markets from world markets. Another example might be a credit subsidy or a fertilizer subsidy. However, to the extent that different commodities have different production functions, the impacts would alter relative profitability and, therefore, commodity supplies which would alter relative prices. Suffice it to say that generic policies would have impacts on world markets—sometimes across the board and sometimes differentially—and, therefore, on other participants in world markets. National policy analysis would have to take these into account.

V MACROECONOMIC LINKAGES WITHIN AND BETWEEN COUNTRIES

Macroeconomic policies pursued by individual countries can impact on world markets and other countries in two ways (McCalla, 1982). First, a tight money policy pursued in one country, which raised interest rates, would alter the competitiveness of that country's agriculture in general (i.e., increase the costs of production) and could alter the composition of output. Thus, macro policy influences a country's excess supply and/or demand functions. Second, macro policy in a large country, such as the United States, could influence other countries through world capital markets which could alter their competitive positions. Further, to the extent that world commodity markets are linked to capital markets, national macro policy could indirectly effect world commodity prices. A brief discussion of each linkage follows.

Macroeconomic policies are defined as those concerned with economy wide aggregate variables including economic growth, employment, inflation, balance of payments, and the national monetary sector. National governments attempt to manipulate policy instruments to accomplish goals couched in terms of these aggregates. These instruments include (a) fiscal policy—sources and expenditures of government revenue, (b) monetary policy—essentially central bank policy regarding the money supply and interest rates, and (c) international policy through exchange rate and commercial policy.

The impacts of domestic macroeconomic policy on the trade position of a particular country are relatively straightforward. We have already discussed the interest rate effect. Additional impacts are the following: (a) Domestic monetary and fiscal policy can influence interest rates which influences capital flows and, given flexible exchange rates, the value of the currency. An appreciating currency makes exports more expensive to world buyers and imports relatively cheaper to domestic consumers. The implications for agricultural trade are obvious, (exchange rate effect); (b) Fiscal and stabilization policies influence the domestic demand for food commodities in predictable ways. High levels of inflation and unemployment reduce real disposable incomes which reduces demand for high-income elasticity products, e.g., meats. In exporting countries, this expands export supply and it contracts import demand in importing countries. The cumulative effect is to cause world commodity prices to fall (demand effect); (c) Fiscal deficits push up interest rates, which constrain resources available for domestic program expenditure and which, as explained above, influence capital inflows and, therefore, currency values. (d) Macro trade policies such as general tariff levels or other restrictions influence both export supply availability and import demand in predictable ways.

It is not difficult to build these kinds of national policy impacts into the kind of commodity trade analysis developed earlier. They are shifters of net supply and demand functions and could be analyzed in a manner similar to the exogenous shocks postulated in earlier sections. The most difficult part would be to develop empirical estimates of the magnitude of the impact of say a change in the U.S. currency value on the supply of U.S. exports. We defer further discussion of these issues until Chapters 5 and 6 where we look at specific policy alternatives.

The second set of linkages is more complex. They are illustrated by reviewing a possible scenario for the 1970s and early 1980s. Very significant structural changes have occurred in the world economy if one compares the early 1980s to the 1960s. They include (*a*) increases in the volume of international trade relative to gross national product (GNP); *(b)* beginning in the late 1960s, the spectacular growth of the European currency market, which now constitutes a world market for short-term capital and increasingly for intermediate-term credit (McKinnon, 1979); and *(c)* the movement from the fixed exchange rate regime of Bretton-Woods to a complex mix of convertible and pegged currencies under a managed flexible exchange rate system.

As the structure has changed, so has the performance of the world economy. Volatility and instability are the best recent descriptors. Despite predictions that a system of flexible exchange rates should lead, after initial adjustments, to stable exchange rates, instability in exchange rates has, if anything, been increasing. Bursts of worldwide inflation in 1973 to 1974 and 1979 to 1980 have occurred followed by a mild global recession in 1975 to 1976 and a deep recession in 1981 to 1983. International flows of capital suggest a highly integrated, if not perfect, capital market where actors adjust portfolios of currencies and variously denominated financial instruments in response to small expected changes in inflation rates, currency values, and interest rates.

Most developed countries, in particular the United States, continued to try to manage domestic policy variables to stabilize their domestic economies in terms of money supply growth and exchange rates, apparently assuming that global integration had not occurred. The result, argued many economists like McKinnon (1982a, b, c), has been to exacerbate global instability.

The impacts of these kinds of developments on world commodity markets are less well understood. The basic question is whether commodity markets are a medium for the transmission of monetary shocks. Most analysis of commodity trade is conducted within a partial equilibrium framework, where domestic supply and demand functions are estimated and then netted to provide components of world aggregate demand and supply functions. While such an approach requires attention to domestic policy and the exchange rate (Chambers and Just, 1979), there is no place for global macromonetary linkages. Lawrence and Lawrence (1981) have explored the more general question of whether there are relationships between changes in international liquidity and changes in primary commodity prices. They explore three possible links. The first is storable commodities as assets in portfolios which might respond to changing monetary conditions. The second is the impact of international transmission of inflation and recession on aggregate demand (Van Duyne, 1979). The third involves considerations of risk, where portfolio holders may adjust assets to achieve some desired level of variance in portfolio returns. Their tentative conclusions are that there appear to be linkages. First, portfolio preferences induce overshooting of storable commodity prices. Second, real disturbances in terms of, say, the money supply have long-lived effects on prices. In general, their work seems to suggest that global monetary expansion puts upward pressure on commodity prices and that these price changes will be more exaggerated than the money supply changes. The converse presumably is also true; thus, current low commodity price levels may have, in part at least, a global monetary explanation (Schuh, 1982).

As noted earlier, macro impacts on agricultural trade can come about in two ways. First, through linkages between global macro variables and international commodity markets, and second, through the impacts of domestic monetary policy on the net trade position of major importers and exporters of agricultural products. Clearly, in the latter case, the position of the United States deserves special discussion in view of the U.S. dominance in both monetary and agricultural commodity markets.

The cumulative impacts of domestic macro policies on international monetary variables and their linkages to commodity markets already has been discussed. Swings in the international money supply are related in a direct and amplified fashion to changes in storable commodity prices. If this tentative finding is coupled with traditional agricultural trade analysis which shows that domestic policy intervention increases world commodity market instability by making excess supply and demand functions more inelastic (Johnson, 1975; Josling, 1981), we have a better explanation, hopefully, of commodity price instability in the 1970s and early 1980s.

If inflation and recession are global phenomena, then the demand impacts through income may be as large or larger than price impacts that come about through exchange rate changes. If they move in the same direction, the impact on particular traders could be severe.

The complexity of the case is best illustrated by focusing on the impact of U.S. macro policy on agricultural trade. The United States in the period 1979 to 1982 pursued a policy of tight money (high interest rates) which induced capital inflows and appreciated the U.S. dollar. The first round impacts on agricultural exports were clear. Dollar appreciation increased the foreign currency cost of U.S. exports (price effect). High interest rates increased the costs of production and storage, which in the short run decreased stocks and increased supplies (supply effect). Global recession reduced the growth of per-capita income, which reduced demand for high-income elasticity goods (e.g., meats) and reduced global aggregate demand (demand effect). Portfolio and asset adjustments caused portfolio holders to move out of commodities (portfolio effect) (Freebairn et al., 1982). All these effects moved in the same direction, which, coupled with U.S. dominance in world grain markets, caused U.S. and world (denominated in dollars) grain prices to plummet. An appropriate scenario also could have been constructed for commodity price escalation in 1972 to 1973 and 1979 to 1980.

For exporters whose currency generally moves with the U.S. dollar, the domestic impacts of reduced prices and contracting exports are the same as for the United States. For the European Economic Community (EC), where their currencies are depreciating vis-à-vis the dollar, their export competitiveness should be enhanced. For grain importers whose currencies are pegged to the U.S. dollar, the exchange rate impact is neutralized vis-à-vis U.S. exports, and therefore, given declines in nominal commodity prices, imports are cheaper. However, exports from competitive exporters whose currency is depreciating (e.g., EC) become cheaper relative to U.S. exports. For countries whose currency is pegged to other depreciating currencies, dollars become more expensive while prices are lower, which produces an ambiguous result. Finally, for inconvertible currency countries that use primary exports to finance food imports or sell gold to buy U.S. exports, their import demand contracts with the rising dollar.

The above scenario is not a complete general equilibrium analysis, but it is sufficient to illustrate the complexity of the interrelationships in agricultural trade when macro dimensions are introduced. Clearly, commodity markets are going to be made more unstable by monetary (macro) instability; and, given the dependence of U.S. agriculture on exports, fluctuations in the U.S. dollar create price and income instability for U.S. agriculture.

While this discussion lacks the neatness required to include these kinds of linkages in analytical partial equilibrium models, we have included it here because it is crucial to developing a complete picture of international market linkages. In Chapter 4 we analyze the 1970s and early 1980s in a case study which will further expand on these linkages.

The analytical techniques developed in this chapter become both a conceptual model for looking at multiple-commodity analysis with and without intervention and building blocks for later analysis. Given that world markets are linked and that most, if not all, countries intervene in agriculture, an understanding of international markets and how they transmit policy and natural shocks is essential. In the next chapter, we use the analysis developed here to look at three real world cases. In Part Two we use the basic models developed in Chapters 2 and 3 for looking at country policy analysis in an interdependent world.

REFERENCES

Abbott P. C. 1979. "Modelling International Grain Trade with Government Controlled Markets," *Amer. J. Agr. Econ.*, **61**:22–31.

Chacholiades, M. 1978. *International Trade Theory and Policy*, McGraw-Hill, New York.

Chambers, R. G., and Just, R. E. 1979. "A Critique of Exchange Rate Treatment in Agricultural Trade Models," *Amer. J. Agr. Econ.*, **61**:249–257.

Freebairn, J. W., Rausser, G. E., and de Gorter, H. 1982. "Food and Agriculture Sector Linkages to the International and Domestic Macroeconomics," in G. C.

Rausser (ed.), *New Directions in Economic Modelling and Forecasting in U.S. Agriculture*, Elsevier/North Holland, New York, pp. 503–547.

Johnson, D. G. 1975. "World Agriculture, Commodity Policy, and Price Variability," *Amer. J. Agr. Econ., 57:*823–828.

Josling, T. E. 1981. "Domestic Agricultural Price Policies and their Interaction Through Trade," in A. F. McCalla and T. E. Josling (eds.), *Imperfect Markets in Agriculture Trade,* Allanheld, Osman, Montclair, N.J., pp. 49–68.

Karp, L. S., and McCalla, A. F. 1983. "Dynamic Games and International Trade: An Application to the World Corn Market," *Amer. J. Agr. Econ., 65:*641–650.

Lawrence, C., and Lawrence, R. Z. 1981. Global Commodity Prices and Financial Markets: Theory and Evidence, Paper presented to the A.E.A. Meetings, Washington, D.C., December.

McCalla, A. F. 1982. "Impacts of Macroeconomic Policies upon Agricultural Trade and Agricultural Development," *Amer. J. Agr. Econ., 64:*861–868.

McKinnon, R. I. 1979. *Money in International Exchange: The Convertible Currency System,* Oxford University Press, New York.

———. 1982a. A Program for International Monetary Stability, Unpublished paper, Stanford University Department of Economics.

———. 1982b. "Currency Substitution and Instability in the World Dollar Standard," *Amer. Econ. Rev., 72:*320–333.

———. 1982c. The World Money Crunch: A Way Out, Unpublished paper, Stanford University Department of Economics.

Rausser, G. C., Lichtenberg, E., and Lattimore, R. 1982. "Developments in Theory and Empirical Applications of Endogenous Government Behavior," in G. C. Rausser, (ed.), *New Directions of Econometric Modelling and Forecasting in U.S. Agriculture,* Elsevier/North Holland, New York, pp. 547–615.

Schuh, G. E. 1982. U.S. Agriculture in Transition, Paper presented to Joint Economic Committee, U.S. Congress 28 April 1982.

Van Duyne, C. 1979. "The Macroeconomic Effects of Commodity Market Disruptions in Open Economies," *J. Int. Econ., 9:*559–582.

Chapter 4

Interdependence in Practice

I INTRODUCTION

The previous chapters developed some analytical tools that, it was argued, would be useful in analyzing international interdependencies. This chapter presents three examples and demonstrates the strengths and limitations of that analytical approach. The first case treated is price instability in the world wheat market in the decade of the 1970s. In particular, we explore how one would include extreme production instability and policy changes of a large actor (the U.S.S.R.) in a single-commodity international trade model. The second case, also in the 1970s, looks at intercommodity relationships focusing on two large actors, the United States and the European Community (EC), and a set of commodity linkages involving corn, soybeans, cassava, sugar, corn gluten, high fructose corn sweetener, and gasohol. In this real world example of substitution, input-output, and complementary relationships, we can historically verify the nature of intercommodity linkages and how policy intervention causes significant and unexpected changes in patterns and volumes of trade. The third case addresses in a simplified fashion the impacts of domestic macro policies on international agricultural linkages and trade flows involving particular countries. It deals with the example of monetary turbulence in recent years as it affected the wheat and cotton markets.

II SINGLE-COMMODITY ANALYSIS: THE CASE OF THE WORLD WHEAT MARKET AND SOVIET PRODUCTION AND POLICY INSTABILITY

The international wheat market in the 1950s, 1960s, and early 1970s can be characterized as a market of stable prices (except for brief price wars in 1965 and 1969) with f.o.b. export prices in Canada and the United States never below $58 per metric ton and seldom above $66 per metric ton. (All prices in this discussion are in nominal U.S. dollars.) Canada and the United States both pursued policies of producer price stabilization and support which included holding stocks to maintain price levels within a narrow band. Several authors have argued that implicit, if not explicit, collusion determined world prices (McCalla 1966; Alaouze, Watson, and Sturgess, 1978). Conditions changed radically in 1972. A confluence of events (combinations of production shortfalls and demand expansions, changes in the Peruvian anchovy catch, devaluations of the U.S. dollar (1971 and 1973), and an apparent change in Soviet policy, among others) caused world prices to explode. Prices averaged $73 per metric ton c.i.f. Rotterdam in 1971 to 1972 (see Table 4-1) and peaked in January 1974 and again in November 1974 at over $230 per ton (U.S.D.A, 1976). Prices in crop year 1973–1974 averaged $196 and 1974–1975 $207 per ton, which was nearly a 300 percent increase over the levels prevailing for 20 years preceding 1972. Since then, prices have continued to fluctuate widely—back down to $131 in 1977–1978 and up again to $215 in 1980–1981 before beginning their steady decline into 1983.

The reason for recounting these events is to set the stage for attempting to apply our single-commodity analytical framework to analysis of the world wheat market from 1968 to 1983. We take a much more simplified approach than that taken by Josling (1980) in his detailed analysis of the period 1968–1969 to 1976–1977. We focus the analysis on significant variability of Soviet Union imports in the 1970s, and their impacts on world markets. The impact has three elements—production instability, changes in policy choice, and stocks policy. Exchange rate changes also enter into the picture.

The Soviet Union (U.S.S.R.) was, until 1971, an exporter of wheat mainly in Eastern Europe. The U.S.S.R. has always been subject to extreme variability in grain production, however, prior to the 1970s domestic consumption was generally adjusted to production variability. U.S.S.R. behavior in the 1970s was marked by periodic large forays into international markets as Soviet policy apparently changed to that of less consumption variability and the use of international markets to make up domestic production shortfalls. This change in policy coincided with rapid increases in livestock feeding and a desire to avoid strong fluctuations in Soviet herd sizes as a consequence of fluctuating grain harvests. For example, by 1970 the U.S.S.R. was feeding 40 million metric tons of wheat to livestock (Schmitz

Table 4-1 World and U.S.S.R. Wheat Statistics

Year	Production U.S.S.R. (mmt*)	Utilization U.S.S.R. (mmt)	Exports U.S.S.R. (mmt)	Imports U.S.S.R. (mmt)	Net imports U.S.S.R. (mmt)	World trade (mmt)	U.S.S.R. net imports (% of world trade)	U.S. Dark Northern Spring 14% (c.i.f. price Rotterdam) (U.S. $/mt†)
1970–1971	79.9	93.6	7.2	0.5	(6.7)	54.8	(12.2)	75
1971–1972	98.8	98.4	5.8	3.4	(2.4)	52.4	(4.0)	73
1972–1973	86.0	99.6	1.3	14.9	13.6	67.4	20.2	100
1973–1974	109.8	95.3	5.0	4.5	(0.5)	62.6	(0.7)	196
1974–1975	83.9	93.4	4.0	2.5	(1.5)	63.8	(2.3)	207
1975–1976	66.2	87.8	0.5	10.1	9.6	66.3	14.5	187
1976–1977	96.9	92.5	1.0	4.6	3.6	63.1	6.7	147
1977–1978	92.2	106.8	1.0	6.6	5.6	72.9	7.7	131
1978–1979	120.8	106.5	1.5	5.1	3.6	72.0	5.0	154
1979–1980	90.2	114.8	0.5	12.1	11.6	86.0	13.5	200
1980–1981	98.2	114.7	0.5	16.0	15.5	94.2	16.4	215
1981–1982	80.0	102.0	0.5	19.5	19.0	101.2	18.8	194
1982–1983	86.0	105.7	0.5	20.2	20.5	98.2	20.9	178
1983–1984	80.0	93.5	0.5	19.0	18.5	100.0	18.5	187‡

*Million metric tons
†Simple yearly average
‡Ten-month simple average
Source: ERS/USDA, Wheat Situation, Washington D.C., various issues.

et al., 1981), up from 5 to 10 million metric tons in the early 1960s. Basic data for the U.S.S.R., world tade, and prices are presented in Table 4-1 for the 1970s and early 1980s.

The Soviets experienced a bad wheat crop in 1970–1971, but the availability of significant stocks (Josling, 1980, p. 17) allowed them to maintain consumption. However, by the end of the 1971 to 1972 crop years, stocks were down to 7 million metric tons relative to 31 million metric tons in 1968–1969. The bad crop of 1972–1973 then faced the U.S.S.R. with the choice of substantially curtailing livestock herds or entering the world market. The U.S.S.R. exported 2.4 million metric tons in 1971–1972. But in 1972–1973 they imported 13.6 million metric tons which represented 20 percent of world imports. The net change in the Soviet position was 16 million metric tons which is more than the 15 million metric ton increase in world trade between 1971–1972 and 1972–1973. Prices reacted strongly as exporters, particularly the United States and Canada, drew down stocks rapidly to meet the surge in world demand. In summary, the data in Table 4-1 shows Soviet performance from 1970. Instability in production was extreme and obvious. Utilization was more stable and net imports switched sharply from export to import and back again between 1970 and 1975 and then steadily grew.

This brief description of world wheat markets and Soviet performance in the early 1970s seems to suggest that the Soviets caused market instability by their performance alone. Such is clearly not the case. In the next few paragraphs we utilize the analytical apparatus developed in Chapter 2 to work through in a stepwide analytical fashion the various factors contributing to circumstances in the world wheat market where a significant change in policy of one actor could contribute to wide swings in prices. We focus on the early 1970s and use our knowledge of how domestic policies influence excess supply and demand functions to construct a verbal model of events. Clearly, it could be captured in a complicated graph but that should be unnecessary given the analytical building blocks from Chapter 2. We look at the major actors in the market.

The analysis begins in 1971. The Soviet Union pursues domestic pricing policies for both producers and consumers which are apparently disjoint from world market prices. In particular, bread prices to consumers are low and nominally fixed. Therefore, in any given year, Soviet import demand is likely to be perfectly inelastic with respect to world price unless there is a foreign exchange constraint. Therefore, the apparent decision to import rather than adjust consumption (after having drawn down stocks) caused a perfectly inelastic excess demand function to shift to the right. Given Soviet size, this contributed to a shift in world demand. In addition over this period (1971 to 1974), the U.S. dollar was devalued twice which, given Soviet sales of gold to purchase imports, potentially further shifted Soviet demand to the right.

The European Community (EC) was still a small importer of wheat in 1971. The EC fixes a guaranteed price to producers and charges that price to consumers. Thus, EC import demand with respect to world prices is also perfectly inelastic. Thus when prices began to rise rapidly in 1972, EC demand did not adjust. In fact, as world prices rose above EC support levels, import subsidies were used to stabilize domestic prices. However, by the end of the period (1974–1975), the EC became a small net exporter of wheat which no doubt contributed to the price fall in the period 1974 to 1978.

Other importers similarly fixed internal producer and/or consumer prices which made their import demand functions highly inelastic. The horizontal summation of all importers' highly inelastic import demand functions yielded a world import demand function that was inelastic with respect to world price. Several of these countries also experienced domestic supply shortfalls in 1973 which when added to Soviet shortfalls and policy changes shifted an inelastic world demand function sharply to the right.

On the supply side, the United States, Australia, and Canada were committed to fixed or guaranteed producer price supports at levels above world price. These prices were generally then passed to domestic consumers. The result, analytically, is for net excess supply functions to be highly inelastic with respect to world price. Thus, our second analytical function can be derived, namely, a highly inelastic world supply function of wheat. However, in 1972, Canada and the United States had significant stocks of wheat. As prices began to rise above support levels, both the Canadian Wheat Board and the Commodity Credit Corporation (CCC) in the United States, who had been sitting on these expensive stocks for years, moved them rapidly into world markets. Thus, in early 1972, there was also a world stock supply function which was perfectly elastic with respect to world price, which until exhausted, moderated world price increases. In addition, in 1973, Australia and other countries experienced a supply shortfall.

The beginning point (1971 to 1972) of our analytical model is now in place—highly inelastic world supply and demand functions (largely because of domestic policy intervention) and substantial stocks held by two major exporters. The result was low but stable prices until mid-1972. Now introduce the dynamics of the situation. When the Soviets experienced a second poor crop in 1972–1973 (after the poor one in 1970–1971), they could no longer draw on internal stocks and major purchases were initiated simultaneously but secretly with major U.S. grain houses. Prices rose $40 per metric ton to $111 per metric ton c.i.f. Rotterdam between August and December but then dropped back to below $100 in early 1973 as stocks were drawn down to meet extremely large Soviet purchases. However, by

May 1973, stocks had dwindled and all the components of our model were in place and prices skyrocketed to record levels, noted earlier, peaking in January 1974 at $236 per metric ton (14 percent hard red Spring c.i.f. Rotterdam).

To recapitulate on how our analytical model is useful, we are able to qualitatively identify the nature of country excess trade functions and therefore horizontally sum them to establish "world" trade supply and demand functions. These, we have argued, were highly inelastic in the international wheat market of the 1970s. We then can shock the model with shifts of individual country excess functions. In 1972–1973, a major shift occurred in Soviet demand because of a basic policy decision to offset a poor crop with imports. However, that shift occurred simultaneously with other events which were simultaneously shifting world supply to the left and world demand to the right. The cumulative result was a price explosion.

One could go further with this analysis because price behavior in the 1970s and early 1980s was very unstable. The period of rapidly rising but unstable prices (1972 to 1974) was followed by a sharp but oscillating price fall in the period from 1975 to 1977, another rapid rise in the period from 1978 to 1980 which was followed by a period of falling prices after 1980. While clearly these price changes have components of their explanation outside of agricultural policy (e.g., the changing value of the U.S. dollar and bouts of global inflation and recession), the basic nature of agricultural policies illustrated in this example create the structural circumstances where, when exogenous shifts, whether from weather or monetary shocks occur, extreme price variability ensues. In this case, we have focused on how one large actor's behavior exacerbated price instability. This was our intent. For a fuller discussion of grain market instability in the period 1971–1972 to 1982–1983, the reader is referred to a recent FAO study (1984).

III MULTICOMMODITY MARKET AND POLICY INTERDEPENDENCE: THE CASSAVA AND CORN GLUTEN CAPER

The preceding case looked at a single-commodity market and the impacts of policy intervention when exogenous weather and policy shocks occurred. The next case looks at multicommodity linkages in a world of policy intervention. We can use the component's parts of the analysis developed in Chapter 3 to reason through this interesting case involving several commodities, several policy units, and substitution, input-output and complementary relationships. It is the case of a policy distortion creating a market for one commodity—cassava—and altering relationships between corn, corn by-products, and soybeans. The story in stylized fashion follows. We then try to dissect it using the analytical framework. Both cassava and corn gluten are imported as ingredients for animal feeds into the European Community (EC). Therefore, the analysis starts with a brief review of developments in the EC in the 1970s. We then look separately at the cassava and corn gluten developments before putting them together in a stylized fashion.

A The Common Agricultural Policy of the European Community

The European Economic Community (EC) was formed in 1958 and a Common Agricultural Policy (CAP) was developed for the original six member countries over the period 1963 to 1968. The basic feature of the CAP was to provide income support to European farmers via increased prices by protecting them from "low-priced" imports. Annually, the Council of Ministers establishes desired prices for, among other commodities, grain. This price, called the *target price*, is a price goal with is sought by managing imports or exports. Related to the target price is the *threshold price* which is the border price necessary to have internal market prices approximate the desired target price. Therefore, if world prices are below the threshold price, a levy (tariff) equal to the difference between threshold and world prices is charged to make the price of imports equal to the threshold price. If world prices fall, the levy increases and vice versa, resulting in the term *variable levy*. Analogously for exports, a variable subsidy (export restitution) is paid to bridge the gap between domestic and world prices.

This mechanism has been applied to grains including feed grains since the beginning of the CAP. In the middle 1960s, European cattle were not, in general, fed high levels of protein concentrates. Thus, nongrain feed ingredients (NGFI) such as soybeans, soymeal, and cassava were not large elements in European rations. Corn gluten (a by-product of wet corn milling for starch, high fructose corn sweetener, and alcohol) was not even a traded commodity. Thus, under pressure from the United States, among others, the EC agreed to bind (leave unchanged) tariffs on these ingredients at low or zero rates. Therein was created a policy distortion—high and substitute and complementary commodities which caused interesting developments in the 1970s.

B The Cassava Market

Nelson, in two publications (1982, 1983), has analyzed the rapid growth of cassava chip and pellet imports into the EC. Much of this section draws on his work. Cassava is a woody, tuberous root crop grown in the tropics (sometimes called tapioca or manioc). It produces high volumes of carbohydrate (energy) per unit of output, but it has very low protein content (about 2 percent). Thus, it is not suitable alone as a livestock feed. However, a ton of dried cassava contains about the same amount of energy as a ton of corn or barley. Thus, "it is possible to prepare a mixture of cassava and soybean meal (roughly, 80 percent cassava) with the same nutrient value as the feed grains, and the feed compounder can feed either a feed grain or the mixture depending on relative prices" (Nelson, 1983, p. 27). Thus, a cassava and soymeal mix is a substitute (within limits) for corn or other feed grains.

The 1970s saw several developments in the European Community. Rapid economic growth caused per-capita incomes to rise, stimulating a rapid increase in the demand for meat. Rising meat prices (partly policy determined) stimulated expansion of livestock numbers (particularly hogs and poultry) and increased the intensity of feeding by using higher protein rations. At the same time the rise in incomes in the nonagricultural sector brought pressure on the Community to raise farm income comparably by raising internal support prices. Thus, commodities under the CAP (including feed grains) experienced price increases throughout the 1970s. As feed grain prices rose, the alternative combination of cassava and soymeal (both entering at fixed low or zero duties) became increasingly price competitive with domestic and imported feed grains. The result was to create a world demand for dried cassava as a feed ingredient where one did not exist before because at world market relationships the cassava-soybean mixture is not competitive with corn. For example, no cassava is imported by Japan, which has generally lower feed grain prices, even though transport rates from Thailand (the principal supplier of cassava) are favorable.

This effect was particularly marked in Germany and the Netherlands, who experienced higher corn prices than in other EC member states through the operation of the "green currency" system. This system was designed to dampen the impact of exchange rate changes on farm prices. Strong-currency countries would find prices decreasing in local currency terms as their exchange rate appreciated. To avoid this impact, common prices within the EC are translated at "green" rates of exchange, which lag behind market rates. The imposition of trade taxes and subsidies (monetary compensatory amounts) is necessary to prevent trade flows from taking advantage of temporary price differences within the common market. Commodities not subject to policy intervention are not included in the system of monetary compensatory amounts (MCAs). Hence, soybeans and cassava, for instance, became cheaper on the German or Dutch markets as those currencies appreciated against the dollar. Corn, which is included in the MCA system, rose in price relative to soybeans. This is illustrated in Figure 4-1. The price of corn is fixed in European Currency Units (CU) irrespective of the world price. If the green rate is undervalued relative to the market rate, an additional tax is put on imports (the MCA). The price of soybeans will, how-

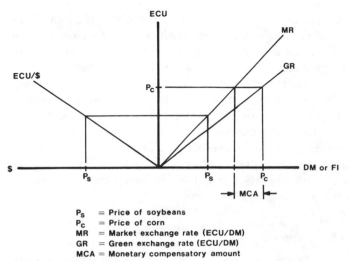

P_S = Price of soybeans
P_C = Price of corn
MR = Market exchange rate (ECU/DM)
GR = Green exchange rate (ECU/DM)
MCA = Monetary compensatory amount

Figure 4-1 Impact of green rate system on relative price of corn and soybeans in a strong-currency country of the EC.

ever, depend upon the ECU/$ rate and the market rate of the DMark in terms of ECU. The MCA will thus increase the relative price of corn on German (and Dutch) markets. If this were a temporary, within-season, effect, the impact would be small. But MCAs have persisted for 15 years, often as high as 10 percent and more for Germany. The effect has been to create unintentionally an extra incentive for the use of nongrain feed ingredients.

The main response to this policy-induced demand came from Thailand which rapidly expanded plantings north of Bangkok. Private sector entrepreneurs invested in land, land clearing, processing, and loading facilities. The rapid expansion also benefited from an expanded internal road network built in part by the United States as part of the southeast Asia defense policy. Imports of dried cassava by the European Community were about $1/2$ million metric tons in 1965, they rose to 1.5 million metric tons in 1973 and then expanded rapidly, peaking at over 8 million metric tons in 1980. Subsequently, the EC has negotiated voluntary constraint agreements with Thailand (the major supplier) and tariff/quotas with Indonesia and other suppliers to hold total imports below 6 million metric tons.

The impacts of those developments go far beyond creating a world market for dried cassava, which would be as far as one could go with single-commodity analysis. First the cassava-soybean mixture is one of complementarity. Therefore, as the demand for cassava increases, so does the demand for soybeans and soymeal. In simplest terms, there was probably an expansion in the demand for soymeal of almost 2 million metric tons. Second, the mixture is a substitute for corn or barley. Therefore, the imports of 10 million metric tons of cassava-soymeal mix reduced EC demand for both domestic and world feed grains by a like amount. Thus, corn exports were less than they otherwise would have been (the EC excess demand function for corn was shifted to the left) and world prices have been lower. The combination of the complementary relationship with soybeans and the substitution relationship with corn, therefore, has contracted U.S. corn exports (and lowered price) and expanded the demand for U.S. and Brazilian soybeans and products, increasing prices of vegetable and animal protein sources. This may explain the ambivalent position of the United States regarding European Community cassava imports which were reducing corn exports but expanding demand for soybeans and products.

C The Corn Gluten Development

Corn gluten is a joint product (by-product) resulting from wet milling of corn for production of high fructose corn syrup (HFCS) and grain alcohol. Two forms of livestock feed came from corn gluten—a high-protein (more than 50 percent) meal and corn gluten feed (about 20 percent protein). The feed is the largest component and has been the dominant product in a rapidly growing export market to the EC. Exports from the United States to the EC rose from almost nothing in the mid-1960s to over 2.8 million metric tons in 1982. The causes of the expansion are a complicated pattern of intercommodity relationships. First, wet milling of corn essentially produces starch and by-products including gluten. In the mid-1960s a continuous process for deriving high fructose corn syrup was developed, which made the sweetener a price-competitive noncrystalline substitute for sugar (Carman and Thor, 1979). Consumption of HFCS grew extremely rapidly in the 1970s, particularly after 1973 as per-capita consumption in the United States grew from 1.5 pounds per year in 1973 to over 20 pounds per capita in 1980. Over the same period per-capita sugar consumption dropped from 103 to 85 pounds per capita. Thus, HFCS has substituted for sugar on nearly a pound-for-pound basis. This is a dramatic case of substitution in consumption. As HFCS becomes available and as the price of sugar rises, the demand for HFCS rises, increasing the derived demand for corn and simultaneously increasing the supply of corn gluten feed. Thus, sugar legislation, in the early 1980s, which via quotas and tariffs significantly increased U.S. sugar prices, expanded the export supply of corn gluten feed.

Second, the wet milling process is also used to generate corn starch for use in production of grain alcohol for gasohol production. Thus, the strong push after the first OPEC price increase (circa 1973) caused increased policy incentives to expand gasohol production. Again, this expanded the demand for corn and expanded the supply of corn gluten feed.

Third, corn gluten feed is a 20 percent protein feed mixture which is a substitute for both corn (10 percent protein) and soymeal (47 percent protein) in high-protein feed rations depending on relative prices. Expanded demand for HFCS and alcohol increased the price of corn, but expanded gluten supplies which, other things equal, reduced its price, making it more competitive with corn. The impacts of these relationships was a rapidly expanding market for corn gluten feed in the European Community.

D The Web of Interdependencies

The cassava and corn gluten stories can now be put together using the analysis introduced in Chapter 3 as an example of a multicommodity policy problem. A diagram of the array of interrelationships is presented in Figure 4-2. In this partial system there are three final demands—fuel, sweeteners, and meat—and three primary products—corn, soybeans, and cassava. Corn and soybeans are substitutes in production in the United States, while cassava and corn are substitutes in production in Thailand. Corn can be used as a feed grain or it can be wet milled to produce starch and corn gluten feed which are joint products in fixed proportions. Cornstarch can be converted either to grain alcohol or high fructose corn syrup (competitive products). Grain alcohol can be a partial substitute for gasoline in the production of fuel. HFCS is a partial substitute for sugar in satisfying sweetener demand. Soybeans produce meal and oil (which is ignored here) in a joint product relationship. Soymeal can be combined in a fixed proportion with cassava pellets to produce a 10 percent protein soy-cassava mix which is a competitive product with feed corn. Corn gluten feed (20 percent protein), feed corn (10 percent protein), and soy-cassava mix (10 percent protein) can be combined in appropriate complementary proportions with soymeal (47 percent protein) to produce high-protein feed rations (30 percent protein) which has a demand derived from the final demand for meat—beef, pork, and poultry—which are substitutes in consumption.

   Now using our partial analysis one can trace through an example of simultaneous exogenous final demand shifts during the period 1976 to 1980. Rising OPEC prices expanded the demand for gasohol. Increases in U.S. sugar support prices expanded the demand for HFCS. Both these demand shifts increased the demand for cornstarch, which simultaneously raised the demand for corn (and corn prices) and expanded the supply of corn gluten feed, lowering its price. At the same time rising incomes in Europe were expanding the demand for meat and, therefore, the demand for imports of feeding stuffs. High feed grain prices in Europe caused feed compounders to seek alternatives and they imported cassava pellets and mixed them with soymeal to produce a substitute for feed grains, expanding the demand for soymeal and raising soy prices but contracting corn demand, lowering corn prices.

   What then are the net effects? First, the demand for soymeal rises, caus-

86

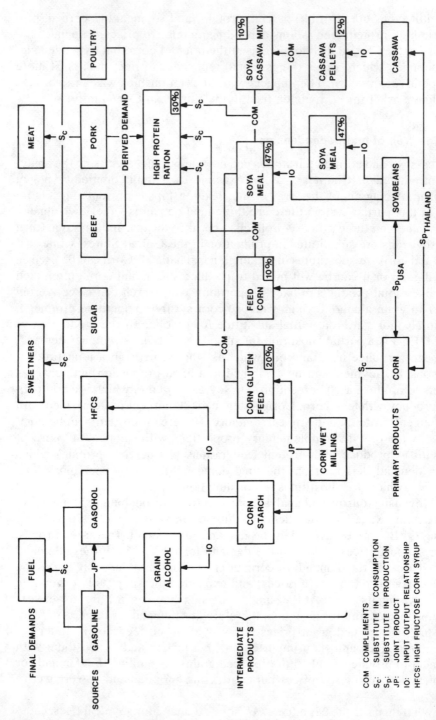

COM   COMPLEMENTS
Sc: SUBSTITUTE IN CONSUMPTION
Sp: SUBSTITUTE IN PRODUCTION
JP: JOINT PRODUCT
IO: INPUT OUTPUT RELATIONSHIP
HFCS: HIGH FRUCTOSE CORN SYRUP

Figure 4-2 Multiproduct linkages in corn, cassava, and soybean complex.

ing soymeal and soybean prices to rise. Second, the increase in soy prices causes an increase in the demand for corn gluten in Europe and the United States but as both the supply and demand for corn gluten are shifting we can say nothing a priori about corn gluten prices. We can say, however, that trade will expand. Third, we cannot say a priori what will happen to corn prices as competing forces are at work—upward pressure from expanded demands for gasohol and HFCS and contracting demand because of cassava substitution in Europe. Finally, we can say that cassava prices rise. Definitive answers with respect to price impacts would require a simultaneous model. However, this analysis clearly shows that the decision of the United States to raise domestic sugar prices, for example, has ramifications for many commodities and many countries because of international interdependence. Analysts should be careful to identify these intercommodity and policy interdependencies in doing policy analysis.

One final part of this saga can be noted even though it does not directly relate to the intercommodity issue. It does, however, relate to international trade policy and its welfare impacts. When the EC negotiated a voluntary export restraint (VER) with Thailand, Indonesia and other suppliers, it was presumably doing so to protect domestic feed grain producers from low-priced import competition. It appears that the EC preferred not to (could not) implement an import quota. The interesting welfare point is that, while under either scenario (import quota or VER) European consumers lose and European farmers gain, who else benefits differs significantly with the choice of instrument. If the EC applied a quota, the quota rent would accrue to importers or if the quota were sold by the EC, to the EC. On the other hand, inducing Thailand to apply a VER allows Thailand to gain the rent in a form equivalent to an export tax (Allen, Dodge, and Schmitz, 1983). Thus, the appearance of not applying a quota is costly in welfare terms to the EC and could make Thai exporters better off than if the EC had not done so.

IV   MACRO INTERDEPENDENCIES: THE CASE OF MONETARY TURBULENCE 1979 TO 1982

Section V of Chapter 3 developed a general scenario about the impacts of monetary and exchange rate instability on commodity markets. This section analyzes more explicitly the circumstances of the early 1980s of an appreciation of the U.S. dollar. It analyzes the impacts on several countries—developed and developing—who have their currencies floating or pegged to the U.S. dollar. Hopefully, it illustrates the impacts on various classes of countries. We start by looking at a single-commodity market. We then add a second where some actors have different net trade positions to see if we can determine the factors that would influence the aggregate impact.

A The Facts about the Early 1980s

Beginning in 1979, the U.S. Federal Reserve Board began pursuing a tight monetary policy which raised domestic interest rates. Higher interest rates attracted capital inflows which appreciated the U.S. dollar. Other countries, with flexible exchange rates, attempted to stabilize their currency by intervention which contracted the world money supply resulting in global recession (McKinnon, 1982). World markets for commodities, e.g., wheat, feed grains, cotton, contracted causing world prices denominated in dollars to fall. United States exports fell in terms of first value and then volume. Some other exporters, such as Canada, also suffered losses while others, notably Argentina, experienced increased export sales. Importing countries in some cases contracted imports while others expanded them as a result of currency realignments. The problem for the analyst is to attempt to disentangle these effects. We attempt to do so by first looking at a stylized analysis of the world wheat market and then turn to the cotton market.

B Developments in the Wheat Market: 1980 to 1983

We begin with the fact that the U.S. dollar appreciated against many hard currencies in the early 1980s. We assume, quite realistically, that wheat trade in world markets is denominated in U.S. dollars ($U.S.). We select for analysis four countries—two exporters, the United States and Argentina, and two importers, Mexico and Egypt. We further assume that the Argentine peso is floating vis-à-vis the dollar as is the Mexican peso while the Egyptian pound (LE) is pegged to the U.S. dollar.

The analysis is presented in Figure 4-3a. The form of the analysis follows the graphic approach used by Longmire and Morey (1983) in analyzing a simpler case. On the export side we assume that before the appreciation of the dollar there was an equilibrium in the world wheat market (solid lines). Argentine domestic supply and demand functions are presented (far left) denominated in pesos (Pesos$_A$). The next panel shows the excess supply function of Argentina denominated in U.S. dollars at the old exchange rate. For simplicity, we present only the U.S. excess supply function kinked at the internal support price. The horizontal summation of the two gives us "world" export supply W_s. There are, of course, other exporters such as Canada and Australia. If their currencies were pegged to the U.S. dollar they would have experiences similar to the United States. If other suppliers had floating exchange rates their experience would parallel Argentina's.

Egypt is a large importer of wheat. Internally, Egypt fixes a low subsidized price to consumers. It also fixes a higher price to producers which is still below world prices. Thus, Egyptian import demand is depicted as highly inelastic. Finally, Mexican import demand denominated in dollars is derived

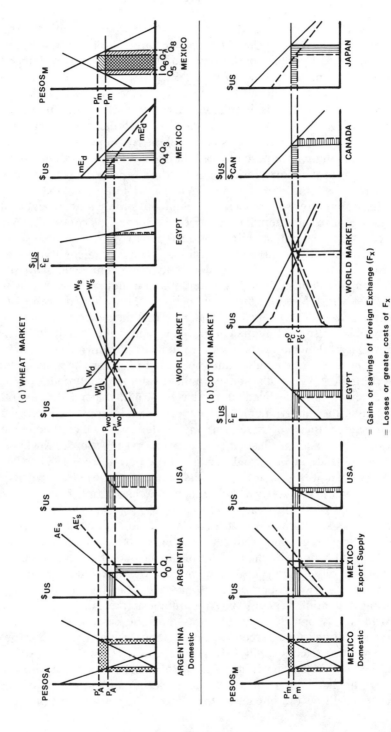

Figure 4-3 Impacts of an appreciation of the U.S. dollar on wheat and cotton markets.

= Gains or savings of Foreign Exchange (F_x)

= Losses or greater costs of F_x

from domestic supply and demand functions which are denominated in Mexican pesos ($Pesos_M$) at the old exchange rate. The horizontal summation of Mexican and Egyptian import demand yields world import demand W_d and an equilibrium world price of wheat P_{wo}.

Now assume that the U.S. dollar appreciates, say, by 30 percent. The impact on Argentina is as follows. Argentina sells wheat in world markets and receives dollars. The appreciation of the dollar means that when export earnings are converted to pesos (which have "depreciated" relative to the dollar) the number of pesos earned increases. This is analytically equivalent to a 30 percent export subsidy on Argentine exports. This is shown as a rotation of Argentine export supply AE_s to AE_s' denominated in dollars. Or stated differently, Argentina is now willing to supply more wheat at any dollar price because the internal peso price has risen. This rotation of Argentina's excess supply function shifts world supply to W_s'.

Conversely, the dollar appreciation is the equivalent of a 30 percent import tax in Mexico, thus raising domestic prices. The result is to rotate Mexico's import demand function denominated in dollars downwards to the left (mE_d to mE_d'). Mexico now is willing to buy less wheat over the full range of world prices denominated in dollars. Egyptian excess demand does not change because the Egyptian pound is pegged to the U.S. dollar. The change in Mexican demand shifts the world demand downward to the left to W_d'.

The new world equilibrium price falls to P_{wo}' denominated in dollars and world trade volume falls, at least in this example. In a broader world market, whether volume declined or increased would depend on several factors including the relative number of exporters and importers where currencies depreciated, their net trade position, the degree to which their currency values changed, and the elasticities of their excess functions. However, in reality, world trade in wheat did decline in the period from 1981 to 1983.

We can now look at the impacts on each of our market participants. At the new world price *Argentina's* exports increase from Q_0 to Q_1 (intersection of AE_s' and P_{wo}'). The quantity of exports Q_1 translates to peso prices off the old excess supply function AE_s and results in an increase in peso prices to P_A'. Clearly, Argentine producers are better off and Argentina gains peso income from exports by the amount of the shaded area. Argentine consumers are worse off. The impact on Argentine foreign exchange earnings depends on the elasticity of import earnings increase. The elasticity of import demand facing Argentina depends on Argentina's market share, the elasticities of world supply and demand functions, and the percentage change in world prices relative to the percentage appreciation of the U.S. dollar (or the shift in Argentine excess supply). In Figure 4-3a, gains in foreign exchange are marked by vertical hatching; losses (from the lower price) are marked by horizontal hatching. In general, the smaller Argentina's share of the market, the less will be the impact of the shift of Argentina's supply function on world prices. Similarly, the more elastic are the world supply and demand functions, the smaller will be the price change. It seems reasonable to assume that Argentina's foreign exchange earnings would rise.

The impact on the *United States* is clear. Exports decline and export earnings decline as the United States sells less at lower prices. Government costs rise as prices fall below support levels. The decline in export earnings is shown as the horizontally hatched area. The impact on *Egypt* is also straightforward. Because we have assumed that the Egyptian pound is pegged to the U.S. dollar, the pound cost of grain does not change. However, the fall in world prices means that Egypt will buy more at a lower price. Given our assumption that the Egyptian import demand is inelastic, the fall in world prices results in a net foreign exchange saving for Egypt.

The impact on *Mexico* is more complex. The fall in world prices is not sufficient for Mexico to buy as much grain as before. Imports fall from Q_3 to Q_4 and foreign exchange (dollar) costs fall as less is purchased at a lower dollar price. However, the domestic impact must also be considered. Domestic peso prices rise to P'_m (read by moving vertically upward from Q_4 to mE_d). Mexican producers are better off while Mexican consumers are worse off. Whether the peso cost of exports increases or decreases depends on the slopes of domestic supply and demand function. In Figure 4-2a, it is the difference between $(Q_8 - Q_5) \cdot P_m$ and $(Q_7 - Q_6) \cdot P'_m$.

In summary, the dollar appreciation results in lower world prices and probably decreased trade. Exporters, whose currency is floating relative to the dollar, benefit. Exporters such as Canada (not shown), whose currencies are pegged (implicitly or explicitly) to the U.S. dollar, would suffer the same fate as the United States—namely decreased exports and decreased prices and, therefore, decreased foreign exchange earnings. Importers whose currency is pegged to the dollar would buy more at lower world prices. Foreign exchange costs would increase if import demand is elastic or decrease if demand was inelastic. Importers with floating currencies involuntarily contract imports (therefore, saving foreign currency) as the appreciation raises domestic prices at the cost of consumers and to the benefit of producers. It is highly unlikely, however, that any country will decide to choose between floating and pegged rates on the basis of one commodity. Therefore, no formal general implication of the "goodness" or "badness" of pegged exchange rates should be drawn from this analysis.

C   The Cotton Market

The second market we analyze is that for cotton. We select cotton for two reasons. First, we can simplify intercommodity linkages by assuming no substitution in consumption and no input-output or complementary relationships. We need only be concerned with substitution in production which, given that the monetary shock hits both wheat and cotton markets, means that prices in the two markets move togehter. Second, cotton is an interesting contrast to wheat because both Mexico and Egypt are exporters of cotton. Thus, we can investigate the multicommodity effects on developing countries of being an exporter in one market and an importer in the other.

The analysis of the cotton market is presented in Figure 4-3b. The participants are Mexico, United States, and Egypt as exporters and Canada and Japan as importers. The analysis proceeds in analogous fashion to that for wheat. Given an equilibrium set of exchange rates, world supply and demand functions are constructed, yielding a world equilibrium price of P_c^o. When the U.S. dollar appreciates, the Mexican excess supply of cotton rotates to the right increasing Mexican supply at any dollar price. The U.S. and Egyptian export supplies do not change. Neither does Canadian demand (pegged implicitly), but Japanese demand rotates to the left given the decline in yen purchasing power relative to the dollar. These changes cause world prices to fall to P_c^t .The results are similar to wheat. *Mexican* peso earnings from cotton increase but whether foreign exchange earnings incrrease depends on the elasticity of import demand facing Mexico. This in turn depends on the Mexican market share, and the percent change in peso value vis-à-vis the percent change in world prices which depend on the elasticities of world supply and demand. Again, our presumption would be that foreign exchange earnings would increase. Both the United States and Egypt suffer losses of exports and foreign exchange earnings. Canada buys more at lower prices, and whether foreign exchange reserves were saved or used would depend on the elasticity of import demand. Japan buys less at a lower foreign exchange cost but domestic consumers pay more resulting in a trade-off between the loss of consumer surplus and saved foreign exchange.

D Both Markets Together

We can now combine our analysis of the two markets and try to determine the aggregate impact of a monetary policy change on various countries. The summary is presented in Table 4-2. We begin with *Mexico*. Mexico saves foreign exchange in the wheat market and could have additional earnings from the cotton market. Mexico in total probably gains foreign exchange. This is a counter-intuitive result in the light of most discussion of the impacts of dollar appreciation on developing countries. On the other hand, welfare, measured in terms of net changes in producer and consumer surplus, is clearly decreased because as an importer the losses in consumer surplus exceed gains in producer surplus.

The impacts in *Egypt* are more ambiguous. Egypt could save foreign exchange on wheat imports if their import demand is inelastic but they clearly lose foreign exchange in cotton as exports and price both decrease. Thus, the pegging of their currency costs them on the export market but

Table 4-2 Impacts of U.S.$ Appreciation: Cotton and Wheat Markets

Country	Mexico		Egypt		United States		Canada		Argentina		Japan	
Exchange Rate	Floating		Pegged to U.S.$		U.S.$		Pegged to U.S.$		Floating		Floating	
Commodity	Wheat	Cotton	Wheat	Cotton	Wheat	Cotton	Wheat	Cotton	Wheat	Cotton	Wheat	Cotton
Trade position (Exp or Imp)	Imp	Exp	Imp	Exp	Exp	Exp	Exp	Imp	Exp	—	Imp	Imp
Impact on excess supply (S) or demand (D) function ← left → right 0 none	↓ D	↑ S	0 D	0 S	0 S	0 S	0 S	0 D	↑ S		↓ D	↓ D
Fx impact + = gain or savings − = cost or loss	+Fx (Savings)	+Fx* (Gain)	∓Fx† (Savings)	−Fx (Loss)	−Fx (Loss)	−Fx (Loss)	−Fx (Loss)	±Fx† (Cost)	+Fx* (Gain)	0	+Fx (Savings)	+Fx (Savings)

*If the elasticity of demand for a single country's imports is elastic
†A savings if the importers demand for imports is inelastic
Fx = foreign exchange

benefits them in the import market. Given that the value of Egyptian wheat imports have been more than twice earnings from cotton, it is still possible that the impact on Egyptian foreign exchange balances cousld be positive mainly as a result of savings on large wheat imports. Egyptian consumers benefit more than producers lose in wheat, but the reverse is true for cotton, thus the net welfare impact is ambiguous.

The impacts on the *United States* are straightforward and expected. The United States loses foreign exchange and it would lead to increased farm program costs which might or might not be offset by U.S. consumer gains. Producers could be unaffected depending on the nature of domestic support programs. *Canada* loses foreign exchange on the wheat market and may gain on cotton imports. Given that the value of Canadian wheat exports far exceeds the value of cotton imports. Canada likely experiences a net loss of foreign exchange reserves. Canadian consumers gain while wheat producers lose. *Argentina*, in this model, is a clear winner at least as far as foreign exchange earning and net national surplus is concerned. Argentine consumers lose however. Finally, *Japan* as an importer of both commodities, saves foreign exchange but experiences domestic welfare losses.

E Summary

Even this simple example illustrates that global generalizations about the impacts of exchange rate changes on individual countries are not legitimate. How exchange rate realignments influence a particular country depends on many variables that the analysis has identified. These include:

1   The combination of export and import commodities
2   The relative values of exports and imports
3   The degree of currency depreciation vis-à-vis the appreciating currency
4   The change in domestic currency value relative to the percentage change in world price
5   Their market share
6   The elasticities of world supply and demand functions which in turn depend on policy intervention in other countries.

This discussion of real world macro impacts can be further elaborated. High interest rates increase the debt service ratios of debtor developing countries, e.g., Mexico and Argentina. Global transmission of inflation and recession contract demand by increasing unemployment and decreasing, or at least reducing, the rate of increase of per-capita income, which would have a demand impact. This would simply exacerbate the results already shown. Finally, as argued in Chapter 3, monetary instability likely increases instability in commodity markets. All these additional effects could be added to this analysis. However, the intent of this chapter was to illustrate the complexity of real world situations and to demonstrate how simple graphical and verbal analysis can help to understand the problem.

REFERENCES

Alaouze, C. M., Watson, A. S., and Sturgess, N. H. 1978. "Oligopoly Pricing in the World Wheat Market," *Amer. J. Agr. Econ.,* **60:**173–185.

Allen, R., Dodge, C., and Schmitz, A. 1983. "Voluntary Export Restraints as Protection Policy: The U.S. Beef Case," *Amer. J. Agr. Econ.,* **65:**291–296.

Carman, H. F., and Thor, P. K. 1979. High Fructose Corn Sweeteners: Economic Aspects of a Sugar Substitutes, Division of Agricultural Sciences, University of California Bulletin 1894, July.

FAO/UN, Committee on Commodity Problems, Intergovernmental Group on Grain. 1984. Impact of National Grain Policies on Selected Countries on World Grain Supplies and Prices, 22 Session CCP:GR 84/3, Rome, August.

Josling, T. 1980. Developed-Country Agricultural Policies and Developing-Country Supplies: The Case of Wheat, Research Report 14, International Food Policy Research Institute, Washington, D.C.

Longmire, J., and Morey, A. 1983. Strong Dollar Dampens Demand for U.S. Farm Export, Foreign Agricultural Economic Report #193, ERS/USDA, Washington, D.C.

McCalla, A. F. 1966. "A Duopoly Model of World Wheat Pricing," *J. Farm Econ.,* **48:**711–727.

McKinnon, R. I. 1982. "Currency Substitution and Instability in the World Dollar Standard," *Amer. Econ. Rev.,* **72:**320–333.

Nelson, G. C. 1982. Implication of Developed Country Policies for Developing Countries: The Case of Cassava. Unpublished Doctoral Dissertation, Stanford University.

Nelson, G. C. 1983. "Time for Tapioca, 1970 to 1980: European Demand and World Supply of Dried Cassava," *Food Res. Inst. Studies,* **XIX:**25–49.

Schmitz, A., McCalla, A. F., Mitchell, D. O., and Carter, C. 1981. *Grain Export Cartels,* Ballenger Publishing Co., Cambridge, Mass.

U.S.D.A. 1976. *Wheat Situation,* Economic Research Service, USDA, Washington, D.C., WS-235, February.

Part Two

National Policy Decisions in an Interdependent World

Objectives, Constraints, and Instruments in National Food and Agricultural Policy

I INTRODUCTION

In this chapter we change our perspective of the world from one of looking at the world in the aggregate to one of looking at the world from the perspective of one country. We look at a nation in terms of its policy objectives, constraints, and possible instruments. To accomplish this we need to discuss the basic policy issues and the role and the nature of food and agricultural policy, and to place these in a usable analytical framework. Using this framework, this chapter looks in a generic way at national objectives and potential policy instruments. We then ask how the international interface enters into the domestic policy calculus through agricultural trade conditions. The chapter concludes by looking at several broad types of agricultural policies, e.g., producer subsidies, consumer subsidies and trade policies, in terms of a single commodity and a single-instrument policy choice in a small open economy. Outcomes are compared to the closed economy case.

II POLICY OBJECTIVE FUNCTIONS AND DOMESTIC AND INTERNATIONAL CONSTRAINTS

Nations either explicitly or implicitly have a national objective function, a set of national goals reflecting collective choices (Hathaway, 1963).

Therefore, the policy problem is to select instruments and choose their values in ways which maximize the national objective function subject to appropriate constraints.

To undertake economic analysis of policies we need to be specific as to these goals. We postulate as a starting point that nations will give high priority to at least the following goals or objectives:

1   An income goal, such as expansion of national product. In the broadest sense, this is a goal of economic and social development; in a narrower sense it would be a goal of growth in GNP or per-capita GNP. The static equivalent is a goal of efficient resource use at a particular point in time.

2   A goal or set of goals relating to the distribution of national product and the changes in GNP. This set of goals could articulate relationships between producers and consumers; between rural and urban sectors; and within each of these categories, distribution between, for example, producers of food grains and producers of export crops.

3   A preference for more stability rather than less in major economic variables such as income, growth rates, and prices.

At any given time, the government attempts to achieve some or all of these goals within two types of constraints—domestic resource constraints and international constraints or opportunities. Domestic constraints clearly include the nation's resource base—both physical and human, previously accumulated capital, the shelf of available technologies, fiscal resources, and foreign exchange reserves. Consideration of international dimensions adds to the policy possibility set through trade, capital flows, and transfers. Trade in goods and services both may expand the possible consumption set and allow more productive resource use as a result of specialization as countries shift production to reflect their comparative advantage. World prices and market conditions, therefore, become critical variables in terms of both exports and imports. Capital inflows potentially expand the domestic resource base and offer possibilities for improved welfare. Capital outflows also could improve welfare if the interest and profit earnings exceed those available from domestic investment of the same capital. Capital flows, along with the trade balance, determine the foreign exchange constraints and influence the value of the domestic currency. Finally, a nation can potentially expand domestic welfare by accepting transfers of goods (e.g., food aid), capital, and technology provided that these do not lead to domestic inefficiencies, inequities, or instability.

In summary analytical terms, national policy makers are faced with constrained optimization problems with multicomponent objective functions which they seek to optimize given domestic and international constraints.

III AGRICULTURAL AND FOOD POLICY ISSUES

The previous section outlined the national policy problem in very general terms. In this section we narrow the focus to agricultural and food policy issues. Agricultural policy decisions, however, occur within the broader policy environment. Figure 5-1 depicts a typical set of national policy issues. Assuming our underlying objective of economic and social development, one can imagine a hierarchy of policy issues represented by the points of the pyramid. National policy issues (A) might include broad concerns of economic growth and employment as well as food supply and social equity questions. Specific agricultural issues (B) include questions of land ownership, technology, and rural incomes. This gives rise to a number of issues which have to do with the interaction of agricultural and national policy objectives. This domestic interface (D) will include questions of the pricing of agricultural products to consumers, the flow of labor from rural to urban areas, investment priorities, and the taxation of rural activities. If we add

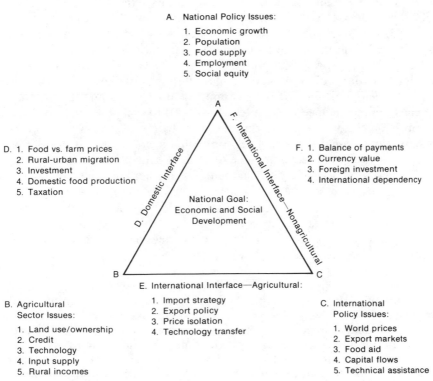

Figure 5-1 National policy pyramid.

another set of issues specifically related to international markets (C), including the behavior of world prices, the availability of concessional commodity flows, and the state of the international capital market, we can distinguish two more interfaces. The interface between national policy issues and these international issues (F) will include the question of the balance of payments, the exchange rate, and the openness of the economy. Most relevant to our present purpose is the interface between agricultural issues and international markets (E). This interface defines the agenda for open economy agricultural policy.

In simplest terms, a country faces four major policy questions with respect to international market interface, *First*, to what extent should the country depend on international markets for portions of its food supply? The degree of international dependence could range from self-sufficiency in normal years and using international markets to cover supply-induced shortfalls to extensive and continuous dependence. Once the degree of dependence is determined, the next question is how is it to be filled—through the commercial market or, in the case of eligible developing countries, via food aid? *Second*, to what extent should agricultural commodity exports be built into the national economic strategy? Agricultural exports could be seen as a major national foreign exchange earner (an agricultural export-led growth strategy), or be sufficient to pay for food imports (agricultural self-reliance), or be used as a disposal site for supply-induced surpluses. *Third*, to what extent should fluctuations of international market prices radiate into domestic markets? The options range from a completely open economy (the transmission elasticity, as defined in Chapter 2, is unity) to complete price isolation (transmission elasticity equal to zero) even though trade may occur. *Fourth*, to what extent should the nation rely on technology transfer or develop indigenous research and technology development capacity?

The policy choice by a particular nation is further influenced by the particular circumstances of that nation. These could be counted as more specific domestic constraints to national policy choice. We simply list them here and develop them further in subsequent chapters. In some cases, these additional constraints are a function of the stage of economic development. The list of the major factors is as follows:

• The role of agriculture in the national economy regarding first, the importance of agriculture to national economic aggregates, such as GNP, employment, fiscal revenue and costs, and foreign exchange balances; and second, the relative importance of food expenditure in consumer budgets, which in turn is a function of per-capita income. The more important both of these are, the more integrated food and agricultural policy should be in national macro and foreign exchange policy. As a generalization, this means that food and agricultural policy should rank higher in and be more integrated into the national agenda in developing countries than in developed countries.

• The openness of the economy and the degree of dependence on the international interface. This latter variable relates to both the levels of agricultural exports and food imports and the importance of capital flows and transfers.

• The relative weights given to growth versus equity or distribution issues. In developed countries this is more likely to be expressed as a concern about agricultural income distribution issues both between agriculture and the rest of the economy and within agriculture. In developing countries the issue may be in terms of the contribution of agriculture to economic growth and the role of the market in encouraging efficient resource allocation.

• The political balance of power between producer versus consumer interests.

• The political philosophy with regard to limited intervention (liberal policy), major intervention (dirigent policy), or complete intervention (central planning).

• The existence of market infrastructure in terms of the efficiency of intermediaries, availability of transportation, storage and processing facilities, and the degree to which production enters the market (degree of subsistence). Again, these variables tend to differentiate developed- from developing-country policy. Centrally planned economies fall somewhere in between.

The above list, though not complete, is sufficient to illustrate the point that even though countries may have similar objectives, their policy approach in terms of instrument selection may be different because of these kinds of factors, most of which are related to the stage of development of the country.

IV THE MEASUREMENT OF POLICY IMPACTS

The above analysis, while useful in a taxonomic way to identify the dimensions of policy choice that require attention, is nonetheless fraught with measurement difficulties of at least three sorts. First, selection of the optimal policy would require us to know the form of a societal welfare function. The economics literature contains not only debate about whether such a function is measurable but whether indeed it exists. Second, it would require the ability to quantify goals, which may be possible for specific objectives such as level of farm income or of export earnings but is much more difficult for qualitative normative variables such as equity and stability. Third, even if we could derive social welfare functions and quantify goals we would also require well-behaved continuous general equilibrium economic models which related instruments to goals in both conceptual and empirical terms.

However, policy makers do make choices and do attempt to quantify them. Frequently, analysts use more pragmatic and partial approaches. In the remainder of this section we discuss the most commonly used partial equilibrium approach, involving the concepts of producer and consumer surplus and the measurement of government revenues, consumer expenditures, and farm incomes. This approach attempts to measure the impacts of a particular policy change on specific goals. We begin with the revenue-expenditure impacts and then add the measurement of consumer and producer surplus to arrive at the net economic impacts.

A   Revenue and Expenditure Impacts of Policy Changes

A policy instrument generally changes market prices and involves government revenues and expenditures. Therefore, one way of looking at the impacts of a policy change is to look at the impacts on producers' gross revenue, consumers' gross expenditure, and on changes in government revenues.

In Figure 5-2, we present the two large countries–one-commodity trade model introduced in Chapter 2. Suppose in the beginning neither government intervenes, so that W_p, the world price, rules in both countries. Country A produces Q_2, consumes Q_1, and exports $Q_2 - Q_1$. Country B produces Q_5 and consumes Q_6, importing the difference ($Q_6 - Q_5$), which is equal to $Q_2 - Q_1$. Now suppose Country A raises the price to producers to D_p by paying an export subsidy. We are interested in being able to identify the impacts of this policy on all concerned in this particular market.

The impact of the policy is to shift outwards Country A's excess supply function, which causes world trade to expand and world price to fall to W_p'. Consumers will have to pay the higher domestic price and the export subsidy amount will be the difference between D_p and the new world price W_p'. Now we can consider the impacts on revenues and expenditures. Producers in Country A now receive gross revenues of $Q_4 \cdot D_p$, an increase over $Q_2 \cdot W_p$. Consumers in Country A now spend $Q_3 \cdot D_p$ instead of $Q_1 \cdot W_p$;

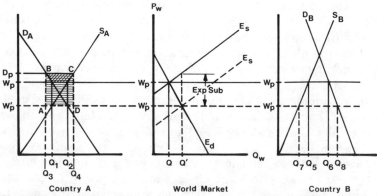

Figure 5-2 Revenue-expenditure impacts of an export subsidy policy.

they will be paying more or less depending upon whether the elasticity of domestic demand is less than or greater than one. Government expenditures in Country A increase from zero to $(Q_4 - Q_3) \cdot (D_p - Q'_p)$. Foreign exchange earnings in Country A change from $(Q_2 - Q_1) \cdot W_p$ to $(Q_4 - Q_3) \cdot W'_p$ which will be greater or less depending on the elasticity of the foreign import demand.

In Country B consumers now spend $Q_8 \cdot W'_p$ instead of $Q_6 \cdot W_p$ which is less if demand is inelastic and more if elastic. Producers receive $Q_7 \cdot W'_p$ which is clearly less than $Q_5 \cdot W_p$. Importers spend $(Q_8 - Q_7) \cdot W'_p$ of foreign exchange compared to $(Q_6 - Q_5) \cdot W_p$ which will be more or less depending on the weighted elasticities of domestic supply and demand.

This analysis yields determinate solutions in terms of the net changes in consumers' expenditures, producers' gross revenue, government costs (or revenues) and foreign exchange costs and earnings, provided that we know the supply and demand functions (or their elasticities) in each country.

B Producer and Consumer Surplus

The positive measurement of revenue and expenditure changes takes us part way to analyzing policy impacts, but does not give an adequate measure of the real income effects on producers, consumers, or the national economy. Producers, for instance, will need to buy more inputs to expand output, and will save costs when they contract. Consumers clearly do not feel better off just because high prices cause them to spend less on a product. Moreover, government revenues are transfers among groups in society, and do not immediately reflect changes in national income. A "normative" element must be added to the accounting of revenue and expenditure and producer surplus. While there continues to be debate on these concepts, one can make a plausible case that partial equilibrium welfare analysis is still the most useful devise for measuring policy impacts (Currie, Murphy, and Schmitz, 1971). Rather than entering this debate, we illustrate how the concepts are used in policy analysis.

The notion of consumer surplus is conceptually straightforward. The demand function represents the various quantities that consumers are willing to buy at different prices. Therefore, a perfectly discriminating monopolist could extract as revenue the whole area under the demand curve by selling to individual consumers at sequentially lower prices. But in a competitive market consumers buy all units for the market-clearing price. Therefore, it can be argued the area under the demand curve above price is surplus utility to consumers, or consumer surplus. This is illustrated in Figure 5-3a. If price is P_0, consumer surplus is area A. If price falls to P_1, the consumer gains are additional surplus equal to area B. We can now say unambiguously that consumers gain from a price fall regardless of the elasticity of demand. All that is required is that the demand function slope downward.

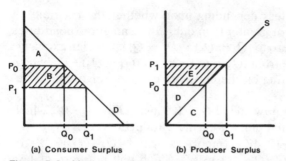

Figure 5-3 Measures of producer and consumer surplus.

The notion of producer surplus follows from neoclassical production theory. The firm's short-run supply function is its marginal cost curve (above minimum average variable cost). Assuming no input price effects, we can horizontally sum individual firm supply functions to get a market supply function. The area under this industry marginal cost will represent the total variable cost. Since producers receive the same price for all previous units, there will be a producers' surplus (or rent) over variable cost as shown by the area above the supply function but below the price. In Figure 5-3b the summation of individual marginal cost curves is shown as S. At price P_0, C is total variable cost and D is *producer surplus*. If price rises to P_1, the gain in producer surplus is given by area E. Compared with gross revenue, both measures unambiguously show that producers gain with price increases and vice versa, but the producers' surplus measure allows one to take into account the extra costs that producers incur in responding to the higher price.

Now, if we return to the case of an export subsidy (Figure 5-2), we can say that, regardless of the elasticity of demand in either country, consumers in Country A are "worse off" (they lost the area under the demand curve between D_p and W_p), and consumers in Country B are "better off" because they gained the area under their demand curve between W_p and W'_p. The result for producers is opposite in sign. If we looked at the country in terms of only producers and consumers, we can say Country A is better off (gains in producer surplus exceed losses of consumer surplus) and Country B is also better off because gains in consumer surplus exceed losses of producer surplus. But we have also to consider the government cost in Country A. The net gain in producer and consumer surplus in Country A is the cross-hatched area in Figure 5-2. The government cost is the area ABCD which is clearly more. Therefore, Country A is worse off by the difference between these two amounts. Country B, however, gains by the full amount of the difference between consumer gains and producer losses, in effect some of the benefits of the export subsidy have been transferred to Country B from the taxpayers in Country A.

This transfer of income from Country A to Country B arises solely because of the world price change, as discussed in Chapter 2. The terms of trade have moved against the exporter and in favor of the importer. The exporter, in this large-country case, has come up against the constraint of the international market. The net cost to the economy, the difference between the net private (i.e., producer and consumer) surplus gain and the government cost, includes two elements. The first is a domestic distortion arising from the excessive use of resources in production of this commodity and the artificial scarcity of the product to the consumer. These "dead-weight" welfare losses are shown in Figure 5-2 as the small triangles under the supply curve and the demand curve, respectively, bounded by the original world price and the new domestic price. The second element is the world price change times the (new) level of exports or the terms-of-trade loss. It can be seen from the figure that this terms-of-trade effect generates the gain to the importing country. In fact, it exceeds the net gain in Country B by the amount of two similar dead-weight welfare-loss triangles, bounded by the price change and the supply and demand curves in that country. The two sets of welfare losses are the cost to the "world" (i.e., the two countries together) of an artificial expansion of trade—or of the transfer of income, if that were the objective of the policy.

V INSTRUMENTS AVAILABLE AND THE MODEL

A country has a large set of specific policy instruments with which it could intervene in the food and agricultural sector. Each country, over time, will develop a unique, complex mix of such policy instruments. To develop an analytical framework for each conceivable policy instrument would be time consuming and would overburden us with detail. Rather what is needed is a generic framework that allows us to deal with general categories of policy. We look at the categories first and then develop a simple model which allows us to look at the impacts of broad policy classes. In the next section we explore the implications of an open versus a closed economy in the small-country case.

Most policies can be analytically conceived as either a tax or a subsidy or a quantitative restriction. In the agriculture-food system taxes, subsidies, and quantitative instruments could be applied at five levels:

- At the fixed (specific) factor or farmer-owned resource level, e.g., a policy to influence land use and availability
- At the level of purchased inputs, e.g., a fertilizer or credit subsidy
- At the final product production level, e.g., taxes or subsidies on wheat or livestock production
- At the consumption level, e.g., consumer subsidies on bread or milk
- At the border (in an open economy), e.g., tariffs and subsidies on trade or quantitative restrictions on imports

Table 5-1 Levels of Intervention, Instruments, and Goals

Examples of instruments	Location of intervention				
	Fixed factor (e.g., land, water)	Input markets	Product market	Consumption or retail level	Border
Public investment in land reclamation or irrigation	X				
Control of inputs					
(a) Land	X				
(b) Other		X			
Research	X	X			
Information and market efficiency	X	X	X	X	
Input subsidy or tax		X			
Guaranteed or fixed prices			X	X	
Direct payments to producers			X		
Consumer subsidy				X	
Quantitative policy					
(a) Supply requisition			X		
(b) Rationing				X	
Export tax					X
Export control					X
Import tax					X
Nontariff barriers					
(a) Quotas					X
(b) Variable levies					X
Stocks			X		X

P = primary goal
S = secondary goal

	Goals			
Growth and efficiency	Equity		Stability	
	Producers	Consumers	Producers	Consumers
P	S	S		
	P			
P	S	S		
P	P	P	S	S
	P	S		
	P	P	S	S
	P			
		P		
		P		
		P		
		S		P
		S		P
	P			
	P		P	P
			P	P

It is relatively easy to match particular instruments at these levels of policy intervention to policy goals. While it would be laborious to try a complete taxonomy, some illustrative examples seem useful at this point. Table 5-1 attempts to identify which goals might be the *primary* target of the instrument. For example, a country investing in an irrigation or a land reclamation project would shift the supply function of land, presumably because of a growth goal. Conversely, a supply management program which tried to reduce acreage would shift the supply function to the left and would usually be paired with an objective of enhancing producers' incomes. Taxes or subsidies could be applied at various levels—the input market, product market, retail market, or at the border. Similarly, quantitative interventions—requisitions, rationing, quotas—could apply at all market levels. Finally, price guarantees or fixed prices (accompanied by necessary complementary instruments) could occur in the product or retail markets. Most agricultural and food policy intervention involves variants of these instruments.

An intervention at any of these levels also has impacts on potentially all other parts of the system. For example, an input subsidy influences land owners, suppliers of inputs, the level of product output, consumer prices, and the net trade position. Further, it has a financial or fiscal impact on the government potentially both in terms of domestic fiscal cost and on foreign exchange balances.

Combinations of policies could give a nation's policy a distinctly producer or consumer orientation. For example, a combination of taxes on land use, inputs and production coupled with subsidies to consumers and no trade barriers could be characterized as a *consumer-oriented* policy. Conversely, a set of input subsidies coupled with high output prices, export subsidies, and import barriers could be characterized as a *producer-oriented* policy.

A   The Simple Closed Economy Model

What is needed is an analytical framework which allows us to look at the impacts of a policy or combinations of policies at the varying levels of the system described above. We start with a very simple model. We begin by assuming a production function involving two complementary inputs—farmer-owned resources (land) and purchased inputs (fertilizer). We assume initially that the product (wheat) is traded only in the domestic market. The demand for the final product (bread) is assumed exogenous, as is the supply of land and the supply of fertilizer. From these relationships we can derive (1) the demand for domestic production of wheat by subtracting the marketing margin from the demand for wheat; (2) the demand for fertilizer as given by the marginal value product (MVP) of that input in wheat production; (3) the demand for land as indicated by the MVP of land in wheat production; and

(4) the supply of wheat, as represented by the industry marginal cost of wheat production.

The model in a closed economy is graphically presented in Figure 5-4. The exogenous relations are in solid lines, the derived functions are indicated by dashed lines. Output is determined by the intersection of the demand for wheat and the supply of wheat. The model also shows that the fertilizer market and the land market are in simultaneous equilibrium with the product market.

From the model we get (1) price of wheat (P_w), (2) the price of bread $(P_w + \text{marketing margin} = P_B)$, (3) the price of fertilizer (P_F) and the quan-

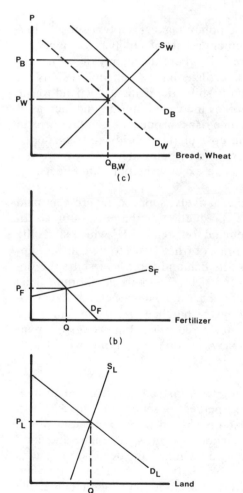

Figure 5-4 Relationships among domestic land, fertilizer, wheat, and bread markets.

tity of fertilizer used (Q_F), and (4) the rental equivalent price of land (P_L) and the quantity of land employed (Q_L). The product market determines gross farm income. Costs for purchased inputs determined in the input (fertilizer) market are assumed to be the farmer's cash production expenses. Therefore, $P_L Q_L$ (Figure 5-4a) in the land market is the residual difference between gross farm income and production expenses which is net farm income. When we probe, as we do next, the impacts of policy intervention at any level, we can immediately determine impacts on net farm income, the well-being of input suppliers, and on consumers.

We first explore the impacts of a few generic kinds of policy interventions in this closed economy model. In the next section, we open the economy to include border instruments.

1 Input Subsidy or Tax Suppose policy makers apply a subsidy to a purchased input, say fertilizer, of 50 percent rebate of supply price. What are the impacts? This is depicted in Figure 5-5b where the supply of fertilizer is rotated to S_F'. The shift in the supply of fertilizer has two effects: It shifts the supply of wheat to the right to S_W' and it shifts the demand for land to the right to D_L'. The new equilibrium involves increased output, and increased use of land and fertilizer. Net farm income rises (producers' gain), returns to fertilizer suppliers increase but at the cost of the subsidy (cross-hatched area) to the government, and consumers gain by being able to buy more at a lower price. A tax on an input would have exactly the opposite effects.

2 Consumer Subsidy or Tax Alternatively, suppose government paid a subsidy to consumers by giving a fixed reduction on the price of bread. In Figure 5-6, this shifts the consumer demand for bread to D_B' which shifts the demand for wheat to D_W'. The market price of wheat rises to P_W' causing supply to increase to $Q_{W,B}'$. The shift in this demand for wheat shifts the demands for both fertilizer and land to the right. The new equilibrium finds farm income increased by the hatched area in the land market, fertilizer producers' gross revenue has risen (also by the hatched area), consumers are better off buying more at the lower subsidized price, but the government pays a subsidy of the cross-hatched area. A tax on consumption would have exactly the opposite effects on all parties.

3 Restricting the Land Input Suppose, instead, government wanted wheat producers to reduce output by 15 percent (a set aside). This is shown in Figure 5-7a where the supply of land is shifted to S_L'. Output declines, consumer prices rise, fertilizer producers lose gross income, and land owners are better or worse off depending on whether the demand for land is inelastic or elastic, respectively. The elasticity of the demand for land depends on the nature of the wheat production function which includes the degree of substitutability of fertilizer for land in the production of wheat. As

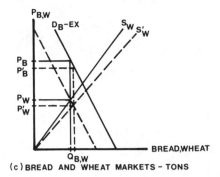

(c) BREAD AND WHEAT MARKETS – TONS

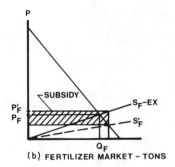

(b) FERTILIZER MARKET – TONS

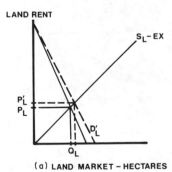

(a) LAND MARKET – HECTARES

Figure 5-5 Impact of an input subsidy on domestic markets.

drawn, it is inelastic and, therefore, land owners gain. A subsidy to land would have symmetrically opposite effects.

For completeness, we could explore other policies such as taxes or subsidies on production or guaranteeing producers a fixed price and paying the difference between the fixed price and market price. But these examples are sufficient to demonstrate the use of the model. We developed the model in a closed economy setting for simplicity and as a base against which to compare open economy policies which follow.

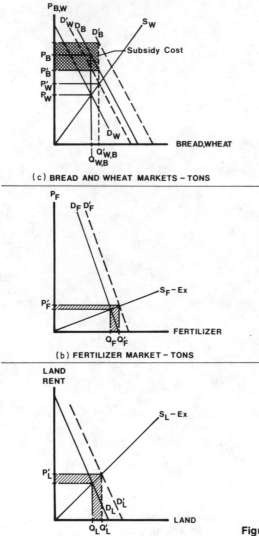

Figure 5-6 Impact of consumer subsidy on domestic markets.

B Open Economy: Small-Country Case

When we expand the model to the open economy case we must distinguish between whether the country is small, i.e., its actions do not influence world prices, or large, i.e., its actions influence world prices because it is a significant portion of the world market. In this chapter we are looking at the small-country case. In both cases, of course, a new set of policy instruments arise, namely, border taxes, subsidies or quantitative restrictions.

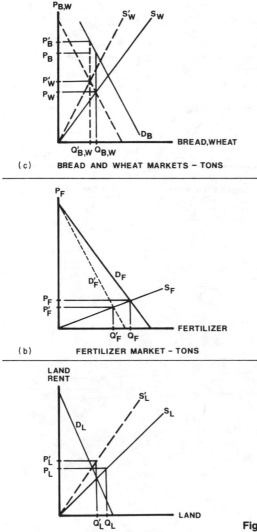

(c)   BREAD AND WHEAT MARKETS – TONS

(b)   FERTILIZER MARKET – TONS

(a)   LAND MARKET – HECTARES

Figure 5-7 Impact of land reduction on domestic markets.

In Figure 5-8 we make the necessary additions. In Figure 5-8*d* we separate out the domestic demand for bread and wheat and show the supply facing domestic consumers (S_{wd}). In Figure 5-8*e* we show world demand (supply) for exports (or imports) as P_w (P'_w). Given the small-country case, it is a perfectly elastic demand function for the domestic country's wheat (if an exporter) or a perfectly elastic supply function of imports (if an importer). S_x is this small country's excess supply function and D_M is excess demand when price falls below autarky price P. Thus, the demand facing domestic produc-

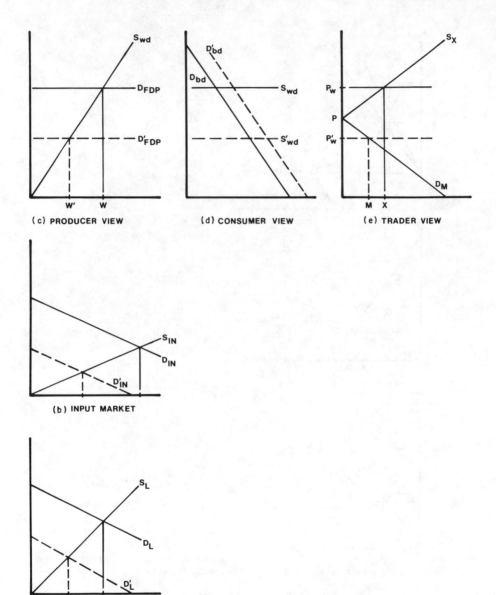

Figure 5-8 Relationships among domestic markets in a small open economy setting.

ers becomes perfectly elastic as shown in Figure 5-8c as does the demand for domestic production (D_{FDP} and D'_{FDP}). In the diagram we depict both the case where our country is an exporter (P_w with solid lines) or an importer (P'_w with dashed lines). We do this to show that the impacts of domestic intervention are identical whether we are talking about an exporter or an importer. A lower world price simply shifts the demand for domestic production downward and along with it (given our model) the demand functions for inputs (to D'_{IN}) and land (to D'_L). The other thing to note is that these latter two functions are now much flatter because of the open economy assumptions of a constant product price. One can look at policy intervention in an open economy using the same sequence as with the closed model.

1 **Input Subsidy or Tax** In Figure 5-9 suppose again our country's government applies a percentage rebate on an input (we operate on the exporter level only for simplicity but clearly the effects are the same for an importer). Again, the supply of fertilizer shifts to S'_{IN} which rotates the supply of wheat to S'_{WD} and the demand for land to D'_L. But note now because of the open economy assumption consumer prices do not change. In comparison to the closed case, the results are different. Consumers do not gain. Output increases more than in the closed case. All the benefits of the subsidy (diagonally hatched area) are captured by land owners (vertically hatched area) and fertilizer producers. Relative to the closed economy cases, resource owners are better off and the government is worse off with the same percentage subsidy on fertilizer. Finally, foreign exchange earnings are increased by the vertical-hatched area in Figure 5-9e. The effects of a tax again would be the opposite. In the case of the importer, the only difference would be foreign exchange savings instead of increased earnings.

2 **Consumer Subsidy or Tax** The case of the consumer subsidy is contained in Figure 5-10. The impact of a consumer subsidy is to benefit consumers at the cost to the government of the subsidy (shaded area) and to reduce foreign exchange earnings (diagonally hatched area) as exports are reduced to meet the increased domestic demand. However, note that there are no effects on domestic producers, land owners, and input suppliers because the demand for domestic production is not altered by the direct consumer subsidy. Thus, in this case and the previous one, policy in an open small economy allows policy makers to specifically target subsidies (or taxes) without spill-over effects on other groups as was always the case in the closed economy model. Producers would not be likely to support consumer subsidies, whereas in the closed case they stood to share the benefits. Again, the case for a tax is the opposite and the effects are the same for importers except that the policy would increase foreign exchange costs.

3 **Restricting the Land Input** Restricting land inputs in the small-country–open economy case benefits no one (Figure 5-11). The policy does not affect consumers. Exporters lose foreign exchange (importers increase

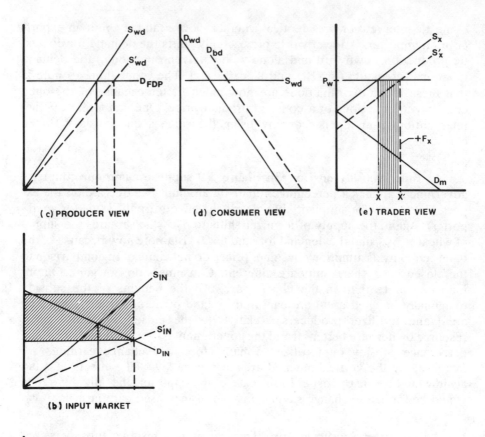

(c) PRODUCER VIEW   (d) CONSUMER VIEW   (e) TRADER VIEW

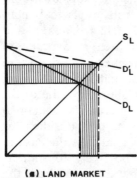

(b) INPUT MARKET

(a) LAND MARKET

Figure 5-9 Impacts of an input subsidy in a small open economy.

foreign exchange costs), fertilizer producers sell less at a lower price (losses are the diagonally hatched area in Figure 5-11b, and land owners lose (diagonally hatched losses plus vertically hatched gains in Figure 5-11a) if the demand for land is elastic (very likely given the perfectly elastic demand

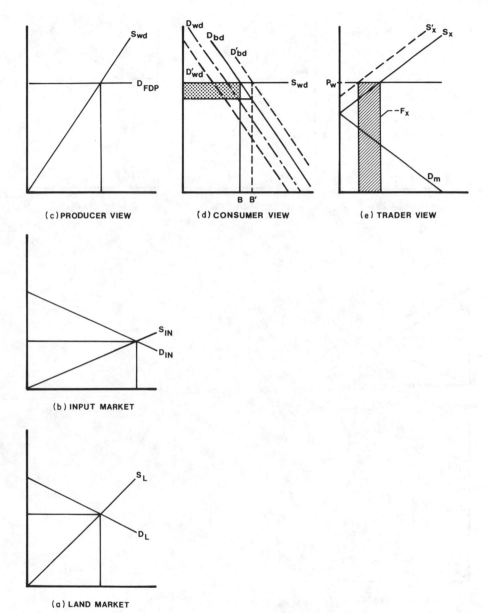

Figure 5-10 Impacts of a consumer subsidy in a small open economy.

for domestic production). Thus, a small open economy country should strike control of land inputs from its arsenal, as in fact most do.

4 Producer Deficiency Payment Suppose now government guarantees

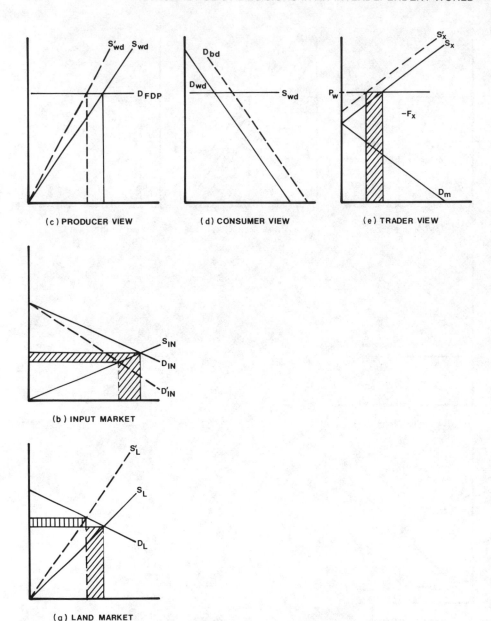

Figure 5-11 Impacts of a reduction in land use in a small open economy

domestic producers a fixed price. As output expands, land owners and fertilizer producers share the gain which is a direct transfer of the deficiency payment cost and exporters earn more foreign exchange. Thus, the case of a production subsidy targets specifically on the agricultural sector with no benefits to consumers.

5 Border Tax or Subsidy Trade offers a country an additional set of policy instruments. In Figure 5-12, we analyze the case of an importer who applies a fixed tariff of t to imports. This shifts the demand for domestic production vertically upward to D''_{FDP} which shifts the demand for land to D''_L and for inputs to D''_{IN}. Production expands with both land owners and input

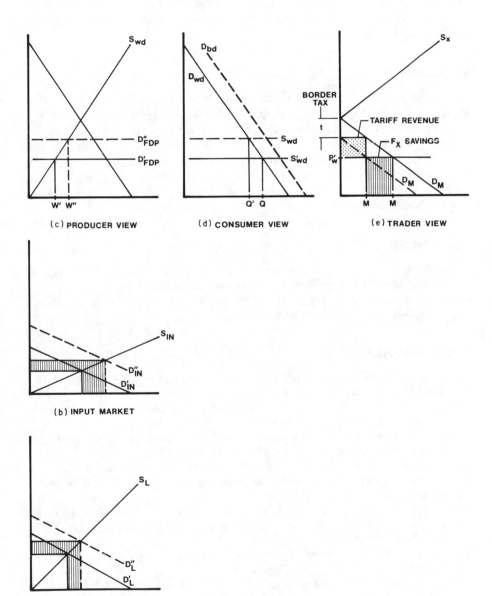

(c) PRODUCER VIEW (d) CONSUMER VIEW (e) TRADER VIEW

(b) INPUT MARKET

(a) LAND MARKET

Figure 5-12 Impacts of a border tax in a small open economy.

producers gaining by the vertically hatched areas. Imports are reduced because of both the contraction in domestic consumption and the expansion of domestic production. Therefore, there are foreign exchange savings (vertically hatched area) and tariff revenue (shaded area) but domestic consumers lose. A quota on imports equal to the reduction in domestic consumption (Figure 5-12d) would have identical effects except that the tariff revenue would go to quota holders as rent. An export subsidy could be similarly analyzed.

VI SUMMARY

We terminate our discussion of the small-country case here even though there are many additional policies that could be considered. In summary, the differences between the closed and open cases are significant. Subsidy or tax policies can be more specifically targeted on producers or consumers and certain policies become undesirable, e.g., supply control of any sort unless it is accompanied by some sort of border control. In the next chapter we discuss the ramifications of being a large country, still using a single-commodity, single-instrument model.

REFERENCES

Currie J. M., Murphy, J. A., and Schmitz, A. 1971. "The Concept of Economic Surplus and Its Use in Economic Analysis," *Econ. J.,* **81**:741-799.

Hathaway, D. E. 1963. *Government and Agriculture: Economic Policy in a Democratic Society,* Macmillan, New York.

ADDITIONAL READINGS

Hathaway, D. E. 1981. "Government and Agriculture Revisited: A Review of Two Decades of Change," *Amer. J. Ag. Econ.,* **63**:779-787.

Infanger, C. L., Bailey, W. C., and Dyer, D. 1983. "Agricultural Policy in Austerity: The Making of the 1981 Farm Bill," *Amer J. Agr. Econ.,* **65**:1-9.

Knutson, R. D., Penn. J. B., and Boehm, W. T. 1983. *Agricultural and Food Policy,* Prentice-Hall, Englewood Cliffs, N.J., chaps. 1 and 2, pp. 3-34.

Lin, W., Johnson, J., and Calvin, L. 1981. *Farm Commodity Programs: Who Participates and Who Gets the Benefits,* Ag. Econ. Report 474, ESCS, USDA, Washington, D.C.

McCalla, A. F. 1977. *Agricultural and Food Policy Issues Analysis: Some Thoughts from an International Perspective,* Special Report, International Food Policy Research Institute, Washington, D.C.

Tinbergen, J. 1966. *Economic Policy: Principles and Design,* North Holland Publishing Co., Amsterdam, chap. 1, pp. 1-26.

Tweeten, L. G. 1979. *Foundations of Farm Policy,* 2d ed., revised, University of Nebraska Press, chaps. 1 and 2, pp. 1-59.

Chapter 6

Large-Country — Single-Commodity Choice: Passive and Active Market Power

I INTRODUCTION

In the previous chapter, analysis focused on small countries (i.e., price takers) in world markets pursuing single-instrument policy choices for one commodity. In this chapter the analysis proceeds to look at the large-country case. Largeness was defined in Chapter 2. What it means for the analysis in this chapter is that exporters face downward sloping world excess demand functions and importers face upward sloping import supply functions. Initially, the analytical framework developed in Chapter 5 is extended to the large-country case where single-instrument policy intervention is explored at the various levels in parallel with previous analysis.

Clearly, in the large-country case, domestic policy choice, even if passively pursued, influences world price and results in international transfers of gains and losses. The next logical step is to explore what would happen if large countries selected domestic policy instruments recognizing international interdependence and chose policies to maximize domestic welfare by manipulating world markets to their advantage. The actions taken by large countries would be unilateral (i.e., acting alone), or collusive (i.e., acting in conjunction with other exporters or importers). The analytical apparatus useful for looking at single-country analysis can be used, with minor modifications, for collusive or cartel action. The basic differences relate to inter-country collusion on matters of market shares and the sharing of profits. We look first at importer possibilities by analyzing the case of the optimum import tariff. For exporters, several possibilities exist: (1) the optimal export tax and the government cartel, (2) the producer marketing board and the producer cartel, (3) the dominant-country price leadership model and the parallel cartel model, and (4) the case of intercountry price discrimination. The latter three options would also be available to importers and could be analyzed by using parallel monopsony analysis. However, this is not done here. In all cases, it is assumed that the export supply or import demand functions facing the large country (or countries) is sloped and may be steeper because of other countries' domestic policy intervention. While not explicitly done in this section, the analysis could be incorporated into the national policy model developed in Chapter 5 and extended to the large-country case in the next section of this chapter.

Fixed policy prices in both exporter and importer markets, leading to more steeply sloped world excess supply and excess demand functions, also increase potential monopoly profits for large international intermediaries. This case is also explored in this chapter. Finally, all the models developed in this chapter are static and involve only some of the large actors (exporter or importers). The reality is that the world is dynamic and could involve attempted simultaneous exercises of monopoly power by actors with opposing interests. The chapter concludes with a brief discussion of a dynamic model.

II OPEN ECONOMY: LARGE COUNTRY—PASSIVE ANALYSIS

We can retain the basic national model developed in Chapter 5 but we need to modify the international interface. In Figure 6-1e, we have net world supply and demand functions representing everyone but the domestic country. But the country of analysis is now large. Therefore, the large country faces a sloping excess function derived from the world market. In Figure 6-1d the vertical price axis intersects a continuum on the horizontal axis with exports to the right and imports to the left. Therefore, we need to construct the world excess function facing the large country. At price W_p, the rest of the world excess supply would just equal world excess demand. Therefore, we have one point on the excess function facing our country. It is on the vertical axis at point A where there would be no demand for the country's output. For prices below W_p, the rest of the world would be a net importer, thus the excess function facing our country is a demand function D_{Ed}. For prices above W_p, the rest of the world has a surplus and would have a net excess supply function E_S. Thus, the excess supply and demand function facing our large country is $E_S = D_{Ed}$. We could, of course, introduce transportation costs and recognize the difference between f.o.b. and c.i.f. prices. In this case, the excess supply and demand function would be discontinuous at the vertical price axis. World prices that fell between c.i.f. and f.o.b. prices

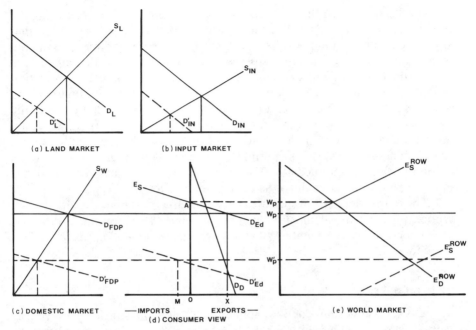

Figure 6-1   Relationships among domestic markets in a large open economy.

would result in the case of autarky. We proceed without this additional dimension, however, recognizing that it exists.

Next, we need to develop our operational demand function for the domestic market, namely, the demand for domestic production. This function is the relevant one for domestic policy makers. It is constructed by horizontally summing domestic demand D_D and the world excess function $E_S = D_{Ed}$. This yields D_{FDP} in Figure 6-1c. As in the small-country case, a shift in world market supply to $E_S^{\prime ROW}$ would switch the country from an exporter to importer (dashed lines in Figure 6-1) lowering demand for domestic production to D'_{FDP} and shifting the demands for inputs and land. It would, however, not alter the general impacts of the policy instruments we are about to analyze. The second thing to note is that this model implicitly says that world prices are set in the domestic market. This comes from the particular construction we are using; it could just as easily be done by aggregating the excess function of this large country into the rest of the world market and having price formed there. The results of either approach are analytically identical. However, we may also note that this may be a bad depiction of world grain and oilseeds markets where the United States is a large actor with a relatively open economy policy and active price formation markets (futures markets).

Having developed the large-country model we can turn to exploring the implications of our set of policy interventions. But we can short-circuit that to some extent. It should now be clear that the closed economy case and the small-country open economy cases are extreme in terms of the slope of the crucial function in this model, namely, the demand for domestic production which in turn influences the slopes of the demands for land and inputs in the large-country case. The demand for domestic production is quite steep (the elasticity of domestic demand for agricultural products is, it is generally agreed, quite inelastic) in the closed economy case. In the small-country, open economy case, it is perfectly elastic. The large-country, open economy case is intermediate. The demand for domestic production has some slope but never as much as in the closed economy case.

Thus, the impacts of policy are qualitatively similar to the closed economy case but we must now include impacts on foreign producers, consumers, and governments. We work through a couple of cases to confirm this conclusion.

A Input Subsidy

As before, assume our country applies a 50 percent subsidy to fertilizer users (Figure 6-2). This shifts fertilizer supply to S'_{IN}, domestic supply to S'_W, and the demand for land to D'_L. The expanded output, contrary to the small

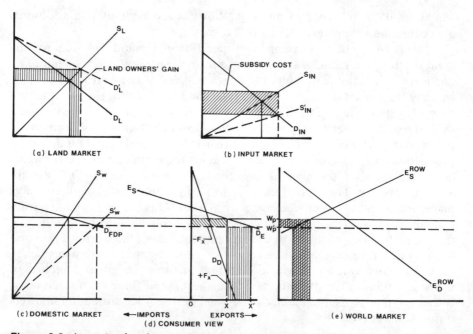

Figure 6-2 Impacts of an input subsidy in a large open economy.

case, causes world prices to fall to W'_p. In the domestic market the results are qualitatively similar to the closed case. However, the distribution of total benefits and costs is more complex. Land owners benefit as before but less than in the open-small case but more than in the closed case (price did not fall as far). Fertilizer producers benefit from increased sales at a higher price. Domestic consumers benefit somewhat but not as much as in the case of the closed economy as some of the benefits are now transferred internationally to foreign consumers. Finally, foreign producers lose gross revenue—selling less at lower prices. This is shown as the cross-hatched area in Figure 6-2e.

B Land Restriction

The case of land restriction is presented in Figure 6-3. The analysis is now becoming routine and potentially tedious so we discuss only the result. This case is akin to the U.S. PIK program of 1983 which we analyze in more detail in Chapter 8. Landowners may or may not benefit depending on whether the demand for land is inelastic or elastic. Input suppliers are worse off as are domestic consumers. Exporters lose foreign exchange earnings if net import demand is elastic (importers increase foreign exchange costs). Foreign consumers also transfer benefits to foreign producers and potentially to domestic landholders. Foreign producers clearly capture part of the benefits of the program.

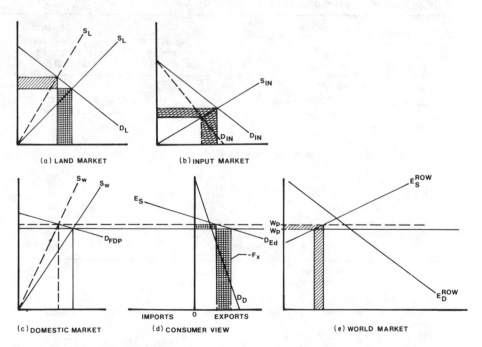

Figure 6-3 Impacts of a reduction in land use in a large open economy.

C Summary

The analysis could proceed with further illustrations but the ones shown are sufficient to show how to use the model for not only the large-country case but the small-country open and closed economy cases discussed in the preceding chapter. A comparative summary is presented in Table 6-1. Readers are invited to use its analysis to explore further possible policy instruments.

It is, however, worthwhile to pause at this stage in our analysis to summarize what we have learned to date using this simple model. These conclusions are useful as we proceed with additional analysis. *First,* outcomes from almost all kinds of single-instrument intervention are different depending on the assumptions regarding openness and size. The *second* conclusion, however, simplifies analysis, namely, that the results are qualitatively the same whether the country is an exporter or an importer. *Third,* a small open country can be the most precise in targeting beneficiaries of policy intervention. *Fourth,* the open economy large-country case is only quantitatively different from the closed economy case in that benefits and costs are now shared with foreign producers and/or consumers. *Fifth,* benefits and the incidence of costs depend crucially on the elasticities of critical supply and demand functions. This conclusion will be used as we now proceed with

Table 6-1 General Results in Large-Country Case

	Input subsidy			Consumer subsidy		
	C	O-S	O-L	C	O-S	O-L
A. Home country						
Domestic producer–land owner rents	+	+	?	+	0	+
Purchased Input suppliers	+	+	+	+	0	+
Domestic consumer	+	0	+	+	+	+
Domestic budget	−	−	−	−	−	−
Home country foreign exchange reserves	0	+	+*	0	−	−†
B. Foreign country						
Foreign land owners rents	0	0	−	0	0	+
Foreign input suppliers	0	0	−	0	0	+
Foreign consumers	0	0	+	0	0	−
Foreign budgets	0	0	0	0	0	0
Foreign country foreign exchange reserves	0	0	−†	0	0	+‡

Symbols: + = positive effect = gain
     − = negative effect = loss
     0 = no effect
     ? = unknown effect *a priori*
*A positive effect on foreign exchange *if* demand facing domestic producers is *elastic.*
†If import demand is *elastic.*
‡If demand for land or inputs is inelastic.

the next set of analyses where large countries attempt to actively exercise market power. Finally, as noted in Chapter 5, the actions of the large country alter international terms of trade. A complete accounting of overall welfare impacts would have to include this as well.

III SINGLE LARGE-COUNTRY EXERCISES OF MARKET POWER

It is clear from the analysis in the previous section that large countries who pursue policy intervention influence world prices even though they are looking only at domestic goals. The logical next step is to ask, Could countries do better in terms of domestic objectives if they manipulated international markets to improve their own position?

This possibility becomes more interesting if other countries are also fixing or guaranteeing internal prices which results in their excess demand or supply functions being more inelastic as was shown in Chapter 2. Fixing internal prices to producers and consumers above world price levels and defending these with quotas, variable levies, or export subsidies results in the excess demand function of an importer or the excess supply function of

Supply restrictions			Deficiency payment			Border tax		
C	O-S	O-L	C	O-S	O-L	C	O-S	O-L
+‡	−	+‡	+	+	+	·	+	+
−	−	−	+	+	+	·	+	+
−	0	−	+	+	+	·	−	−
−	−	−	−	−	−	·	+	+
0	−	−	0	+	+	·	+	+
0	0	+		0	−	·	0	−
0	0	+	0	0	−	·	0	−
0	0	−	0	0	+	·	0	+
0	0	?	0	0	?	·	0	−
0	0	−	0	0	−	·	0	−

0 = no effect
C = closed economy
O-S = open-small country
O-L = open-large country

an exporter becoming more inelastic while simultaneously increasing domestic production. The result is to lower world prices and increase quota rents or tariff income. A question naturally arises, Could the importer(s) or exporter(s) select the level of internal prices such that the country(ies) maximizes domestic welfare? The analysis proceeds first with the single-country case and then extends it to collusive action. Importers are treated first before turning to the exporter case.

A Importer Exercise of Power

1 **Single Importer Exercises of Power—Optimum Tariff**   If an importing country is large in international markets, it faces an upward sloping net import supply function from the rest of the world. Enke (1944) demonstrated that a single importer would improve domestic welfare by imposing an optimal import tariff to maximize domestic monopoly rent. In the simplest case, suppose a country has no domestic supply of a commodity (e.g., United States for coffee or tea) and faces an upward sloping world supply function. The case is demonstrated in Figure 6-4. Domestic demand is D–D. World excess supply is S_w. Because the importer wishes to maximize domestic monopoly rent, it behaves as a monopsonist and sets the marginal import cost (MIC) (shown by the curve marginal to S_w) equal to demand, charges domestic consumers P_d, and buys Q_{im} from the world market at P_{im}. Gross tariff revenues or "quota rents" are $P_{im}P_dAB$. Consumers lose P_dACE of consumer surplus from the price rise. The net gain to the country is $P_{im}EDB - ADC$. The gain becomes less the flatter the world supply func-

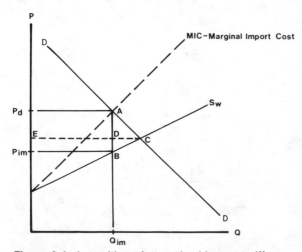

Figure 6-4 Imposition of an optimal import tariff.

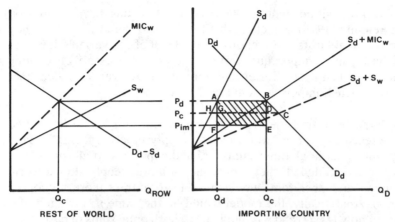

Figure 6-5 Optimal import tariff in the presence of domestic supply.

tion (it disappears in the small-country case) and conversely greater the steeper the world supply function. The outcome would be the same if there were domestic producers and the national authorities wished to exploit domestic producers as well. In this case, one would simply add domestic supply to S_w. Now, of course, there would be a domestic producer loss of some portion of BDC. Thus, this case would not be optimum from the national point of view.

Suppose, however, that the domestic authorities wish only to exploit foreign suppliers and raise prices to domestic consumers (a producer-oriented policy) and there exist domestic producers. This case is depicted in Figure 6-5. Domestic demand is D_d-D_d, domestic supply is S_d, and world excess supply is S_w. Our country operating as a monopsonist is interested in MIC_{ROW}. Analytically, we horizontally sum MIC_w and S_d to derive the function $S_d + MIC$. The country sets this equal to demand and chooses the domestic price of P_d at which consumers consume Q_c. Domestic producers produce Q_d at price P_d. The difference $Q_c - Q_d$ is imported. To induce exporters to supply $Q_c - Q_d$ (equivalent to $0 - Q_e$) the importer has to pay P_{im}, which is determined by the price vertically below the intersection of MIC_w and D_d-S_d. The optimal tariff is $P_{im} - P_d$ and tariff revenue is ABEF (cross-hatched area). For a proof of the optimality of this solution the reader is referred to a paper by Carter and Schmitz (1979).

Clearly, the country gains. Consumers lose P_dBCP_c; producers gain P_dAHP_c; and the government gains ABEF. Therefore, the net gain is (GDEF) − (BCD) − (AGH). All these are in comparison to the passive or competitive solution of P_c (where $S_d + S_w = D_d - D_d$). Of course, this statement of gains is contingent on the assumption that exporting coutries do not retaliate. The proposition depicted here is one that has been argued by Carter and Schmitz (1979) who claim that the EC and Japan acted as if they were setting optimal tariffs in the choice of the level of the variable levy and the size of the Japanese import quota. We are not here necessarily accepting the empirical conclusions of Carter and Schmitz. However, it is clear that conceptually, at least, importers could do so and gain.

2   **An Importer Cartel**   Action by a single importer would be limited by the slope (elasticity) of the world excess supply function facing it. That excess function is net of all other importers and exporters. If all (or at least all large) importers colluded, they would face a more steeply sloped world supply function and, therefore, would be able to extract more monopoly profits (rents). Analytically, the model would be the same as in Figure 6-4 and 6-5 except now D_d-D_d and S_d would be the horizontal sums of participating importers' domestic supply and demand functions. Importing countries participating in the cartel would gain monopsony rent at the expense of foreign producers but also from their own domestic consumers.

However, two new problems do arise for the importer cartel. First, countries might have different cost relationships, thus the optimal price for the cartel would be different for at least some of its members. Some mechanism would be necessary to allocate cartel rents differently than the imports to induce members to abide by cartel price. Second, enhanced prices could shift some members from being importers to being exporters raising the problem of intracartel trade. If it was permitted, overall cartel revenue would decline. If it was not, the low-cost members would face costs of export subsidies and would be tempted to break the cartel by paying slightly higher prices to exporters. Whether or not it would pay several large importing countries to collude would depend on the magnitude of increased monopsony rents versus the costs of organizing and administering a cartel. The reality of world agrricultural markets is that there is no high importer concentration, thus, potentially making the costs of collusion high.

3   **Implications of Importer Power**   Several comments are in order. First, gains to the importer(s) are greater the steeper the slope of the world supply function. This is equivalent to saying gains are greater the larger the particular importer(s) is (are) in terms of market share. Second, government gains are greater, the larger the share of domestic consumption that is imported. The converse is also true, namely, domestic producers gain more the larger their share of domestic consumption. Third, as noted before, the gains are conditional on no retaliation. Finally, note again that the optimal import tariff clearly benefits producers and the nation as a whole but at the expense of consumers unless the government uses the tariff revenue to compensate consumers. Full compensation is possible only if imports are a significant proportion of domestic consumption as can be seen by inspection of Figure

6-5. Therefore, producers and government fiscal authorities would argue in favor of optimal tariffs on the basis of net national welfare. Consumers would lobby against it on the grounds that such policies reduce their consumer surplus.

In terms of the world market, implications of importer power are that world prices are lower and trade volumes contract. In the absence of exporter intervention, foreign consumers gain and foreign producers lose.

B Exporter Exercises of Power

The set of options open to exporters is larger than for importers. It is also a subject that has received more attention (McCalla, 1981). In particular, the cartel question has been analyzed in a recent book (Schmitz, McCalla, Mitchell, and Carter, 1981). Our intent is not to enter into the debate as to what is the appropriate characterization of world markets. Rather, our approach is to look at a selected set of analyses of the implications of exporter(s) market power. Assuming that exporters attempt to operate to set world prices to maximize national welfare, how could they go about doing so and what are the implications of the attempt?

We consider four cases: (1) the optimal export tax, (2) the producer marketing board, (3) price leadership by the dominant country, and (4) price discrimination. In the first three cases, we consider first the single-country case and then extend it to a cartel analysis. In the last case we look at only the cartel case.

1 Optimal Export Tax

(i) Single Country Consider first the case of a large country that seeks to maximize national welfare by applying an export tax. The objective function is to maximize the sums of producer and consumer surplus and net treasury benefits. Figure 6-6 presents the analysis. Domestic supply and demand in the exporting country are S_d and D_d, respectively. The exporters excess supply is E_s in the rest of the world (ROW) (Figure 6-6b). The net difference between the sum of all other exporters and importers supply and demand functions is E_d (world net import demand facing the exporter). For the exporting country to operate as a monopolist, the relevant decision function is the marginal export revenue (i.e., the curve marginal to world excess demand, MR_{Ed}). This is equated to E_s and Q_e is chosen as the optimal export quantity, charging export customers P_i. The tax rate is $P_i - P_d$ and this rate times $0-Q_e$ is tax revenue gained from foreign importers. This is BCFG in Figure 6-6a.

The price necessary to induce domestic producers to produce $0-Q_e$ in excess of domestic consumption is P_d. Producers produce Q_p and domestic consumers buy $0-Q_d$. The market clears and on net the exporting country is better off. How can we show this? The free trade price would be P_c (where

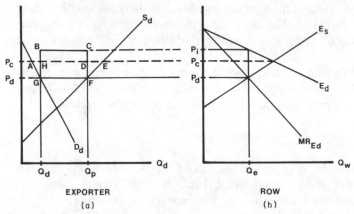

Figure 6-6 Imposition of an optimal export tax.

$E_s = E_d$). Relative to that price, producers have lost P_cEFP_d in producer surplus. Consumers have gained P_cAGP_d and the government has earned BCFG in tax revenue. Net gain is (BCDH) − (AHG) − (DEF) which is positive for export tax levels below a certain limit under the large-country assumption of this model. Therefore, the country is better off but are producers in the exporting country better off? In the absence of any transfer of tariff revenue to producers they are unequivocally worse off. It turns out that even if all the tariff revenue was transfered to producers it is not necessarily true that producers are better off. Carter, Gallini, and Schmitz (1980) show the conditions under which some of the consumer gain would have to be taxed for producers to gain even if they received all of the tariff revenue.

(ii) Government Cartel   The problem with actions by a single country to raise the price charged to importers by the implementation of an export tax is that there is a free-rider problem that increases in significance the less dominant the single country is in world markets. Other exporters can slightly undercut current market price. However, as E_d already contains other countries' supply functions, longer-run price cutting in the normal sense is not analytically permissible. Further, P_i being above P_c (competitive price) could induce supply expansion in subsequent years as other countries shift into the particular commodity. Therefore, there would seem to be incentives for exporters to form a cartel. This seems a particularly interesting possibility in many agricultural markets (e.g., wheat, coarse grains, soybeans, coffee, tea) where exporter concentration ratios are high.

Analytically, we can continue to use the analysis in Figure 6-6, only now E_s is the sum of individual-country excess supply functions. If it is assumed that cost structures in exporters are similar (identical), no problems of aggregation occur. However, operational rules which are enforceable would be required. These would be, first, that P_d is passed back to domestic markets for both producers and consumers. The monopoly profits earned by the cartel, if paid to producers, would need to be in a lump sum payment so as to not stimulate production beyond Q_p in each country. Second, countries would have to agree to sell to all importers at P_i. There would be a strong incentive for individual countries to raise P_d slightly and undercut P_i to sell additional output. This is the free-rider problem. Therefore, penalties for cheating would have to be devised to force compliance. The possibilities for these are discussed in Schmitz et al. (1981). Third, a means of monitoring the behavior of members would be required to detect cheating. However, if all these rules could be enforced, the cartel members would be better off, though as indicated in the single-country case producers would not necessarily be better off.

Of course, the volume of world trade would be less as producers in importing countries would respond to higher prices and expand production. In addition, noncartel exporting members would be encouraged to expand production. It is also possible that the higher prices could shift low-cost importers to become exporters. Thus, the long-run stability of the cartel would always be in question. In terms of gains and losses, consumers in the exporting country and producers in the importing countries are better off. Producers in cartel countries may be better off when they receive compensation. Consumers in importing countries are worse off.

2 Producer Marketing Board

(i) Single Country The optimal export tax model had one deficiency from the producers' point of view, namely, unless all of the tax revenue plus, in some cases, some of the consumer gain is given to producers by the government, they are not necessarily better off. An alternative is for producers in a single country or several countries to band together in a producer marketing board and gain monopoly rent at the expense of both domestic and foreign consumers. This case is what Schmitz et al. (1981), call a producer cartel as opposed to a government cartel, the previous case. Figure 6-7 presents the analysis. Domestic demand is D_d, net import demand is E_d, and domestic supply is S_d. The producer monopolist would horizontally sum $D_d + E_d$ to total demand, take the marginal to total demand (MR to total demand), and equate it to S_d. The optimal level of sales is Q_o sold at price P_o. $0-Q_d$ is consumed domestically and $Q_d - Q_o$ is exported. Relative to free trade, producers are better off. They extract $P_o EFP_{ft}$ from domestic consumers and EDAF from foreign consumers. This gain more than offsets their loss in producer surplus of ABC. Foreign and domestic consumers are clearly worse off and the government gains no revenue.

However, there is one major problem. If producers pass price P_o to themselves, they would want to produce Q_p, not Q_o. Thus, some method of allocation or rationing of supply would be necessary. If, for example, the monopolist was the Canadian Wheat Board acting for producers, the board,

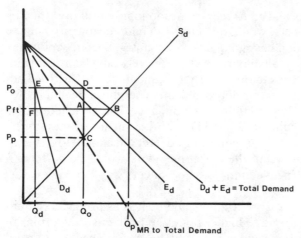

Figure 6-7   Export tax to maximize producer profits.

either via marketing quotas or production limits, would have to constrain production to Q_o or face a problem of accumulated storage.

    (ii)   *Producer Cartel*   Again, the same model could be applied to a collection of producers by making S_d and D_d the sums of domestic supply and demand of members. As with the government cartel, problems of price maintenance, detection of cheating, and enforcement of sanctions would be required. But the producer cartel has additional problems. In the government cartel case, if the lower internal price P_d were enforced, no excess supply would result. However, in the producer case, P_o is the producer price. Therefore, each country would have to restrain production to Q_o. Therefore, the cartel would have to allocate production quotas to members. How could it do this? One approach would be to apply the familiar multiplant monopoly model where production is allocated such that the marginal cost of production of the last unit is the same in each country, i.e., where P_p is equal to supply in each country (assuming country supply is the horizontal summation of producer marginal cost curves). This is also the only solution which maximizes cartel profits. If costs were similar in each country this rule could also allocate cartel profits on the basis of production shares. However, if costs were significantly different, it might pay the cartel to bribe high-cost producers not to produce. This clearly would require a profit or rent allocation rule in addition to a production allocation rule. These and other issues are discussed in detail in Schmitz et al. (1981), and are not extended here.

In sum, the impact of an exporter cartel of either sort would be to reduce world trade and raise world prices. Exporters would have problems of enforcing production reduction in each member and, for the producer cartel, allocation rules among members would be required for both profits and market shares. A cartel would be an international distortion but whether it would be more distorted than is currently the case because of domestic policy intervention is a question of empirical analysis comparing two second-best situations. Finally, as the Schmitz et al. (1981) analysis suggests, there could be short-run gains to cartel members but long-run sustainability in the face of cheating and nonmember production expansion would be more problematical.

3 Price Leadership Model It is often argued that the United States as a dominant exporter is both a price setter in world temperate zone grain and oilseed markets and is at the same time a residual supplier. The next model investigates this type of pricing arrangement of exporter market power both for the case of a single country and as a cartel model with a fringe of competitors.

(i) Price Leadership by a Dominant Country The approach to this issue applies the dominant-firm oligopoly analysis familiar to all students of intermediate microeconomics. The analysis is presented in Figure 6-8. Assume that one country, say the United States, is a large exporter of a commodity. United States supply is S_d. Let ED_{ROW} be the summation of net import demands of all importers. Suppose also that there are a set of small exporters who are content to sell all they can at the price the United States sets. Let ΣS be the sum of their supply functions. Finally, let us assume that the United States is willing to let the fringe sell all they can at whatever price the United States sets. Therefore, the demand function facing the United States

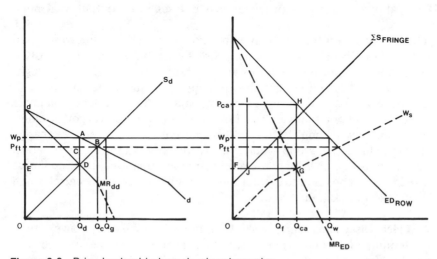

Figure 6-8 Price leadership by a dominant country.

is $d-d$ which is the horizontal subtraction of ΣS from ED_{ROW}. If the United States wants to maximize national returns it equates the marginal revenue to $d-d$ (MR_{dd}) to U.S. supply S_d to determine the optimal output Q_d. The United States charges W_p (off $d-d$) which is world price. At that price the fringe of competitive exporters sell $O-Q_f$. This plus $O-Q_d$ (O_f-Q_w) satisfies world demand of Q_w. The United States sets world price but simultaneously is a residual supplier. If producer price is set at P_p, the United States is better off compared to the competitive situation P_{ft} because the net loss in producer surplus (BCD) is more than offset by the net gain in monopoly rent $W_p A C P_{ft}$. Also, the fringe is better off selling a larger quantity at a higher price. Consumers globally are worse off.

There are several ways the United States could price domestically. It could charge an export tax equal to $W_p - P_p$. This case would be identical to the optimal export tax discussed earlier. Or a mandatory supply control program could be implemented to restrict supply to Q_d. Or if W_p is paid to U.S. producers, they would like to produce Q_g not Q_d and some form of supply control would be necessary. If this were a paid diversion program, some of the benefits of supply control would be transferred to other exporters. If these additional diversion costs exceeded the net benefits, i.e., $(W_p A C P_{ft}) - (BCD)$, then the United States might prefer the competitive solution of P_{ft} and Q_c without supply control costs. At the competitive price other exporters are clearly less well off.

(ii) A Price Leadership Cartel It appears, therefore, that it might be both in the interests of the United States and the fringe to come together and form a cartel. If they did this, they would want to equate W_s (the horizontal sum of S_d and ΣS) to the marginal to ED_{ROW} (MR_{ED}), charge P_{ca} with output Q_{ca}. This is, of course, the exporter cartel case discussed in Section 6-III-B-1 above. The fringe produces less but sells that output at a much higher price.

The real question then is, Why don't exporters get together to form an Organization of Grain Exporting Countries? Two possible reasons are often advanced. First, importing countries are not homogeneous. Some are high-income developed countries that already support domestic agriculture with high prices, e.g., EC and Japan. They presumably have perfectly inelastic net demands for imports and are ripe for exploitation. However, other countries are poor (low-income LDCs) and may have severe foreign exchange constraints. This latter group would be greatly disadvantaged by a cartel. The second reason is that there are a few large multinational intermediaries who would be in a position to extract the monopoly rents of the cartel. Each possible reason is examined in turn.

4   Price Discrimination Model   If nations have market power, they could attempt to improve export earnings or accrue foreign exchange savings by discriminating between markets or suppliers. The basic conditions for price discrimination are well known—markets must be separable (i.e., products sold in the low-price market must not be able to be resold in the high-price markets), demand and supply functions must be sloped, and the elasticities in the separable markets must be different. Here we treat only the exporter price discrimination model. However, there is a similar analysis that could be applied to importers facing several suppliers with different elasticities. We limit our analysis to the cartel case though the analysis could be used also to look at the single-large-country case.

Consider first the case of the government (export tax) cartel. Suppose in the world market there are four classes of importers: high-income developed countries who support domestic producer prices above world price via variable levies or quotas; centrally planned (and other) economies who buy sporadically, through state trading agencies, in periods of domestic production shortfall (e.g., the U.S.S.R.); middle-income developing countries with no foreign exchange constraint; and low-income developing countries whose import demand elasticity is at least -1. Would an exporter cartel be better off to charge prices to the developed countries equal to domestic support prices (i.e., extract all levy income or quota rent), charge all the traffic will bear to the centrally planned economies, and sell to low-income LDCs at domestic price? In terms of Figure 6-6, we could consider developing countries as part of domestic demand and add the low income LDC demand to D_d and subtract it from E_d. This would make the E_d function more steeply sloped, increasing the monopoly rents available to the exporter cartel. A more detailed analysis would be to disaggregate developed-country, centrally planned, and middle-income LDCs, horizontally sum their marginal revenue functions, and equate that sum to E_s. Using conventional price discrimination models we could determine the profit-maximizing price in each market.

In the case of the producer cartel, disaggregation could be bimodal—(i.e., domestic consumers versus foreign consumers) or it could be further disaggregated into the four (or more) international market segments outlined above. This analysis is presented in Figure 6-9. The four markets identified in the previous paragraph plus the domestic market make up the model: Developed Countries (DC) (Figure 6-9a); Centrally Planned Economies (CP) whose demand is perfectly inelastic until a foreign exchange constraint becomes binding—for prices above that level demand has unitary elasticity (Figure 6-9b); Middle -Income LDCs (MY) and Domestic or Cartel Consumers (DM) who are assumed to have regular demand functions (Figure 6-9c and d); and finally, in Figure 6-9f, low-income LDCs (LY) who are assumed to be bound by a foreign exchange constraint, and therefore whose demand function has unitary elasticity.

The cartel horizontally sums the marginal revenue functions in Figure 6-9a to d (ΣMR) and equates this to cartel or domestic supply (S_{DM}). [The marginal revenue function (ΣMR) is not the marginal function to total world

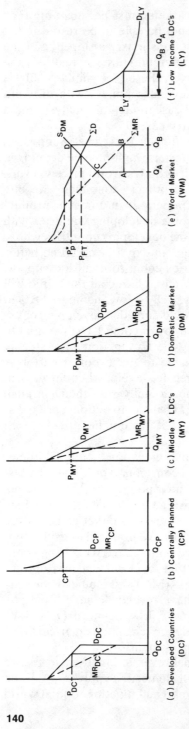

$*P_P$ = Weighted Average of P_{DC}, P_{CP}, P_{MY}, and P_{DM}

Figure 6-9 Price-discriminating producer cartel.

140

demand because the marginal revenue for the unitary elastic LDC demand is zero.] The optimum level of output is Q_A (zero to low-income LDCs) allocated such that marginal revenues are equal in each market. Thus, Q_{DC} is sold in the DC market at price P_{DC}, Q_{CP} is sold in the CPs for P_{CP}, Q_{MY} is sold in the MYs for P_{MY}, and Q_{PM} is sold in the cartel (domestic) market for P_{DM}. This is the rent (profit)-maximizing solution for the cartel. But how does one get the revenue back to producers without stimulating output in excess of Q_A? The low-income LSCs offer a possible alternative to supply management. Suppose P_p is the weighted average of prices in the four markets to the left of the world market. Paying producers P_p would induce producers to produce Q_B (without supply control). The difference between Q_B and Q_A could be exported to the LY countries at price P_{LY}. This would be a rational alternative if the direct and implicit economic cost of the necessary supply control program necessary to restrain output to Q_A exceeded ABCD in Figure 6-9e. Perhaps this explains why overseas shipments of PL480 grain in the United States may be rational even if there is a net loss on those particular shipments.

Producers would clearly be better off with Q_A and P_P relative to free trade (P_{FT}). World prices are higher and no longer uniform and importers are exploited relative to their own interface with world markets. That is, countries who completely isolate their markets (e.g., the U.S.S.R.) pay the highest price—a sort of "free trader" justice. It would be a relatively simple matter to expand the model to include the cartel as the dominant seller with a fringe of competitors. This is left to the reader.

5 Implications of Exporter Power   This completes our discussion of exporter market power. Several comments are in order which apply to all approaches. First, the more importing countries that fix or guarantee internal prices, the greater the potential gains to exercises of market power. Second, the steeper the excess demand function facing exporters, the greater the disparity between free market and cartel prices, necessitating, in cases of producer cartels, greater supply control efforts. In the case of government cartels, the result is lower domestic prices which in the case of feed grains would benefit domestic (cartel member) livestock producers. Third, again the models assume no retaliation by importers. Fourth, and finally, the static one-sided nature of the models has some limitations. We return to the point in the last section of this chapter.

IV   A DIGRESSION ON MIDDLEMEN MARKET POWER

Our discussion of international markets has to date not dealt explicitly with the fact that numerous intermediaries or middlemen who perform functions of space, time and form transformation exist between producers and consumers. If middlemen are small and competitive firms, their omission is not serious as we could simply assume that the demand functions being used are derived demands facing producers.

But suppose middlemen were large and few in number. Could they exploit exporters and importers? And, would their potential for monopoly profits be enhanced by domestic policy intervention? We treat each question sequentially in this section. The current structure of international grain markets suggests that the analysis may be of some interest (Gilmore, 1982).

We can use our single-commodity, large-country analysis developed in this chapter. Suppose, for simplicity of analysis, there is a single trading intermediary (monopolist/monopsonist) who is the only one who can provide a necessary service, e.g., a shipping cartel controls (owns) all grain shipping capacity such that all exporters sell to him and all importers buy from him. What decision rules would the intermediary follow to maximize his monopoly/monopsony rents? Figure 6-10 presents the analysis. In Figure 6-10a, we assume there are two exporters, A and ROW, and two importers, B and ROW (Rest of the World) and that there is no policy intervention. With competitive middlemen, world price is P_w. Now, suppose there was a single monopolist/monopsonist middleman who seeks to maximize monopoly rent (profits). His profit-maximizing position would be determined by the intersection of the marginal revenue to world excess demand E_d–MR_{ED} and the marginal supply cost function (MSC_{ES}) to world excess supply function (E_s). The optimum level of trade is Q_T', less than free trade Q_T. The middleman buys from exporters at P_E and sells to importers at P_I. His profits are the double cross-hatched area. He has extracted producer surplus from exporting countries and consumer surplus from importing countries.

More realistically, suppose countries are already intervening in world markets (Figure 6-10b) such that exporter A is fixing minimum prices to producers and consumers of P_s and paying an export subsidy of the cross-hatched area. This kinks the excess supply function and results in E_s'. Similarly, importer B establishes P_s' as an internal support price and defends P_s' with a variable levy equal to the difference between P_s' and P_w'. This also kinks the excess demand function and results in E_d'. The results of both interventions increase the slopes of E_s' and E_d' in the relevant range. World price falls to P_w' (compared to P_w) and trade contracts slightly to Q_T'' (compared to Q_T in Figure 6-10a). Importer B collects revenue equal to the diagonally hatched area. The result is a partial transfer of A's export subsidy to B's treasury. The solution is shown by solid lines.

Now, suppose we impose upon the case (Figure 6-10b) of intervention, the monopolist/monopsonist middlemen intervention (shown by dashed lines). Then equate MSC_{ES}' to MR_{ED}', charge importers P_I', and buy from exporters at P_E'. The results are interesting. The middlemen's profits (double cross-hatched area in Figure 6-10b) increase as a result of intervention ($\pi' > \pi$), prices to exporters fall to P_E' ($P_E' > P_E$), exporter A's subsidy costs increase by the shaded area, and ROW_E is virtually pushed to self-suf-

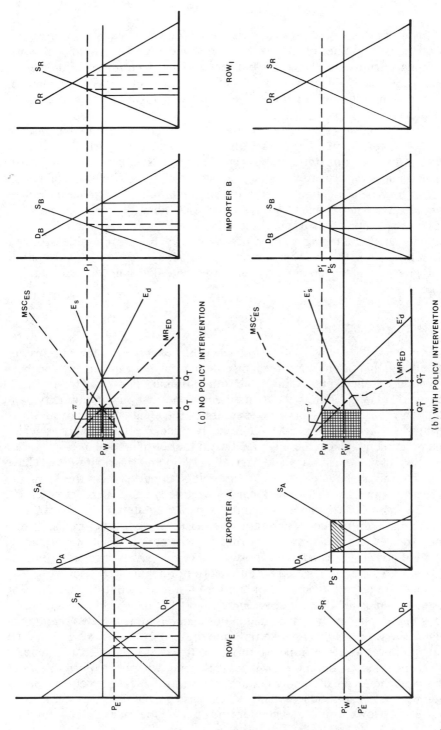

Figure 6-10 Exercise of market power by international middlemen.

143

ficiency. Prices charged importers rise to P'_I. The middlemen capture all (or in other cases, some) of importer B's levy income. The volume of world trade declines to Q'''_T. Thus, the existence of intervention plus middlemen with market power decreases the benefits (increases the costs) of domestic intervention and some of these losses of country benefits accrue to the middlemen.

This analysis demonstrates the possibilities for middleman(men) market power. Some have argued that it exists at least partially (Gilmore 1982). However, this static analysis would suggest significant profits for new entries unless there were barriers to entry, possibly information costs. Further, it may be a function of the fact that actual middlemen act as well as handlers for state traders who strike price-quantity deals. Finally, as handlers and intermediate purchasers in uncertain markets, handling large volumes and arbitraging price differences may be a preferable strategy. Therefore, while the analysis may be somewhat academic, it does illustrate that price fixing by countries makes the potential gains to such action larger.

V THE DYNAMIC REALITY

All the preceding analysis of the impacts of the exercise of market power by exporter(s), importer(s), or middlemen, acting singly or in concert, has been premised on one group acting while others remain passive. However, the real world of large-country, large-middlemen, international-commodity trade could involve the simultaneous and interdependent actions of all three groups. To analyze this case requires dynamic feedback analysis which defies simple graphics, the main analytical tool of this book.

Recent works by Karp and McCalla (1983) and Paarlberg (1983) have attempted to apply game theory to international markets. As the Karp and McCalla analysis is explicitly dynamic, we briefly summarize its potential.

The model is a dynamic Nash noncooperative difference game of the international corn market. There are three large players, two importers and one exporter. Several variants are run: (1) when all three actors attempt to exercise power, (2) when one exporter and one importer engage in competitive warfare, and (3) when either an exporter or an importer tries to act as a monopolist but with reaction functions built into the control analysis. The results, even using a simple econometric model of the world market, are interesting. For the analysis included in this chapter, three conclusions are relevant. First, in the dynamic setting, monopsony behavior by an importer leads to lower levels of import tariffs than reported by Carter and Schmitz (1979) in the static optimum tariff case. Second, when an exporter faces an importer, the levels of export tax and import tariff, respectively, are lower than when each acts independently to exercise power. Thus, power interaction leads to lower prices and greater trade than in the case of unilateral exercises of market power. Third, strategic opportunities are plausible in the dynamic case. For example, the exporter may well pay export subsidies in early years to force out other competitors and then raise prices in later years.

VI SUMMARY

This chapter has dealt with the large-country, single-commodity case. We have dealt successively with passive and active policy intervention for both importers and exporters. The analytical techniques used were first our single-commodity national model with an international interface. Second, we applied static monopoly, monopsony, and cartel analysis to importer, exporter, and middlemen exercises of power in a static setting. Finally, we discussed briefly dynamic analysis. The overall conclusion is that explicitly recognizing power increases the reality of our analysis without unduly complicating our analytical framework. Clearly, the market power analysis could be incorporated into the domestic factor/input market model. But, we still are far from the real world of multicommodities, multiple instruments, and multiple goals. This is the subject of the next chapter.

REFERENCES

Carter, C., Gallini, N., and Schmitz, A. 1980. "Producer-Consumer Trade-offs in Export Cartels," *Amer. J. Agr. Econ.,* **62:**812–818.
———— and Schmitz, A. 1979. "Import Tariffs and Price Formation in the World Wheat Market," *Amer. J. Agr. Econ.,* **61:**517–522.
Enke, S. 1944. "The Monopsony Case for Tariffs," *Quart. J. Econ.,* **58:**229–245.
Gilmore, R. 1982. *A Poor Harvest,* Longman, New York.
Karp, L. S. and McCalla, A. F. 1983. "Dynamic Games and International Trade: An Application to the World Corn Market," *Amer. J. Agr. Econ.,* **65:**641–650.
McCalla, A. F. 1981. "Structural and Market Power Considerations in Imperfect Agricultural Markets," in A. F. McCalla and T. E. Josling (eds.), *Imperfect Markets in Agricultural Trade,* Allenheld, Osmun and Company, Totowa, N.J., pp. 9–28.
Paarlberg, P. L. 1983. Endogenous Policy Formation in the Imperfect World Wheat Market, unpublished Ph.D. Dissertation, Purdue University.
Schmitz, A., McCalla, A. F., Mitchell, D. D., and Carter, C. 1981. *Grain Export Cartels,* Ballinger, Cambridge, Mass.

ADDITIONAL READINGS

Gould, J. P., and Ferguson, C. E. 1980. *Microeconomic Theory,* 5th ed., Richard D. Irwin, Homewood, Ill., chap. 12, pp. 316–347.
Mansfield, E. 1982. *Microeconomics,* 4th ed., W. W. Norton, New York, chap. 12, pp. 330–359.

Chapter 7

Policy Choices, The Reality: Multiple Instrument, Multicommodity, and Multiple Goal

I INTRODUCTION

The real world of food and agricultural policy choice faces policy makers with the problem of simultaneously dealing with all of the issues that we have dealt with separately in previous chapters. First, countries undoubtedly have *multiple objectives*. The impact of a policy instrument, therefore, involves trade-offs among competing objectives unless by chance the instrument has complementary impacts on all targets (objectives). Second, countries almost always use *multiple instruments,* i.e., taxes on some commodities, subsidies on others and other types of quantitative intervention on still others. Third, countries always produce *many commodities*. Thus, consideration of all the relationships discussed in Chapter 3 of substitution and complementarity in production and consumption as well as input-output relationships must be considered. Fourth, countries are seldom pure exporters or importers. Rather, they export some commodities, import others, and do not trade in yet another set of goods. Therefore, they will tend to have a mixed trade strategy. Fifth, some countries are large while others are small, in terms of world markets; moreover, it is likely that a country will be large in some world markets and small in others. This is further complicated by the fact that a country could be a large exporter (importer) of one product while being a small importer (exporter) of another product. Sixth, the agricultural and food sector, and policies pertaining thereto, exist within a broader national and international macro environment. Thus, macro policies are important to the nature and effectiveness of food and agricultural policy.

The task of this chapter is to try to synthesize the various partial tools developed earlier to look more comprehensively at country policy choice. In particular, use is made of (a) multicommodity, multicountry international market analysis (Chapter 3); (b) the individual country model, for both the small country (Chapter 5) and the large country (Chapter 6); (c) the welfare measures of economic surplus, and revenue and expenditure balances (Chapter 5); and (d) some further notions regarding instrument and goal trade-offs developed in this chapter. The task is to synthesize these into a verbal-qualitative model of the real world of policy choice.

The chapter begins by discussing the issues involved when one has multiple instruments and more than one goal. An outline of one perception of the real world of country policy choice is presented next. It tries to develop a broad conceptual road map through the real complexity of policy choice in three stages. First, it looks at necessary policy instrument linkages that come about because of multiple goals, an open economy, macro constraints, multiple commodities, and size variables in a static setting. Second, it looks at policy in a dynamic fashion where exogenous variables of technical change, macro policy, and changing demand patterns may force additional policy actions on countries which are far from their original intentions. For example, switching from importer to exporter with import-oriented instruments in place greatly complicates the policy problem. Finally, the chapter looks at how policy actions in other countries, transmitted through international markets, may force or constrain national policy choice in the game which might be called competitive interactive policy choice with fixed national goals. The approach attempts to remain analytical, but the multiple linkages make diagrammatic analysis of limited value. Rather than resorting to general equilibrium mathematical models, the purpose is to assist the reader to reason through the analysis assuming that the basic analytical components developed earlier and in this chapter are clearly understood and available for use. A few examples are used to place the analysis in context at some points, but the real world of actual policy choice is reserved for the three case studies in the next chapter.

II MULTIPLE INSTRUMENTS AND MULTIPLE GOALS: TRADE-OFFS AND COMPLEMENTARITIES

Countries try to simultaneously satisfy goals of growth, stability, and equity by the selection of instruments and instrument levels to best achieve these goals within their national constraints. But surely this is too simplified a view of the world. Only in the extreme case would goals be independent of each other and individual instruments uniquely influential on a single goal. This is the case of independence of both instruments and goals. The more likely case is where "the same instrument influences more than one objective and the same objective can be influenced by different instruments" (Kirschen and Associates, 1974, p. 259). Clearly, some *goals* could be complementary, i.e., change in an instrument moves them both in the same direction, and some *instruments* could be complementary for particular goals. In either of these cases, if the relationship between goals and/or the instruments is fixed or at least linear, the two goals or instruments can be redefined for analytical purposes as single goals or instruments. If, however, the relationships are nonlinear, a problem remains—again, the more likely case.

But in reality it is more likely that goals conflict and that instruments do not always move in the same direction on a particular goal or set of goals. Therefore, policy making involves trade-offs and policy analysis must likewise analyze such trade-offs. This section illustrates a few such possibilities and illustrates that economic analysis itself is not sufficient to determine the optimal policy. In addition, community welfare functions are needed which include not only the appropriate goals but the weights society attaches to each goal.

The analysis begins with the case of more than one goal and a single instrument. As a general rule, the number of effective instruments must be equal to or greater than the number of goals. Therefore, a single instrument can be targeted for only one goal. However, policy makers are still interested in the impacts that instrument may have on the other goals. Figure 7-1 presents some simple graphics. Figure 7-1*a* is the case of a positive interrelationship between instrument and goal. An increase in the instrument's value, say, level of price support, unidirectionally increases a goal, say, growth in output. Figure 7-1*b* depicts linearly complementary goals which both increase in fixed proportions with increases in the value of the instrument

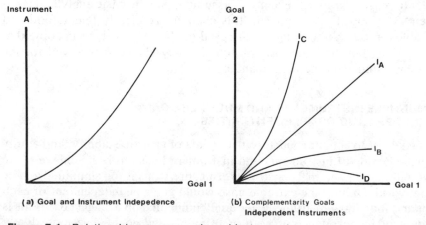

(a) Goal and Instrument Indepedence

(b) Complementarity Goals
Independent Instruments

Figure 7-1   Relationships among goals and instruments.

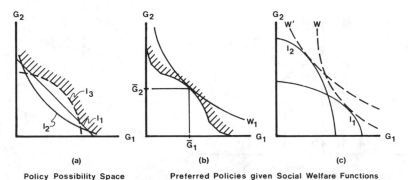

        (a)   (b)   (c)

Policy Possibility Space   Preferred Policies given Social Welfare Functions

Figure 7-2 Policy possibility space and social welfare functions.

variable I_A. This case is also trivial as we can construct another goal as a linear combination of goals 1 and 2. But there is no a priori reason why complementarity should be linear. Also in Figure 7-1b, I_B illustrates that increases in the instrument value eventually lead to greater attainment of goal 1 but no further improvements in goal 2. I_C is the opposite case. I_D is the case where early doses of the instrument lead to improvements in both goals but more and more of the instrument leads eventually to a lesser accomplishment of goal 2. This could be the case of increasing levels of tariffs where G_2 is national income and G_1 is income of domestic producers.

The more realistic case is where a single instrument has positive impacts on one goal but at the expense of the other goals. Figure 7-2a depicts three different kinds of possible trade-off functions—linear, convex, and concave. The policy possibility space is to the left of (i.e., inside) the external envelope of instruments I_1, I_2, and I_3. If we postulate that there is a set of community indifference curves, the selection of which instrument and at what level would be at the point of tangency of the frontier to the highest indifference curve, as is shown in Figure 7-2b. Even if two instruments both were concave (to the origin), they could have different relative impacts on the two goals as is shown in Figure 7-2c. Thus, the selection of which instrument would depend on the shape of societies' welfare function, e.g., $W - W$ or $W' - W'$ in Figure 7-2.

The case of three goals and one instrument is also interesting. Figure 7-3a illustrates three goals. The impacts of the instrument I_1 are competitive between G_1 and G_2 and G_2 and G_3; G_1 and G_3 are, however, complementary. Say G_1 is more equity as one moves to the right, G_2 is more growth as one moves upward, and G_3 is more stability as one moves to the left from the origin. Thus, the selection of I_1, at value I_1^0 simultaneously determines the level of accomplishment of all three goals—G_1^0, G_2^0, and G_3^0. Selection of an alternative value of I_1, say I_1^1, would yield less growth (G_2^1) but improvement in both equity (G_1^1) and stability (G_3).

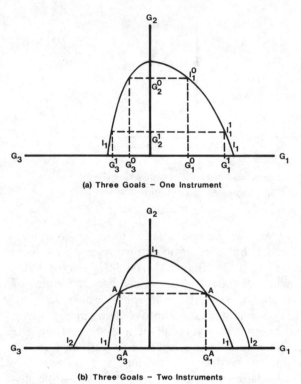

(a) Three Goals – One Instrument

(b) Three Goals – Two Instruments

Figure 7-3 Policy trade-off frontiers with multiple goals.

Suppose there were two different instruments available, say, I_1 and I_2 in Figure 7-3b, each capable of yielding point A. If more growth (G_2) was desired, instrument I_1 would be preferable because the amounts of stability (G_3) and equity (G_1) which would have to be sacrificed would be less than for I_2. Conversely, if more equity and/or stability were desired relative to the current situation then I_2 would be preferred because the amount of growth sacrificed would be less. But there is no a priori reason that these trade-off frontiers should all have similar shapes. If there were a third instrument which gave you more stability but less equity with more growth, then no single instrument would be a clear choice even given policy makers' relative preferences. One could choose a particular instrument if for a given level of growth I_2 gave more of both equity and stability than I_3. But if I_3, relative to I_1, gives more equity (G_1) but less stability (G_3) while I_1, relative to I_3, gave the opposite—namely, more stability and less equity, then without a community preference function we cannot choose between the instruments even though G_1 and G_3 are complementary goals.

The preceding analysis has involved three goals and a set of independent instruments and has discussed how policy analysis would proceed to select among instruments when only *one* can be used. Now suppose policy makers can pursue two instruments simultaneously. To illustrate the approach consider two goals, G_1 and G_2, and two instruments, I_1 and I_2. Again, these could be complementary instruments. In Figure 7-4a assume the economy is at initial position A. A specific alteration of I_1 would move us to say B. While a specific dose of I_2 would move us to C. The combination of I_1 and I_2 would, given that the impacts of I_1 and I_2 are linear, follow the principles of vector addition and yield point D. In fact, any point along the ray A–D is possible for proportionate increments of I_1 and I_2.

But suppose I_1 and I_2 are competitive, i.e., I_1 increases G_1 but decreases G_2 (say movement from A to B in Figure 7-4b), and that I_2 increases G_2 but decreases G_1. Again by vector addition, the combination of policies would achieve point D which is more of both. In fact, C and B are extreme points on a multiple-instrument goal trade-off frontier that goes through D. All points along the frontier are theoretically possible given different combinations of increments of I_1 and I_2. Now given a community indifference curve, policy makers could choose which vector combination of I_1 and I_2 would be preferred. If that occurred at D, we would have an optimum combination of instruments. We can also add a policy budget constraint. If I_1 and I_2 both involve fiscal costs, then how far out on vector AD one could go, i.e., how high a community indifference curve one could reach, would be determined by the budget constraints (Ballenger, 1984, chap. 5).

Generalization beyond two goals and two constraints is difficult graphically but conceptually possible. Full information would require us to know not only the direct impact but also the cross impacts of instruments on objectives.

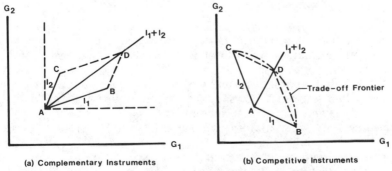

(a) Complementary Instruments   (b) Competitive Instruments

Figure 7-4 Policy choice with two goals and two instruments.

III THE GENERAL PROBLEM OF NATIONAL POLICY CHOICE

The analysis proceeds based on the following set of assumptions which are common to all the cases that follow in this chapter. The first assumption is that all countries interact to some extent with world markets. Thus, all cases are open economy cases. Discussions of the case of autarky, to the extent it is introduced, is for comparative purposes. This assumption squares very well with reality. Few countries are completely isolated from world markets. However, the degree of interaction can and does vary widely. The second premise is that all countries have generally similar goals which apply to food and agricultural policy. Countries may articulate more specific objectives for the agricultural sector but they are expected to contribute to these general goals. It is also assumed that all countries produce and trade more than one commodity (all that is necessary to illustrate the intercommodity issues is that there be two commodities per country) and that all countries export some commodities, while they import others. Therefore, considerations of trade-offs among border policies must be considered. Finally, it is assumed that all countries use more than one instrument.

Given this list of assumptions, national policy makers face a complicated maze of policy choices pursuing several goals with multiple instruments affecting more than one commodity and with potentially differential impacts on producers, consumers, and the nation (at least the nation's fiscal and foreign exchange budgets). Life is further complicated by the net trade position of each commodity and by whether the country is large or small in some or all of the international markets in which the country participates. In an open economy, policy instruments can either be internally directed or operate at the border. The task in this and following sections is to begin to work through the problem in a sequence of events building in additional dimensions as we proceed.

Let us begin by reviewing in more detail the flavor of the nature of relationships between goals and instruments. We have argued that most countries pursue at least three general goals:

1 Growth, which can be defined more narrowly as increasing national product by more efficient use of existing resources and expansion of the resource base.
2 Equitable distribution of income and wealth. This goals implies attention to groups within a society. For simplicity three groups are identified:
   a Producers—who prefer more income to less
   b Consumers—who want to maximize utility and therefore, prefer lower prices to higher prices
   c Taxpayers—who prefer less government expenditure to more
   In the context of food and agriculture policy, this goal would seek to enhance producers' incomes, minimize consumer expenditure on food,

and do it at minimum budget cost. The possibilities of conflict and trade-offs are obvious.

3 Stability—producers prefer stable incomes and prices to unstable ones of the same average level and consumers prefer stable prices to unstable prices.

These goals are listed across the top of Table 7-1. On the left are listed some of the many possible instruments that are available to a country's policy makers. We categorize them as (a) internal noninterventionist, i.e., ones that are not directed at influencing market price, (b) internal interventionist, which do influence price, and (c) external or border instruments. A quick scan of the table suggests some notion of the trade-offs involved even before multiple commodities, multiple instruments, differing net trade positions, and country size are added. In the next sections we look at how policies may necessarily have to be linked; how policy choice over time may force and/or constrain future policy choice, and how other actors (nations) influence a country's policy choice. These approaches draw upon all the preceding partial analyses in an attempt at verbal, qualitative general equilibrium analysis.

IV POLICY LINKAGES

Earlier analysis of single instruments and single goals (Chapters 5 and 6) allowed us to treat exporters and importers alike. However, the introduction of multiple combinations of goals, instruments, and commodities requires us to treat them separately from now on. The reality is frequently that internal instruments used to accomplish domestic goals have necessary border counterparts. Further macro constraints in terms of domestic budget costs and/or foreign exchange balances must be included. We also comment on the implications for policy choice of multiple commodities and the size of the country.

Our approach to dealing with the reality of our multidimensional policy problem is to proceed through a number of cases. The first case is presented in considerable detail, so that the reader gets a flavor of what steps are necessary for comprehensive policy analysis. The steps are as follows: (1) identify if exporter or importer, or both, and of what commodities; (2) explicitly identify the goal or goals sought, e.g., consumer or producer orientation action; (3) identify some of the internal policy instruments available; (4) identify border instruments which could either substitute for internal instruments or which are required complements to internal policy; (5) identify and analyze impacts of macro variables or constraints; (6) determine whether additional instruments are needed to manage macro concerns; (7) determine impacts on goals other than those identified (goal trade-offs); (8) look at the intercommodity implications in two parts—first, intercommodity relations

Table 7-1 Goals and Instruments

Instruments	Growth and efficiency	Equity		Stability		Budget minimization (Taxpayers) Domestic cost
		Prod.	Cons.	Prod.	Cons.	
A Internal						
1 Nonintervention						
a R + D	+	+ or 0	+	+ or −	+ or −	−
b Market efficiency and information	+	+	+	+	+	−
c Anti-monopoly	+	+	+	−*	−*	−
d Public investment (e.g., irrigation)	+	+	+	+	+	−
e Crop insurance	+	+	0	+	0	0
2 Intervention						
a Price fixing (internal supports)	−	+	−	+	+	0
b Direct payments and deficiency payments	−	+	+	+	+	−
c Marketing boards and orders	−	+	−	+	+	0
d Compulsory food requisition	−	−	+	+	+	−
e Domestic stocks	+	0	0	+	+	0

+ positive effect on goal as defined
− negative effect
0 no effect
*Under the assumption that imperfect markets are more rigid in terms of prices.

within the target policy set and second, implications for commodities outside the policy set; and (9) finally, determine how the policy analysis would need to be modified if the country were large in world markets.

Table 7-1   Goals and Instruments (cont.)

		Goals				
						Budget minimization (Taxpayers)
	Growth and	Equity		Stability		Domestic
Instruments	efficiency	Prod.	Cons.	Prod.	Cons.	cost
B External (border)						
a Export tax	−	−	+	0	0	0
b Export subsidy	−	+	−	0	0	−
c Export and import restrictions for domestic stability	+	+ or −	+ or −	+	+	0
d Import tax:						
Fixed	−	+	−	0	0	+
Variable	−	+	−	+	+	+
e Import quotas	−	+	−	+ or −	+ or −	0
f Free trade	+	+ & −	+ & −	−	−	0

A   Case 1: Producer-Oriented Exporter Policy

The first case is of an exporter of the relevant commodities, e.g., grains. The country wishes to pursue a producer-oriented policy to accomplish goals of increased producer prices (and incomes) and increased price stability, i.e., internal producer prices P_p will be enhanced by intervention. Consumer prices P_c will be allowed to rise also so that both are above world price W_p ($P_p = P_c > W_p$). Internal instruments could include guaranteed minimum or fixed producer prices accomplished by intervention purchases which are either stored or exported (e.g., United States pre-1965 on grains and EC post-1975 on wheat). The pursuit of this constellation of instruments would require border instruments as well. These would include export subsidies and/or food aid and also would require import constraints (tariffs, quotas, etc.) to prevent other exporters from taking advantage of higher internal prices (e.g., exports to the United States from Canada). Macro considerations would also be important, e.g., if there were a budget constraint on the costs of export subsidies and/or food aid, then additional instruments to control cost such as supply management [e.g., control of land input (United States) or marketing quotas (Canada)] might also be required to limit producer response to higher prices.

The combination of internal, border, and additional instruments could result in increased production of the target commodities at the expense of other agricultural output. This could impact on national income in a negative fashion if resource misallocation resulted. One would also have to be cognizant of intercommodity effects both within the policy set and those not included. Within the set, the policy analyst would have to analyze substitution, input-output, and other linkages. For example, if all grains are included, relative policy prices would have to be selected which were consistent with desired levels of output, i.e., if more feed grains are desired with less wheat, price relatives would have to reflect this. For commodities not included, such as livestock, increased grain prices would presumably lead to decreased herd size and rising livestock prices which would have impacts on consumer prices. Also, if policy was pursued in the grain sector to stabilize as well as raise prices, the livestock sector would also be stabilized. This produces a policy trade-off between more stability and lower returns in the livestock sector. Finally, suppose the exporter is large in some or all of the international markets for the commodities in the policy set. If price supports and export subsidies are used without supply control, world prices would be depressed as larger exports (resulting both from expanded production and reduced consumption) entered world markets. This would increase the costs of food aid and/or export subsidies and could force supply control in subsequent periods which, if restrictive enough, could raise world prices again.

Thus, even this simple case of an exporter wanting to support and stabilize grain prices above world prices requires a complex set of instruments and an approach to policy analysis using all the tools developed earlier in this book even to identify the broader qualitative impacts of policy intervention. Empirical modeling would require a large quasi-general equilibrium approach.

B Case 2: Producer- and Consumer-Oriented Exporter Policy

Suppose an exporter has goals to (1) support producer prices but allow consumers to buy at world prices ($P_p > P_c = W_p$) and (2) stabilize prices. Internal instruments include some policy which sets target prices at the desired level and pays the difference between target and world price in a direct or deficiency payment. The only required border instrument is import restrictions to prevent in-country farmers from acquiring grain on world markets to qualify for greater internal support. Export subsidies are not required nor are acquisitions and stocks unless the latter are held for stabilization purposes. Budget constraints could force an additional policy of supply management. Impacts on the efficiency are again in terms of levels of price support and the degree of resource misallocation. Intercommodity effects within the grains are the same as in Case 1. However, now the impact on the livestock industry and meat consumer is the opposite, namely, costs fall and prices fall because of expanded output. If goals of income improvement and stability for livestock producers exist, they are simultaneously improved by the deficiency payment approach. Finally, being large makes the policy more expensive (in the absence of supply control) because the deficiency payment is equivalent to an indirect export subsidy which depresses world prices. This could also reduce foreign exchange earnings if excess demand is inelastic. Again, effective supply control could raise world prices (see Chapter 6).

C Case 3: Producer Support–Consumer Subsidy Exporter Policy

Both Cases 1 and 2 are more representative of high-income, developed-country, producer-oriented policies. Suppose now an exporter has goals of supporting producer price and subsidizing consumers ($P_p > W_p > P_c$) while also stabilizing prices. Internal instruments would include price supports or deficiency payments and consumer subsidies. Import restrictions at the border would be required. Macro costs could require supply control and consumer rationing. Nonincluded goal and intercommodity impacts are similar to the first two cases as are the implications of being large.

D Case 4: Consumer-Oriented Exporter Policy

The final exporter case is akin to many developing-country exporters where the goals are to keep consumer prices low and reduce government cost by keeping producer prices low ($W_p > P_p \geq P_c$). The internal instruments available include input subsidies (if farm income is also a goal) to induce sufficient production to generate exports and consumer subsidies. However, in this case, a single border instrument, namely, the export tax, could do the job. If one wanted internal stability, a variable export tax could be used. Export quotas or other forms of control, e.g., state trading, export licenses, and foreign exchange controls, could also be used. Macro impacts now could include loss of domestic revenue (internal producer tax), increased domestic costs (food and input subsidy costs), and losses of foreign exchange. Nonincluded goals and intercommodity impacts are now the opposite to the cases where producer prices are held above world prices, namely, resources shift out of production of included commodities (unless there are mandatory deliveries, e.g., Egypt) causing expanded output of those which are substitutes in production. The implications of largeness are also the opposite. A large country could force up world price by use of an export tax or export restrictions, thereby reducing somewhat the cost of the program and could gain foreign exchange if world demand is inelastic. However, other exporters share the benefits.

E   Cases 5 to 8: Producer-Oriented, Producer-and-Consumer–Oriented, and Consumer-Oriented Importer Policies

In a parallel fashion we can think of four comparable importer goal sets: producer-oriented $(P_p = P_c > W_p)$, producer-and-consumer–oriented $(P_p > W_p = P_c$ and $P_p > W_p > P_c)$, and consumer-oriented $(W_p > P_p = P_c)$. We discuss them only generally, as much of the analysis proceeds similarly but with opposite impacts.

For example, an importer wishing to raise internal prices above world prices could do so with only border instruments such as unit or *ad valorem* tariffs, quotas, licenses, or state trading. If stability was also the goal, variable levies or quotas or state trading would suffice. Now macro dimensions could be revenue generating and foreign exchange saving. Largeness would allow the possibility of setting import tariffs to maximize national welfare (Chapter 6). Intercommodity effects would again impact through relative policy prices and policy prices versus nonpolicy prices. Highly distorted internal prices could have negative impacts on the goal of growth and efficiency. Obviously, consumers lose. If there was internal supply instability, intervention prices and stockholding might be required if border instruments could not be managed with sufficient precision.

If importers were concerned with consumer welfare as well, alternatives would include deficiency payments (which could be financed with import levies), consumer subsidies, input subsidies, and state trading. If importers wish to keep consumer prices below world price, consumer subsidies and import subsidies would be required. In the final case where producer and consumer prices are below world prices, some mechanism of inducing domestic production such as input subsidies and forced deliveries (Egypt in the 1960s and 1970s) might be required. In general the greater the gap between producer and consumer prices the more expensive the domestic cost of the program, which could trigger budget and foreign exchange constraints (as discussed in Chapter 8 for the case of Egypt).

We could go further but it seems clear now that a careful comprehensive policy analysis would be required in each of the almost endless sets of possible goal, instrument, and commodity combinations. The intent here was to demonstrate one conceptual approach using combinations of simple analytical tools. In both the exporter and importer cases, large countries, in addition to considering direct international impacts of their policy action, would also have to be cognizant of the intercommodity and interpolicy connections in international markets discussed in Chapter 3.

F   Exporter-Importer Cases

The above cases treated only countries that were exporters or importers but not both. Clearly, many countries (particularly large ones) are both exporters and importers of different commodities (e.g., United States, Canada, EC, Australia, Brazil, Pakistan, Egypt), sometimes even of the same commodity (e.g., U.S. meat, EC wheat and sugar). Analysis of these cases, while somewhat more intertwined, could proceed using the same tools and the same sequential approach taken here. The additional complications result from additional instrument-goal trade-offs and more complex intercommodity effects. In Chapter 8 we treat the case of Egypt on cotton and wheat which embodies some of these issues, so we defer further discussion until then.

V THE IRREVERSIBILITY OF TIME: OR DO CURRENT POLICY CHOICES FORCE OR CONSTRAIN FUTURE POLICY CHOICE?

All the previous analyses have focused on static analysis of increasingly complex webs of policy choice. Further, in most instances, the analyses started with a no-policy position. Yet in reality, both of these assumptions are at variance with real policy choice. Countries tend to become involved in food and agricultural policy in incremental steps over time. Further, once intervention is implemented, it usually is in place for some duration, in fact, some would argue that "old policies never die, they are just added to." This has two implications for policy analysis. First, once policy instruments are in place, exogenous variables such as technology and income can change the situation. These exogenous variables in conjunction with others interact with policy variables and alter the structure of the food and agricultural sector. These changes alter the commodity composition, the size of farms, and many other variables which in turn influence all aspects of policy choice. Second, real policy analysis generally involves beginning with an existing policy apparatus and, therefore, involves incremental changes in instruments. Inevitably, this then involves a choice among second-best solutions. In this section we treat both of these issues with some simple examples which clearly have real world counterparts. We build on our cases in the previous section.

Technological change alters input-output relationships in individual commodities and the mix of commodities. Further, as is often argued, technological change occurs more rapidly under stable and enhanced prices (Cochrane, 1979). Consider first the case of an exporter who is supporting internal prices above world prices (Case 1) in time period t_0 without supply control. The result is that in subsequent time periods, supply functions shift to the right. This has two impacts. First, increased output increases the cost of internal instruments. Second, in the large-country cases, or if technological change is occurring simultaneously across several small countries, there is downward pressure on world prices which increases costs of export subsidies and/or food aid. Thus, overall program costs rise. Eventually, they may hit budget constraints which require additional instruments to try to manage supply. In the United States, for example, supply control efforts have focused on managing the land input. Constraints on land inputs coupled with high and stable prices induce intensification and more rapid technological change which further exacerbates the original problem of excess supply. In addition, once a country becomes involved in agricultural interventions, program benefits become capitalized into land values, and strong vested interests become potentially seriously disadvantaged should, for example, price supports be discontinued.

Consider next the case of an importer who is initially deficit in most commodities and who decides to implement a policy mechanism to restrain imports to enhance domestic prices. The process of technical change could shift aggregate supply to the right more rapidly than population and income changes shift demand. The outcome would be reduced imports, which reduces income from the program. More critically, it could eventually shift the country from importer to exporter which immediately shifts policy from a revenue generator to a fiscal cost. Thus, budgetary costs begin to rise putting pressure on for additional instruments (e.g., co-responsibility levies) to constrain cost. This is not too abstract a description of events in the European Community (EC) for wheat, dairy products, sugar, and meat over the 1960s and 1970s.

Consider also the case of a low-income developing country or a centrally planned importer who for various reasons fixes consumer (and producer) prices at low nominal levels. As incomes grow and population increases, demand shifts to the right rapidly. Low producer prices discourage technological change which means domestic supply increases lag behind demand, increasing the import bill. Efforts to increase domestic production by raising producer prices, while retaining low consumer prices, increases domestic costs (Egypt, Poland, etc.). Thus, the trade-offs between foreign exchange and domestic fiscal costs become crucial (Chapter 8).

Simultaneous, but uneven rates of changes in technology, income, and population create difficulties over time for national policy makers who may have constrained their present options by previous policy choice. Two simple examples illustrate this obvious point. First, the adoption by the EC of the Common Agricultural Policy (CAP) mechanism of internal target prices defended by variable levies was a simple and effective device *as long as the EC was an importer,* but when the EC switched to being a surplus producer, it proved nearly impossible to switch to more export-oriented policy instruments and to implement effective supply control. The obvious alternative of lowering support prices runs into extreme domestic political opposition from vested interests and those that have purchased land on the expectation of continued high prices.

The second example is Egypt where an industrialization, import substitution strategy of development dictated low nominal wages. Given that food was the dominant component of disposable income, low food prices became locked in as an element of development policy. Over time, rapid population growth and rising incomes pushed demand for bread rapidly to the right. Low producer prices caused production to fall as economically rational Egyptian farmers shifted to more profitable nonprice-controlled crops. The result was an explosion in both foreign exchange and domestic budgetary costs. But food riots in Cairo and many other countries attest to the political difficulty of breaking into the vicious cycle of cost escalation. Thus, by the early 1980s, food subsidy costs in Egypt were a major drain on public expenditure.

The time horizon of policy choice must be long enough to recognize the power of exogenous shifters. But if policy choice today is constrained by yesterday's decisions, the policy analysis problem involves second-best choices which requires pragmatic policy analysis. We leave it to the reader to use any or all our models in a comparative static way to look at the impacts of shifts of supply and demand functions over time.

VI INTERNATIONAL PRESSURES ON NATIONAL POLICY CHOICE

So far we have been looking at individual policy units (e.g., countries) and their domestic policy choice in an interdependent world. In that process we have shown that policy intervention alters excess supply and demand functions and, therefore, inevitably world prices. These changes in world prices impact on producers and consumers in other countries leading to potential pressure, internationally induced, for domestic intervention.

To illustrate the point, consider the following simplest of cases. The analysis is shown in Figure 7-5. Suppose we start with a situation where there is no intervention. Assume two exporters, A and B, and two importers, C and D. Aggregate excess supply is E_s, excess demand is E_d, and world price is P_w. Suppose Country B implements a target price of P_B and pays producers a deficiency payment equal to the difference between P_B and world price. Assume also, that Country A has guaranteed producers this year's price P_w for next year. The result of B's intervention is to kink the total excess supply function to E_s' which causes world price to fall to P_w'. The impacts are clear: Country A pays an export subsidy (area G), Country B pays deficiency payments (area H), and in importing countries C and D, producers are worse off but consumers (and the economy) are better off.

In round 2, now importer C producers demand and receive a guaranteed price of P_c. This kinks the total excess demand function to E_d', world prices fall to P_w''; costs increases in B (area I) and producers in A and D are worse off while importer C pays the deficiency payments to producers (area J).

In round 3, producers in both A and D demand and receive the original world price on the argument that they should not be disadvantaged by intervention in other countries. Assume that in A, a state trading agency buys at

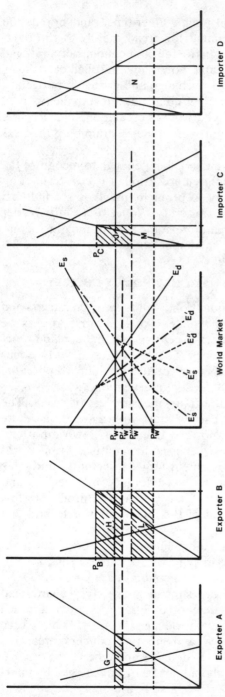

Figure 7-5 International transmission of domestic policy effects.

162

P_w, sells domestically at that price, and will pay an export subsidy, this further kinks E_s to E_s''. In importer D, P_w is guaranteed and is defended with a variable levy. The result is to make E_d steeper (E_d''). The intersection of E_d'' and E_s'' yields a world price of P_w'' which further increases the export subsidy cost of Country A (area G + K). Country B's deficiency payment cost increases again by area L; Country C's deficiency payment increases by area M; only Country D's government benefits by gaining tariff income (area N).

What has this analysis shown? First, sequential interventions in response to Country B's intervention have reduced world prices and increased the costs of Countries A, B, and C's farm programs. Second, part of the benefits have been transferred to Country D and consumers in Countries B and C. Third, if other countries also respond to defend producer prices, costs in Countries A, B, and C will continue to rise. As in the previous sections, Countries B and C may make one or both of two responses—to charge domestic consumers the same price as producers receive (shifts burden from treasury to consumers) and to implement supply control. What then prevents successive and competitive interventions from driving world prices to zero? Two things are apparent. First, national treasuries are not bottomless. Therefore, alternative additional measures are devised to limit costs, e.g., PIK and co-responsibility levies. Second, the dynamics of the market may have expanded demand sufficiently rapidly to maintain nominal but not always real prices as happened in the grain market through most of the 1970s.

This simple single-commodity case illustrates the point that domestic actions in one country may force interventions in other countries. Thus, it is clear why the tendency is that, once intervention has begun, more is likely to occur. This is in fact the history of international agricultural markets in the post–World War II period.

VII SUMMARY

The analysis in this chapter is both closer to the real world of policy choice and further away from neat, simple policy analysis. The attempt has been to illustrate how the simple tools of economic reasoning and graphic analysis can be used conceptually to sort through increasingly complex policy scenarios. Obviously, the real world of policy intervention is even richer in the kinds of instruments used. However, the purpose was to illustrate a sequential way of looking at problem conceptualization and policy analysis. It is a necessary intermediate step before proceeding to empirical analysis. In the next chapter three actual cases are presented to complete this part of the book which has been concerned with national policy choice in an interdependent world.

REFERENCES

Ballenger, N. S. 1984. Agricultural Policy Analysis for Mexico: Sectoral and Macro Impacts, unpublished doctoral dissertation, University of California, Davis.

Cochrane, W. W. 1979. *The Development of American Agriculture,* The University of Minnesota Press, Minneapolis, Minn.

Kirschen, E. S. and Associates. 1964. *Economic Policy in Our Time*; vol I: *General Theory*, Rand McNally, Chicago.

ADDITIONAL READINGS

Economic Report of the President and Annual Report of Council Economic Advisers. 1984. Food and Agriculture, chap. 4, pp. 112–144.

Farrell, K. R., and Runge, C. F. 1983. "Three Dimensions of U.S. Agricultural Policy," *Policy Research Notes*, Issue 16, ERS/USDA, pp. 13–19.

Hoover, M. 1981. "A Framework for Analyzing Agricultural and Food Policy in the 1980's," *Amer. J. Econ.,* **63**:328–332.

Martin, Marshall A. 1981. "Reconciling Agricultural Pricing, Environmental, Conservation, Energy, and Structural Concerns," *Amer. J. Agr. Econ.,* **63**:309–315.

Rayner, A. J., and Reed, G. V. 1978. "Domestic Price Stabilization, Trade Restrictions, and Buffer Stocks Policy: A Theoretical Policy Analysis with Reference to EEC Agriculture," *Eur. Rev. Agr. Econ.,* **5**:101–118

Schuh, G. E. 1976. "The New Macroeconomics of Agriculture," *Amer. J. Agr. Econ.,* **58**:802–811.

Senauer, Benjamin. 1982. "The Current Status of Food and Nutrition Policy and Food Programs," *Amer. J. Agr. Econ.,* **64**:1009–1016.

Wallerstein, B. 1980. "Foreign-Domestic Intersections in U.S. Food Policy," *Food Policy*, **5**:83–96.

Chapter 8

National Policy Choice in Practice

I INTRODUCTION

The previous three chapters have developed some analytical tools useful in analyzing national policy choice in an interdependent world. This chapter presents three historical real world case studies which demonstrate how the analytical tools can be used. The first case is of single-commodity, large-country analyses. The subject is the Payment in Kind (PIK) program implemented in the United States in 1983. Both wheat and corn programs are discussed not as interdependent commodities (which they are) but as two related but different case studies of the impact of a large country acting for national reasons (passive-large) but having significant world impacts. The second case looks at intercommodity multiple-instrument and macro interrelationships where the country is an exporter of one and a major importer of the other. The case of Egypt was chosen because it is a country with interventions of every conceivable sort. Further, it allows study of macro constraints as well. The third case is of the EC–New Zealand dairy products cartel which addresses the question of market power in commodity markets. The intent in presenting these cases is to lend reality to the book's approach and to test its usefulness.

II LARGE-COUNTRY-PASSIVE, SINGLE-COMMODITY
ANALYSIS: THE CASE OF PIK

A Background

The United States has pursued price and income support programs for major national commodities almost without exception since the Agricultural Adjustment Act of 1933. The principal instrument used has been to attempt to manage the quantity produced (supply) by persuading producers to reduce acreage. The inducements have varied from high minimum prices with acquisition at that price [loan rate plus Commodity Credit Corporation (CCC) assumption of commodity collateral upon loan default] to more complex arrangements of target prices, direct payments, and loan rates which characterized policy under legislation passed in 1973, 1977, and 1981. Throughout the 50-year period, yields have increased significantly and the United States has had frequent difficult bouts with stocks in periods of falling and low prices. Also, during the period, the importance of export demand changed markedly as has the structure of agriculture.

Phenomenal growth in agricultural trade, particularly in food grains, feed grains, and oilseeds and oilseed products, marked the period from 1972 to 1980. During this period, U.S. market shares in wheat, corn, and soybeans increased as the United States captured a more than proportionate share of the growth. Circumstances changed in the early 1980s. The U.S. dollar appreciated sharply against other currencies as U.S. monetary policy tightened in an attempt to reduce high rates of inflation. Tight money and inflation led to a major recession in the early 1980s. Demand for commodities slackened and U.S. market shares dropped because of the appreciaton of the dollar, slackening demand and expanded output in major export competitors. Finally, conditioned by high rates of inflation, the Agriculture and Food Act passed in 1981 contained legislated increases (through 1985) in target prices at roughly the then prevailing rate of inflation.

The just recounted factors plus others resulted in the United States accumulating very large stocks of wheat, corn, sorghum, rice, and cotton by the end of 1982. Falling prices, rising costs, and an election year resulted in cries for drastic intervention to shore up prices and incomes for U.S. farmers. The result was the PIK program announced in January of 1983. The novel part of the program was that within the framework of the 1981 act, farmers would be generously compensated for withdrawing additional land from production in actual commodities drawn from government stocks, thus the payment-in-kind title. This program represented one in a long line of U.S. domestic programs implemented for domestic reasons which had international impacts which in part thwarted U.S. goals. It is, therefore, an excellent case study of large-country passive policy which was discussed in Chapter 6. The nature of U.S. policy circa 1981 and PIK is first outlined. Then the models developed in previous chapters are applied to the year

1983 to illustrate the impacts of large-country action. The analyses treat both corn and wheat because the outcomes of the program were very different largely because of the random element of weather.

B The 1981 Act and PIK

Beginning with the 1973 Food and Agriculture Act, U.S. policy has involved two crucial prices. These are target prices, set presumably to represent a socially desirable price for producers on the basis of cost of production and socially desirable returns to efficient producers, and the "loan rate" which is in effect a minimum guaranteed price. It is called a loan rate because of the way the floor is implemented. If producers sign up for the commodity program, they may put some or all of their production up as collateral at time of harvest and receive a loan determined in dollars per unit of output, e.g., $3.50 per bushel of wheat. If before the end of the crop year, market price rises above the loan rate, the farmer can redeem his loan by paying back the loan plus modest interest charges. On the other hand, if market price falls below the loan rate, the farmer defaults on his loan. He keeps the money and the government forgives him his loan and interest charges. Therefore, it is called a nonrecourse loan which is in effect a minimum price guarantee. The loan rate is set below the target price and is generally set at expected world market price.

How the program functions is illustrated in Figure 8-1 where the target

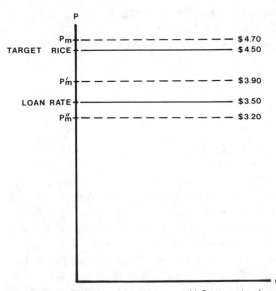

Figure 8-1 Relationships between U.S. target prices and loan rates.

price and the loan rate are shown at say $4.50 and $3.50 per bushel, respectively. If a farmer participates and the market price is P_m ($4.70) at the end of the year, presumably he would redeem his loan and sell his entire output on the free market at $4.70. If the market price is P'_m ($3.90), the farmer would still redeem his loan and sell it on the market. However, he would be compensated in the form of a direct payment (deficiency payment) from the treasury of $60 per bushel [the target price ($4.50) minus the average market price ($3.90) for each bushel produced up to the average yield per acre for his district]. If the market price is below the loan, say P''_m ($3.20), the farmer rationally would default on this loan and keep the $3.50 per bushel and receive a deficiency payment of $1.00 per bushel (target price–loan rate) on average yield.

This same mechanism was preserved in the 1981 Agriculture and Food Act. It is clear that as market price falls and/or target prices are increased, the cost to the government rises in terms of deficiency payments. Cost is also sensitive to the proportion of producers participating. If market prices fall below the loan rate, additional costs are interest foregone and storage costs for the commodity acquired through loan defaults.

The scene is now set to analyze the year 1983 and PIK. As noted earlier, the rising dollar and a global recession caused grain prices denominated in dollars to fall in the early 1980s (see Chapter 4). United States exports declined because of a soft market, increased export supplies from competitors, and the strong dollar which resulted in a loss of market share. This coupled with increasing target prices legislated into the 1981 Act, two very good crops in 1980/81 and 1981/82, and the limited supply control provisions of those years' programs resulted in burgeoning stocks and escalating budget costs. The stage was set for PIK.

When announced in January 1983, the objectives of PIK were to (ERS/USDA), 1983):

- Reduce production and stocks simultaneously
- Minimize direct government outlays
- Increase farm incomes
- Ease storage problems
- Improve conservation practices

Prior to its announcement, the government had already announced general programs for commodities including wheat and corn, the commodities of interest here. To be eligible for target prices and access to loans, wheat farmers would have had to agree to reduce acreage 20 percent—15 percent as the price of admission and 5 percent as a paid diversion. Corn producers also had to reduce acreage 20 percent—10 percent without compensation [Acreage Reduction Program (ARP)] and 10 percent in paid land diversion (PLD). Sign-ups had been low, thus for PIK to be effective, it was argued, it would need additional incentives. For wheat, these were that if farmers agreed to reduce acreage a further 10 to 30 percent (beyond the initial 20 percent) they would be compensated at 95 percent of average yield in wheat for each acre removed. Corn producers would be compensated at 80 percent of average yield for each acre entered into the program. In both programs, farmers could offer to remove their entire acreage for some percentage of average yield which they submitted as a sealed bid to the U.S. Department of Agriculture (USDA).

At the end of the sign-up period, over 80 million acres were signed up to be removed from production, nearly 35 percent of eligible acres and about 20 percent of total U.S. crop land. The largest sign-ups occurred in rice, corn, and wheat. The level of sign-up surprised everyone and was claimed to exceed official estimates of participation by a factor of two.

Curiously, the analysis that preceded the announcement of PIK paid limited attention to international implications. Use of the model developed by Chapters 5 and 6 should have suggested otherwise. The case of a large country attempting to reduce land inputs is reproduced in Figure 8-2. From initial equilibrium, farmers are paid to reduce acreage of wheat S_L' which shifts wheat supply to S_W' and reduces the demand for fertilizer to D_F'.

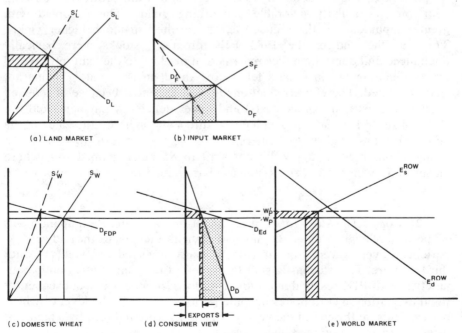

Figure 8-2 Impacts of the U.S. Payment-in-Kind program.

World prices rise to W_p'. The results are clear—landowners lose the shaded area in rent but gain the cross-hatched area plus the payments (in-kind) for removing the acres. Variable input suppliers lose gross revenue (by the shaded area). Foreign suppliers gain by the cross-hatched area in Figure 8-2e. United States foreign exchange earnings are less by the shaded area in Figure 8-2d and increased by the cross-hatched area. They would increase only when world excess demand is inelastic. Consumers in the United States and the rest of the world clearly lose.

Given this analysis, how could one assume that world impacts would be insignificant? It came from the assumption that as stocks were transferred from government stocks (essentially isolated from the market by high stock release prices) to farmers' hands that they would replace reduced production almost one for one and therefore supply would not shift to the left as the model suggests. What actually happened differed greatly between wheat and corn.

C The Results of PIK

1 Wheat All the winter wheat was planted prior to the announcement of PIK. Thus, the 95 percent payment rate was higher than for other commodities to induce wheat producers to plow up wheat. Approximately 35 percent of eligible acres of wheat were signed up. However, the crop year was particularly favorable concerning yields. This, coupled with greater input use on the reduced acres, resulted in much higher yields. Thus, at the end of the 1983 PIK program, stocks were basically unchanged and domestic prices remained at or close to the loan rate. World prices denominated in dollars fell below the loan rate and U.S. market share declined. Therefore, reductions in cost expected because of reduced stocks (interest and storage costs) and lower deficiency payments did not materialize. In fact, farm program costs, direct and indirect (the value of the commodity assets given to farmers), were the highest in history. Thus, in terms of our model, supply did not shift to S_w' but remained somewhere closer to S_w which when stocks released are added resulted in lower world prices.

2 Corn The story for corn is almost the opposite. Participation was 38 percent of eligible acres. But, instead of yields increasing, the midwest experienced a very severe drought which in many areas reduced yields by one-third or more. This stochastic shift to the left of the supply function in conjunction with PIK resulted in a rapid run-down of stocks and subsequently rapid escalation in corn prices in some periods almost to the level of wheat prices. Thus, at the end of the year, corn stocks were reduced by a factor of three and prices continued high.

D　The Messages from the PIK Analysis

Several messages emerge from this simplified analysis of PIK. *First,* for a large country to ignore international ramifications is hazardous. Had the United States explicitly considered desired changes in world prices, it might have designed a program to raise world prices just to the loan rate so as to not induce additional supplies from other suppliers. *Second,* stochastic elements in the form of weather can have significant impacts on the outcome of particular programs even within the same country and in the same year. *Third,* the model allows the explicit identification of gainers and losers both domestically and internationally. These, of course, are modified by stochastic elements but at least we could use the model to plumb the impacts of the extremes of poor versus excellent crops. *Finally,* even though the analysis has not explicitly included the intercommodity linkages developed in Chapter 3, they clearly could be included. The bottom line is that although real world policy analysis is inherently complex, simple models can be very useful in disentangling the multiple effects.

III　MULTIPLE-COMMODITY, INSTRUMENT, AND GOAL INTERACTIONS: THE CASE OF EGYPT

The second historical case study relates to Egypt in the late 1970s and early 1980s. The objectives are (1) to further refine the model with two commodities, several instruments, and multiple goals; (2) to develop policy trade-off frontiers between two macro variables, local currency costs and foreign exchange balances, given domestic food and agricultural goals; and (3) to demonstrate the absolutely crucial role that empirical analysis must play in real world policy analysis. However, empirical analysis must be preceded by a clear conceptual understanding of what is really happening.

　　Egypt provides a rich environment within which to explore these trade-off questions. Almost every conceivable form of intervention has been and still is being tried. The importance of the food and agricultural sector to the national economy, the importance of trade, and currency inconvertibility, makes exploring the fiscal and foreign exchange trade-offs interesting. Inconvertibility means domestic currency and foreign exchange holdings are not direct substitutes; thus the differing impacts of policy change on these two accounts must be understood.

　　The approach begins with static analyses of individual commodity programs, both at the production and consumption levels, with the objective of deriving a fiscal–foreign exchange trade-off frontier. This is done by changing particular program parameters and tracing out their implications. Two cases are studied—cotton/textiles and wheat/bread. After deriving a direct-effects frontier, the intercommodity effects are explored by examining the impacts of, for example, a change in producer prices for wheat on the cotton trade-off function. It is derived from a much more detailed paper to which the reader is referred for more detail (McCalla, King, and Carter, 1982).

A Egyptian Food and Agricultural Policy

The Egyptian agricultural sector provided, in 1981–1982, nearly a fifth of GNP and over a third of the gainful employment, and it was a significant factor in fiscal and foreign exchange budgets. A complex web of explicit and implicit taxes and subsidies have resulted in resource transfers from the production sector to the consuming and government sectors. Policies with respect to producers have generally been those of maintaining prices below world market prices. Thus, an implicit tax is levied on, for example, export crops such as cotton which is exported at world price. The tax revenue appears in foreign exchange accounts. In parallel fashion, low farm wheat prices contribute to a consumer subsidy. However, in the years under study, subsidized consumer prices have been below producer prices resulting in an explicit consumer subsidy. Some of this is paid from the domestic fiscal budget and some requires foreign exchange allocations for wheat imports. Historically, the agricultural sector has been a net foreign exchange earner but by the late 1970s massive increases in food imports have shifted that balance to a net foreign exchange deficit.

Consumer subsidies have increased to such an extent that the fiscal cost of subsidies is a very important part of Egyptian public finances. A significant number of consumer commodities are rationed and/or subsidized. Commodities which are rationed and subsidized include cooking oil, sugar, rice, and tea. Commodities which are subsidized and loosely rationed (where quantities per family are guaranteed except in times of supply shortage) include beans, lentils, frozen beef, poultry, and flour. A third category is subsidized but unrationed. Bread is the major item under this policy. The government (the Ministry of Supply) is involved in wholesale and retail distribution of these commodities as well as many nonsubsidized, but price-controlled commodities such as many fruits and vegetables.

Policies relating to agricultural production are equally pervasive involving complex combinations of production mandates, product requisitions, government purchases at fixed prices, and various price ceilings. As this analysis focuses on cotton and wheat, a more detailed discussion is presented as background. Historically, *cotton* has been a major foreign exchange earner for Egypt. The area to be planted to cotton is centrally determined, based in part on anticipated foreign exchange needs. Area is assigned to governorates, districts, and villages. Production from the mandated area is purchased by the government at prices generally well below world prices. A portion of the requisitioned cotton is sold to domestic mills at a fixed price between farm price and world price. The remainder is exported, with the foreign exchange earnings accruing to the government. Inputs for cotton are provided at subsidized prices.

Until the late 1970s, *wheat* was also a requisitioned crop with mandated delivery quotas. Since then the government has offered support prices for wheat which, while increasing, still remain below world prices. Domestic wheat production has been either stable or declining in recent years. Domestic consumers are guaranteed unlimited quantities of bread at very low fixed prices. Population has grown at over 2.5 percent annually, resulting in increases in consumption such that Egypt imported nearly three-quarters of her wheat needs. The imports are of two types—commercial imports and concessional imports (PL480)—which involve low down payments and long payment periods, making the current costs very low.

B Characteristics of the Actual Trade-Off Functions

Simple supply and demand diagrams, with program parameters included, can be used to derive actual trade-off functions between domestic fiscal costs or revenue and foreign exchange earnings (or savings) or costs.

  1 Cotton The cotton program is depicted in Figure 8-3. A positively sloped supply function is postulated. Evidence suggests that, even with cotton requisitions, farmers do respond to price. Thus, to get an increased requisition quantity, requisition price must rise. A perfectly elastic world demand function at world price (P_{wo}) is specified based on the findings of Monke and Petzel (1984) who found significant interfiber-length competition in world markets at least between short, medium, and long staple cotton. This questions the conventional notion that Egypt can behave as a monopolist in the extra-long staple (ELS) market. Even if the world demand function is not perfectly elastic it does not significantly alter the analysis. Finally, it is assumed that the allocation to domestic mills is constrained by mill capacity and is sold at a fixed price (above requisition, but below world price) (Ikram, 1980, pp. 264–265). Domestic demand is shown as D_d in all parts of Figure 8-3.

The analysis begins with Figure 8-3III which represents the base program. Requisition price (P_{req}^c) is below domestic mill price (P_d^c) which, in turn, is less than world price (P_{wo}^c). Producers produce $0-Q_i^c$. Domestic mills receive $0-C_d^c$ and $C_d^c-Q_i^c$ is exported at world price. Gross revenue (in pounds) to the Egyptian government for domestic sales is A + B. Payments to producers (in pounds) are A + C. Net fiscal cost is B − C. Foreign exchange earnings are C + D. B − C and C + D are the coordinates of point III on the Fx–L.E. diagram which is one point on the fiscal–foreign exchange trade-off frontier shown in Figure 8-3V. The four quadrants repre-

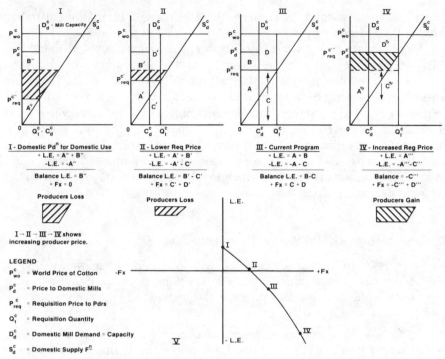

Figure 8-3 Impact of changes in Egyptian cotton policy on foreign exchange and domestic budget balances.

sent all possible combinations of changes in foreign exchange costs (−Fx) or earnings (+Fx) and budgetary revenue (L.E.) or costs (−L.E.)

In Figure 8-3II, requisition price and quantity are lowered with the allocation to domestic mills remaining unchanged. Net L.E. position improves—less acquisition costs and higher profits on domestic sales—and foreign exchange earnings decline, yielding point II on the trade-off function. In Figure 8-3I, price is reduced to just produce for domestic mill capacity. The result is no Fx earnings but a substantial profit in L.E. This is shown as point I. Finally, if requisition price was increased to, say, domestic mill price (Figure 8-3IV), production increases as do exports (+Fx), but domestic costs also increase, yielding point IV in Figure 8-3V. I, II, III, and IV are four points on a continuous trade-off function with movement from I → IV occurring with increased requisitions and requisition price, the principal policy instrument of the Egyptian government. Static producer surplus losses or gains relative to the current situation are shown as the cross-hatched areas. It should be noted for completeness that this analysis does not consider the changes in alternative crops that could be grown as cotton acreage changed. Thus, they are only *partial* producer losses or gains. Trade-offs could also be drawn between producer-consumer surplus with alternative policies.

2   **Wheat**   A parallel analysis of wheat, which depends heavily on a paper by de Janvry, Siam, and Gad (1981), is presented in Figure 8-4. The base program is depicted in Figure 8-4III. Egypt is eligible for PL480 wheat on long-term credit terms. Therefore, the current foreign exchange cost is very low. This current cost is some proportion β of world price (βP_{wo}^w) and as de Janvry et al. (1981), argue it is below domestic consumer price. Given that domestic sales of PL480 wheat generate L.E. profits, it is assumed that the government will import all that is available. (It should be noted, however, that if the United States did not divert grain into PL480, world commercial prices could be lower, reducing foreign exchange costs of commercial imports.) Assume PL480 imports are $Q_I^w - C_d^w$, the foreign exchange cost is G, and domestic revenue is G + H. Consumer prices of bread are assumed fixed at P_c^w. Given domestic demand D_d^w, domestic consumption is C_d^w. The

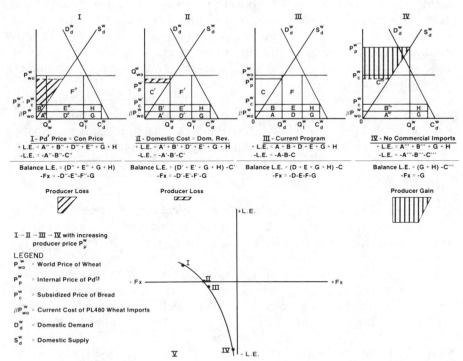

Figure 8-4 Impact of changes in Egyptian wheat support price on foreign exchange and domestic budget balances.

policy question becomes how much to produce domestically and how much to import commercially. The critical policy variable then is the domestic support price to Egyptian producers (P_p^w). As it rises, domestic production substitutes for imports, yielding a Fx–L.E. trade-off.

In Figure 8-4III (the depiction of the base program), $0-C_d^w$ is consumed at P_c^w yielding L.E. revenue to the government of $A + B + D + E + G + H$, $0-Q_d^w$ is produced, given a support price of P_d^w, with an acquisition cost of $-A - B - C$. The net L.E. balance which is $(D + E + G + H) - C$, consistent with de Janvry's et al. (1981) findings, is modestly negative. $Q_d^w - Q_I^w$ is imported at world price (P_{wo}^w) at a foreign exchange cost of $D + E + F$ and $Q_I^w - C_d^w$ is imported under PL480 at a current foreign exchange cost of G. Therefore, $(D + E + G + H) - C$ (<0) and $D + E + F + G$ (<0) give the coordinates of point III on the trade-off function.

As with cotton, the domestic producer price of wheat is changed to trace out the function. In Figure 8-4II and I producer price is lowered yielding points II (breakeven on L.E.) and I on the frontier. In Figure 8-4IV producer price is raised to eliminate commercial imports which, as would be expected, greatly increases the domestic L.E. cost of the program. Thus, the function is negatively sloped as producer prices are increased moving from point I towards IV showing a decrease in foreign exchange costs but an increase in domestic costs. Again, the cross-hatched areas show changes in producer welfare relative to the current program. Analysis of changes in world price, consumer price, and shifts in the wheat supply function are deferred until later.

The analysis could proceed to additional commodities but these are sufficient examples to illustrate the use of trade-off functions in looking at cross-program effects. The two derived functions are imposed on one another in Figure 8-5. Under current programs, cotton earns $+Fx^c$ and costs $-L.E.^c$ and wheat costs $-Fx^w$ and $-L.E.^w$. Next we explore the direct and cross effects of program changes.

3 Interprogram Effects   Here, the analytical model is used to explore the cross effects of program changes on domestic and foreign exchange budgets. Suppose the foreign exchange earnings from remittances and oil decline because of the global recession and the government of Egypt wants to investigate the implications of increasing the requisition (and requisition price) of cotton to expand exports and increase foreign exchange earnings. The *direct* effect of that change can be read directly off the cotton trade-off function in Figure 8-5. An increase in requisition price would increase production and increase exports, therefore, moving from point III towards point IV. Foreign exchange earnings would increase as would L.E. costs. If the function was estimated econometrically, it could be used to determine the relative trade-off, the ratio $+\Delta Fx^c/(-\Delta L.E.^c)$. Given policy-maker

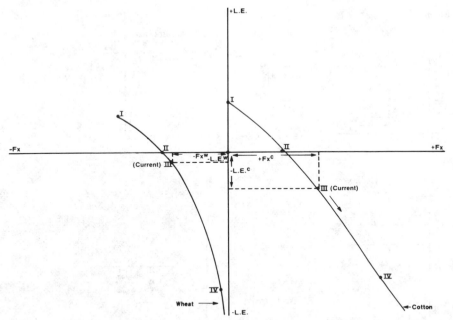

Figure 8-5 Trade-off between foreign exchange and domestic budget balance: Egyptian wheat and cotton.

weights on the relative importance of availability of domestic currency vis-à-vis increased foreign exchange, something could be said about the desirability of the change.

But that would only look at the direct effects of the change. Clearly, with an aggregate land constraint in the short run, an increase in cotton area means a reduction in the area of other crops. It is these cross effects as a result of production substitution that are derived in Figure 8-6.

The individual commodity supply functions were drawn as a function of that commodity's price *ceteris paribus,* i.e., the quantity of wheat produced Q_d^w as a function of the producer price of wheat P_p^w $[Q_d^w = f(P_d^w)]$. In reality, the supply function of wheat is $Q_d^w = f(P_d^w, P_{req}^c, \ldots)$ where other prices are shifters of the wheat supply function. A change in, say, cotton program prices (assuming through a complex cropping pattern adjustment, positive changes in cotton plantings have a negative impact on wheat area, that is, $dQ_d^w/dP_{req}^c < 0$) will shift the wheat supply function as is illustrated in Figure 8-6a. An increase in the program price of a competing crop shifts the wheat supply function to the left, that is, $S_d^w \rightarrow S_d^{w'}$. The result is a reduction in domestic production (and L.E. costs) and an increase in imports, $-Fx$. This is a point $S_d^{w''}$ on a new trade-off frontier. A fall in the price of a competing

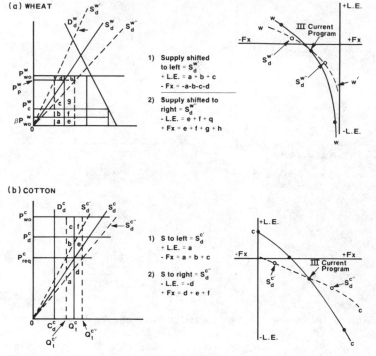

Figure 8-6   Cross-commodity effects of program changes: Egyptian wheat and cotton.

crop shifts the supply of wheat to the right ($S_d^{w''}$) and has the opposite effect, that is, $-$L.E. and $+$Fx, and yields point $S_d^{w''}$ on the new function. Repeats of this would trace out a new trade-off frontier $W'-W'$ which is different from the original frontier. Recall the original frontier was drawn with a fixed cotton price and varying wheat prices. This one is drawn with a fixed price of wheat but with changes in cotton prices. Therefore, the function is rotated through the original program point (III on $W-W$).

In Figure 8-6b the exercise is repeated for changes in the cotton trade-off function for changes in other program parameters. Again, supply shifts rotate the Fx–L.E. trade-off function through the current program point III to trace out the broken-line function. Repeating a similar set of adjustments in the allocation to domestic mills traces out a similarly shaped function moving to the southeast as allocations to domestic mills decrease.

The analysis can now be used to look at both the direct and cross effects of a particular program change. In Figure 8-7 it is hypothesized that there is an increase in the cotton requisition (and requisition price). The direct effect is to move along the L.E.–Fx trade-off function from III to III' resulting in an increase in foreign exchange earnings of $+$Fx^c and an increase in domestic currency cost of $-$L.E.^{c}. But an expansion of cotton supply hypothetically shifts to the left the supply function of wheat (through indirect cropping pattern adjustments) causing movements to a new point y' (from y) on the new wheat function. Wheat production falls reducing domestic acquisition costs ($+\Delta$L.E.^{w}) but increasing imports ($-\Delta$Fx^w).

The direct and cross effects of the change in the cotton program can be summarized as follows:

$$\Delta Fx = +\Delta Fx^c - \Delta Fx^w$$
$$\Delta L.E. = +\Delta L.E.^w - \Delta L.E.^c$$

In the absence of empirical estimates of these functions, the policy makers would not know whether there are net gains or net losses in either foreign exchange earnings or budgetary L.E. outlays resulting from the cotton program change.

C   Implications of Analysis

In addition to the derivation of these trade-off frontiers, the static partial analysis allows identification of impacts on producers (farmers), and on rural

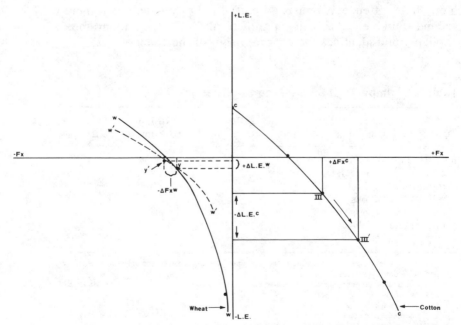

Figure 8-7   Direct and cross effects of increasing Egyptian cotton requisitions.

and urban consumers. These are summarized for the case in Table 8-1. Few definitive a priori statements can be made about the effects on individual targets, let alone aggregate net impacts. If the analysis attempted to look at simultaneous changes in more than one program, the outcomes become more uncertain a priori.

The use of a conceptual model alone to look at particular Egyptian policies does not provide definitive policy answers. However, it is a necessary step in more effective policy analysis for two reasons. *First,* it focuses explicitly on what must be an important trade-off for macro policy makers, particularly if balances in the budgets are sharply different, e.g., a large domestic budget deficit and significant foreign exchange surpluses. Adjustment of domestic program parameters could assist in simultaneously improving both situations. But more importantly, it should help agricultural policy analysts to make these implications explicit in their analysis.

Second, the analysis permits looking at both direct and cross effects of program changes and forces consideration of the implications of the cross elasticities even in individual commodity analysis. While the approach is not fully a general equilibrium one, it is much broader than a single-commodity partial approach. It ought to be obvious that a succession of cross effects could have one of three impacts on the net outcome: (1) accentuate the direction of change, (2) offset change so as to negate the outcome, or (3) more than offset the direct effect and move the outcome in the "wrong" direction. Yet, all too often, economists do partial policy analysis as if there were no second-round effects. This approach allows taking them into account explicitly and identifies the expected sign of the change.

Table 8-1 Impacts of Single-Program Changes

Changes	Impacts	Farmers	Rural consumers	Urban consumers	L.E.	Fx
Increase in cotton requisition price: other programs unchanged	Direct effects: Cotton	+	0	0	−	+
	Cross effects: Wheat	−	−*	0	+	−
	Net	?	−	0	?	?

+ = increased producer surplus; increased consumer surplus; positive change in net balance of L.E. or Fx accounts
− = decreased producer surplus; decreased consumer surplus; negative change in net balance of L.E. or Fx accounts
0 = no change
? = outcome uncertain a priori
*The contraction of wheat production raises the free market price of wheat in rural areas.

IV INTERNATIONAL PRICE FIXING: THE CASE OF THE DAIRY MARKET

A Background

The international dairy market represents perhaps the most clear-cut case of the cumulative effect of national farm policies on the conditions of world trade. Dairy production is a favored activity in most industrial countries, often seen as a key to maintaining the income of small farmers because the scale of technology and the marketing system are geared to these farmers. The dairy cow is a highly efficient converter of grass and roughage, as well as concentrated feedstuffs, into palatable and nutritious foods. The continuity of production over the year, by phasing the cow's breeding cycle, contrasts with the seasonality of crop harvests and provides a steady income flow. The price paid to the producer is, in most industrial countries, aimed precisely at the needs of the small farmer with a strong orientation towards income maintenance.

Unfortunately, for policy makers, the milk price set for small farmers is often very profitable for the larger farmers, who over the past 30 years have increased herd size and yield per cow by the use of better breeding stock and new technology. This has led to output which cannot readily be absorbed on domestic markets. To prevent increased production from weakening the position of small farmers, governments have implemented market management for milk and milk products by controlling the quantities going to the (generally more price inelastic) liquid milk market, and by setting support prices for milk products through government purchases, import controls, and subsidies to users of such products. This has contributed to a situation where milk products are highly priced on domestic markets but find few outlets at the international level.

International trade in milk products is primarily in butter, cheese, and skim milk because liquid milk, by reason of its bulkiness and perishability, does not lend itself to international trade. These are also the commodities which bear the brunt of the surplus problem in developed-country dairy sectors. But the market overseas for such products is limited, thus the few commercial outlets for milk products can quickly become overburdened with surplus products sold with the aid of subsidies. The gainers from this situation are those countries—the Soviet Union is the best example—that can absorb surplus dairy products without facing criticism from domestic farm interests and incorporate them into the domestic food supply system as and when they are available. The chief losers are those countries, exemplified by New Zealand, which have genuine low costs due to ideal conditions for pasture production, and would otherwise be able to satisfy a significant part of world demand.

The dairy market is thus dominated by the unwanted surpluses of countries who have, by high domestic prices, encouraged excess production, and who choose not to allow domestic consumers (through, say, a deficiency payment system) to reap the benefits of expanded milk output. Recently, the costs of moving such surpluses onto world markets has been more apparent. Hence, the countries that engage in dumping dairy surpluses on world markets have a strong financial interest in keeping up the world market price. Such price fixing also strikes a responsive chord in the more efficient exporters.

This part of this chapter discusses the recent attempts by exporters, in particular, the EC and New Zealand, to maintain dairy product prices on world markets above the levels which would otherwise obtain. Another potential exporter, at present domestic price levels, is the United States. The United States has not at present entered significantly into the world dairy market, choosing other methods of surplus disposal. But as will be seen below, the connivance of the United States is necessary for the operation of price fixing. In effect, there has been an implicit triopoly in this market.

The benefits and costs to parties concerned can be examined using the analysis of Chapter 7. The emphasis is on the markets for butter and for skim milk powder; cheese, though an important traded product, is much less homogeneous and has a wider distribution of both production and consumption, and other products such as casein, lactose syrup, and butter oil are of lesser importance to the story.

B International Trade in Butter and Skim Milk Powder (SMP)

1 The Actors The market for butter and SMP, and the place of the EC, New Zealand, the United States and the U.S.S.R. in that market, is shown in Table 8-2. Notable is the dominance of the EC in butter exports, with a 1981 market share of nearly 60 percent, followed by New Zealand with 24 percent of exports. The EC also imports butter from New Zealand, under a long-standing quota arrangement; if this trade were put directly onto the world market by New Zealand, the share of that country would rise to 35 percent and that of the EC would drop to 46 percent. The U.S.S.R. in 1981 accounted for 53 percent of world imports. Exports of skim milk powder are also dominated by the EC, with 56 percent of the market, with the United States and New Zealand together making up another 32 percent. Imports of SMP are more widely distributed, with countries such as Mexico and other countries in Latin America and Asia taking considerable amounts of this product. The U.S.S.R. imported 15 percent of the SMP on world markets.

2 The EC Dairy Policy Given the dominant market position of the EC in these products, the natural place to start an analysis of the market is with EC policy. The Common Agricultural Policy (CAP) of the European

Table 8-2   Trade in Butter and Skim Milk Powder, Selected Countries' Imports and Exports, 1981

	Butter exports		Butter imports		SMP exports		SMP imports	
	Quantity (tmt)	Share (%)	Quantity (tmt)	Share (%)	Quantity (tmt)	Share (%)	Quantity (tmt)	Share (%)
EC	484	57.1	92	17.6	551	56.1	10	1.9
US	54	6.4	2	0.4	155	15.8	1	0.2
NZ	203	23.9	—	—	163	16.6		
USSR	18	2.1	275	52.6	—	—	80	15.0
Other	89	10.5	154	29.4	113	11.5	444	82.9
Total*	848	100.0	523	100.0	982	100.0	535	100.0

*Total of 34 major producing and trading countries.
Source: USDA/FAS, "Foreign Agricultural Circular," *Dairy*, May 1982.

Community is designed to provide producers in the 10 member states with a stable and protected market for their output, with the aim of increasing incomes and encouraging rural development. Two mechanisms dominate the CAP: a set of minimum import prices for most of the temperate-zone products which keep foreign supplies from undercutting domestic markets, and a series of fixed intervention prices which offer producers a guaranteed outlet when surpluses would otherwise depress the market. Prices are set in common for all members, and trade is at least, in principle, free within the Community. Revenue from import levies goes into the common budget and expenditure on support buying comes from the common purse. In practice, little trade moves into the EC at these price levels; the quota for New Zealand butter [87,000 tons is imported into the United Kingdom (UK), as a concession to New Zealand] being the main exception. More important to the European dairy farmer is the intervention policy. The EC authorities calculate, on the basis of processing costs and conversion ratios, a set of prices for butter and skim milk powder that would allow dairy factories to pay farmers an agreed price for raw milk. Agencies in each country then agree to buy all offered butter and SMP at these intervention prices.

The surplus acquired by the intervention agencies must then be disposed of in some way. The two outlets available are the internal market, with the aid of a consumer subsidy, or the international market, with an export subsidy. Both methods have been tried. Domestic subsidies have ranged from general distribution schemes, in one or more countries, to targeted sales aimed at the elderly and at institutions, and subsidized sales of SMP and skim milk for animal feed. Such internal schemes are costly. Foreign subsidies, ironically, cost less to the taxpayer—the wider market is more responsive to small price cuts—even though they represent an overall economic loss to the EC. But even with such market discrimination, the disposal of butter and skim milk powder has on occasion taken up one-third of the total expenditure on the CAP and one-quarter of total EC spending on common programs in agriculture and elsewhere. Hence, by the early 1980s, the financial cost of the EC dairy policy represented a major problem for the EC as a whole. Eventually, in 1984, an attempt was made to restrain dairy production. But the price-fixing agreement that is the subject of this discussion was an attempt to use the international market to reduce this policy cost.

3   New Zealand Policy   New Zealand is blessed by abundant natural pastures which it has exploited effectively to give it an important export trade in milk and meat products. For many years, much of this trade went to the UK, with whom New Zealand had close historical ties and preferential access agreements. Upon the accession of the UK to the Community in 1973, New Zealand found its access limited to the agreed quota (mentioned above) for butter; similar arrangements have since been concluded for lamb. New Zealand was forced to search for other outlets for its agricultural exports. As a result of generally low production costs and of the size of the export market relative to total production, export subsidies have been both less necessary and less forthcoming than in other countries. A comparison of support prices in New Zealand, the United States, and the EC gives some indication of the difference between the relatively low level of protection in New Zealand compared with the United States and the EC (Table 8-3).

Both domestic policies and trade policies are less heavily dominated by government intervention in New Zealand than in Europe or the United States. The government sets a price for milk going for liquid consumption

Table 8-3 Comparison of Producer Support Prices
NZ, EC, and US, 1981–82
($/mt)

	Butter	SMP	Milk*
NZ	1,696	703	119
US	3,351	2,072	282
EC	3,828	1,595	292

*For manufacturing.
Source: Bazley, P. 1983. An Economic Analysis of Domestic Dairy Policies and Their Implications for the International Dairy Market, unpublished honors thesis, Stanford University.

and operates a quota system for this part of domestic production. A consumer subsidy keeps the "town milk" price low relative to farm returns. Manufacturing milk, by contrast, is sold on the domestic market, or to the New Zealand Dairy Board for export at a price largely fixed by the industry itself. Producer associations operate a fund which accumulates in times when prices are firm and pays out money to farmers when prices are weak.

   4   The United States and the U.S.S.R.   The United States operates a dairy policy based on both the purchase by the Commodity Credit Corporation (CCC) of dairy products at floor-price levels and the organization of some of the fluid milk market through federal marketing orders. The milk marketing orders encourage producer groups to arrange with milk handlers and processors minimum prices for milk going to different end uses. The CCC does not, in general, engage in subsidized exports to the same extent as the EC intervention agencies. Domestic "donations" of dairy products have been the main source of surplus disposal, though considerable amounts of SMP have found their way onto world markets through trade and food aid.

   The Soviet Union is the largest dairy producer. It also has the distinction of facing reduced production. It is, thus, a large potential importer. Its imports so far appear to have been opportunistic rather than reliable. In 1973 it went to the world market for 230,000 metric tons of butter—many times its normal purchases, at a time when the world price was exceptionally low. Since 1979, the U.S.S.R. has been somewhat more regular in its butter purchases, even at more normal world prices. SMP purchases also have been significantly increased since 1979. The Soviet Union, unlike the United States, the EC, and New Zealand, has the luxury of engaging in trade without too much concern for internal market conditions. The trade function is essentially one of supplementing domestic food supply from whatever source is available. Surpluses from the West assist the Soviet trade agencies to lower the cost of food supplies. Soviet purchases of these surpluses help the agricultural policies of the West and avoids even greater trade problems for these countries. The future of the dairy market is, in part, related to the continuation of the Soviet Union's willingness to be a dumping ground for surpluses.

   5   The International Dairy Agreement (IDA)   The problems of instability and low prices in dairy product markets have been around for some time. The EC, always a proponent of international commodity agreements, took the opportunity of the last GATT round of trade negotiations to interest its trading partners in an International Dairy Agreement. The agreement, signed in 1979 as a part of the outcome of the Multilateral Trade Negotiations (MTN), provided for the establishment of minimum export prices for some dairy products, notably butter and SMP. No explicit trade quotas or coordinated storage policies were agreed upon: instead, countries who signed the agreement (including the EC, United States, and New Zealand) undertook to respect the minimum prices specified in the IDA.

Under different circumstances, this story could well have been about the success or failure of the IDA to bring stability and firmer prices to the world dairy market. In fact, the world prices have been at levels almost *double* the IDA minimum levels since 1980. The agreement has yet to be tested. The only effect of the IDA has probably been to facilitate and legitimize the coordinated behavior of the dairy product exporters. The story is one of collusive action by these exporters which has been much more effective than envisaged in the modest minimum price provisions of the Agreement itself.

C The Triopoly at Work

The success of any attempt to raise prices on an international market depends upon the willingness of exporters to restrict sales. In the short run, this can be accomplished by increasing stock levels; in the longer run, some form of output control is necessary. The implicit agreement among the EC, New Zealand, and the United States to support international dairy prices has the air of short-run success clouded by the threat of long-term failure. Table 8-4 shows the production, export, and stock accumulation (closing stock—less opening stock) levels for the United States, the EC, and New Zealand. The United States experienced steady increases in both butter and SMP production and, in the face of static consumption, moved this surplus into stocks and into exports. EC production of these commodities has fluctuated around a rising trend, and exports peaked in 1980. In New Zealand, production of butter has been steadily falling while SMP production has gradually increased.

The elements of coordination among policies can be seen by looking at the extent to which production changes are translated into stock and export effects. It follows from the basic market-clearing identity (see Chapter 2) that changes in these variables, together with consumption and imports are related. Table 8-4 shows the year-to-year changes in production and their distribution to exports and stocks (consumption and import changes are omitted for clarity). The United States put its production increase in butter into stocks in 1980 but into exports in 1981 and 1982. The EC and New Zealand choose to reduce stock accumulation and emphasize exports in 1980, despite a fall in production. This presumably set the scene for coordination in the following two years: the world market was under pressure from the additional exports. In both 1981 and 1982 the situation was reversed. Exports declined (except for a small increase in 1982 for New Zealand) and stock accumulation was increased. The United States did not apparently participate in this action in these two years. However, the Unit-

Table 8-4 Production, Exports and Stock Accumulation, Butter and Skim Milk Powder; USA, EC, and NZ, 1979–1982 (tmt)

	United States			EC			New Zealand		
	Production	Exports	Stock changes	Production	Exports	Stock changes	Production	Exports	Stock changes
A Butter									
1979	447	—	−7	1,988	405	+17	255	192	+18
1980	519	—	+57	1,956	549	+152	255	231	−20
1981	561	54	+57	1,895	505	−124	247	203	+27
1982	595	90	+56	2,060	395	+175	235	210	+60
B SMP									
1979	412	84	−45	2,160	570	+50	174	141	+30
1980	527	131	+46	2,074	574	−19	169	172	−15
1981	593	155	+138	2,090	502	+72	181	163	+8
1982	670	170	+201	2,240	347	+323	183	185	−12

Source: Bazley, P. 1983. An Economic Analysis of Domestic Dairy Policies and Their Implications for the International Dairy Market, unpublished honors thesis. Stanford University.

ed States could have reduced its own stocks onto the firmer export market. It was a passive observer, an accomplice by inaction, to the supporting of the market price.

The skim milk market tells something of the same story, though less dramatically. Exports were expanded in 1980, even though New Zealand and the EC had experienced a drop in domestic production. The United States participated in the stock build-up, by increasing its rate of stock accumulation in 1981 and 1982, but also expanded exports. The action of the EC and New Zealand to reduce exports in 1981, despite production increases in the EC, was weakened by this action. New Zealand apparently decided to leave the export contraction to the EC in 1982.

It would take a deeper analysis to determine how much of the export restraint in 1981 and 1982, in contrast to the expansion in 1980, was due to the exporters' actions as against demand shifts in the importers. The amount of planning of the export squeeze, and the role of the United States in such planning, is not on public record. But there clearly was a beneficial coincidence of actions not entirely explicable by purely domestic events. The implication is that the EC and New Zealand were trying to raise world prices through their trade policies in a market where they dominated supply (butter) and to a lesser extent in a market where all three were important exporters (SMP). Figure 8-8 is an attempt to describe the rationale behind such a move. The world export supply curve, aggregated over the major exporters, presumably has two distinct segments: the "commercial" supply, at high world prices, above EC (and United States) domestic support price levels (P_1)—if prices were this high, unsupported exports would begin to be readily available; and the "subsidized" supply, at price levels below domestic support levels—where supply is greater than it would be if no subsidies were

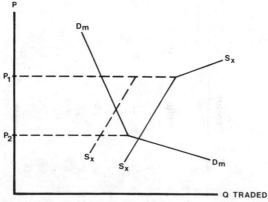

Figure 8-8 Effects on the world dairy market of the build-up of exporter stocks.

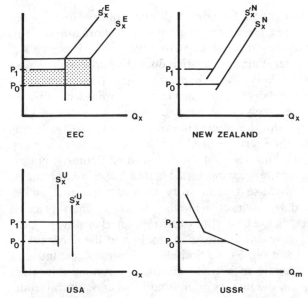

Figure 8-9 Impact on major trading countries of an increase in the world dairy price.

available. The demand also, less clearly, probably has two sgements: a steeper portion where countries buy those dairy products than can be absorbed easily onto domestic markets; and a "bargain basement," where importers such as the U.S.S.R. (and outlets such as food aid) can absorb large quantities if the price is right (below P_2). The world price probably varies somewhere above or below this demand curve kink—the aim of the exporters presumably is to climb up the portion above P_2. A supply shift to S'_x would accomplish this. However, if the supply constraint is merely due to a stock build-up, then in the next period there is a likelihood that prices would collapse once again. Permanent supply reduction would be needed to keep price above P_2, unless the demand curve were to shift to the right.

The effect on the four countries considered here is represented in Figure 8-9. The price rise resulting from export restraint in the EC and New Zealand, coupled with a small increase in U.S. supply, could raise prices from P_0 to P_1 in the figure. The EC clearly benefits financially from the lower cost of export subsidies (shown as shaded area). There may, however, be extra costs in a later time period as the stocks are released onto domestic or world markets. The EC did, in fact, experience a decrease of over $1 billion (37 percent of total export subsidy costs) between 1980 and 1981, though this was also due to higher world prices (caused by increased demand) as well as to a cut in export quantities. This undoubtedly saved the CAP from financial crisis and postponed adjustments to the dairy and other commodity regimes. New Zealand stands to gain in producer revenue in the short run—in this case, the benefit working its way through contributions to the Reserve Account and in a higher producer-maintained price floor. Export earnings rose by 30 percent in 1980–1981 relative to the previous year and by a further 13 percent in 1981–1982. Skimmed milk powder export earnings rose by 55 percent and 6 percent, respectively, in these two years. The value of U.S. dairy exports rose similarly, with the emergence of butter exports (including sales to New Zealand) and the increase in skim milk powder sales abroad, reducing program costs and taking some of the pressure off domestic policy. The country to lose most from the price increase was the U.S.S.R.. It remains to be seen whether this will cause that country to revert to being an occasional buyer in world dairy markets, moving in only when price is unusually depressed. If that is the case, the exporters' market power could be very short lived. In any case, the build-up of stocks and the apparent inability of the United States and the EC to find effective means of control of output suggest that this example of active coordination among exporters may become just a footnote in the history of international agricultural trade.

REFERENCES

Bazely, P. 1983. An Economic Analysis of Domestic Dairy Policies and Their Implications for the International Dairy Market, unpublished honors thesis, Stanford University.

de Janvry, A., Siam, G., and Gad, O. 1981. Forced Deliveries: Their Impact on the Marketed Surplus and the Distribution of Income in Egyptian Agriculture. Agricultural Development Systems: Egypt Project, Economics Working Paper No. 38 (revised), University of California, Davis, September.

ERS/USDA. 1983. An Initial Assessment of the Payment-in-Kind Program, special report of the Economic Research Service, Washington, D.C., April.

Ikram, K. 1980. *Egypt: Economic Management in a Period of Transition,* Johns Hopkins Press, Baltimore.

McCalla, A. F., King, G. A., and Carter, H. O. 1982. Conceptualizing Macro and Intercommodity Linkages in Egyptian Food and Agricultural Policy, Agricultural Development Systems: Egypt Project, Economics Working Paper No. 106, University of California, Davis, December.

Monke, E. A., and Petzel, T. E. 1984. "Market Integration: An Application to International Trade in Cotton," *Amer. J. Agr. Econ.,* **66:**481–487.

Part Three

International Policy Decisions and Collective Goals

Chapter 9

International Objectives, Institutions, and Programs

I INTRODUCTION

The world of international agricultural policy is inhabited by pragmatists, whose life blood is the cut-and-thrust of intergovernmental meetings; by idealists, frustrated by the inability of governments to look beyond their own self-interest to work for the common good; and by statisticians, eager to meet the insatiable need for facts. Calls for action, backed up with descriptions of the issues, fill the agendas for international meetings. Delegates to those meetings come prepared with arguments to defend their country's records, to suggest action that others might take, and to pass judgment on the latest proposals for international cooperation. In a small proportion of these meetings, genuine negotiation takes place and commitments are undertaken. More often, resolutions are passed which have little or no immediate impact on national policy decisions. In such an area the analytical approach to policy seems to be of secondary importance. To attempt to explain international policy in other than an institutional and ad hoc way is risky. Into these muddy waters we now plunge.

The premise of this chapter is that international policy has both definable objectives and instruments to achieve those objectives. These goals are themselves the product of a chain of reasoning, each link of which can be subject to analysis. For instance, the objective of price stability in world grain markets is presumably premised on the observation that grain output is variable, that the structure of world markets is such that this variability is translated into price instability, that such price variations impinge particularly heavily on low-income developing countries, and that action taken at the international level can alleviate such impacts. Similarly, the objective of increased developing-country agricultural output rests on the assumptions that the capacity exists in developing countries for meeting a higher proportion of their own needs, that this is desirable as a contribution to overall development as well as to the objective of improving nutrition, and that international assistance can stimulate such extra production.

The dissection of such objectives is as important in international policy as in national policy. Economic analysis can help to clarify both the links between high-level goals and program aims and the alternatives available to improve the performance of the world food system. The analysis of policy, however, requires a framework within which to adapt the concepts found useful for the examination of national policy alternatives. Perhaps the simplest framework is to use directly the analogy with national-level policy decisions. Government policies in the national environment can be thought of as providing public goods, correcting divergences, changing income distribution, and establishing property rights, in pursuit of national objectives. Similarly, one can ask the question, "What do governments acting internationally, do?" Governments, acting in concert, can presumably fulfill four similar functions:

1 Provide "global goods" that are underproduced by individual governments although desirable by all. World market stability and the security of food supplies could be examples of global goods inadequately provided by uncoordinated action.

2 Correct divergences, where "local" efficiency (at the national level) does not yield "global" efficiency in resource use and distribution. The social cost of labor at the national level, for instance, may be different from its social cost when that labor is viewed as a global resource.

3 Change the distribution of income or assets, according to some agreed criteria. International coordination is presumably required to effect income transfers in a deliberate way, and to avoid undesirable income transfers arising from national policies.

4 Define rules and property rights. Such definition is a necessary function in an interdependent world, and cannot be met by uncoordinated national action.

The task of international policy analysis is to model such collective government behavior in a way which assists good policy decisions. As in the national case, one can also distinguish positive analysis from the analysis of the welfare effects of such policies.

The chapter starts with a definition of international policy and then moves to a discussion of policy objectives at the international level and to a discussion of some of the major institutions involved in policy deliberations. A concluding section summarizes some of the programs of those institutions, prior to the analysis of these measures in the following two chapters.

II DEFINITION OF INTERNATIONAL AGRICULTURAL POLICY

Much of national agricultural policy, as seen in previous sections of this book, has international significance. Some is even *designed* to influence world markets, prices, and the situation in other countries. However, to be considered an "international policy" an action would have to contain the following elements:

- Agreed objectives among countries. These objectives may not be any more specific than in national policies. Often they will be couched in words designed to mean more to the diplomatic rather than the lay world. But they do reflect gaps between desires and reality and can be a useful guide for analysis.
- Discussion of common action or rules in an international forum. Most international policy operates through national instruments: exceptions are agencies which can administer programs in consultation with national governments. This makes them a part, though a separable part, of national policy actions. Without the concert of rules or actions, what would otherwise be an international policy becomes merely an exercise in diplomacy.
- Monitoring of activity in compliance with agreement. Even if an objective is agreed upon and the common rules are accepted, no international policy of significance can avoid some form of monitoring. This forms a large part of the task of international agencies (along with administration)—particularly with regulatory policy. Monitoring is, of course, only as effective as the major national actors wish it to be.
- Joint finance, coordination or administration. Most effective international policies will have an element of common finance—even if only for the administrative costs inherent in the policy. Some will set up specific agencies for administration or coordination; others will be administered from within existing agencies. Where international transfers are involved the policy includes a decision as to how and from where it is financed, and this is often a key consideration in the success of the policy action. It also represents the most clear-cut distinction between national and international policy.

III INTERNATIONAL OBJECTIVES

National policy actions were analyzed in the last section in terms of agreed goals, a set of beliefs about reality, the identification of gaps to be filled by policy, and the choice of instrumentalities available to improve the situation. These actions were heavily constrained by other competing goals, by the lack of total effectiveness of instruments, and by the economic environment including the actions of other countries. The instrumentalities themselves were discussed with respect to their efficiency in an open environment. A similar task awaits the student of international policy. Objectives have to be defined against the background of perceptions of reality, instruments have to be examined for their ability to promote desired ends, and constraints have to be acknowledged as they impinge upon the process of decision making. The efficiency of policy instruments in turn requires a satisfactory calculus of gains and losses to improve the quality of decisions.

A discussion of global objectives can get somewhat rarefied. Most people, and many governments, would subscribe to the preeminent aims of world peace and prosperity. The higher-level goal of peace can be translated into an objective in the food and agricultural sphere through the proposition that the elimination of hunger promotes harmony both within and between nation-states. Both as a cause and a consequence, rising prosperity is associated with adequate nutrition: people with adequate incomes usually avoid poverty-related malnutrition and well-fed people are in a better position to contribute to economic growth. To many, the eradication of hunger exists as an aim quite separate from income growth.

Rising prosperity itself can be thought of as part of a more general development objective, including both the improvement of efficiency in resource allocation, the steady growth in incomes, and the transformation of the presently poor countries into full participants in economic progress. This goal is associated, with reasonable justification, with the development of the agricultural sector in low-income countries, but it also includes the better allocation of resources in developed-country economies. Stability of the world economy, itself difficult to define, can also be classified as a broad objective which lends legitimacy to attempts to stabilize particular aspects of the economy, such as commodity prices and export earnings. Instability is considered to distort long-run decisions on resource allocation and weaken confidence in the working of markets. And equity, even more elusive than stability from the point of view of an operational definition, is certainly a major concern in intergovernmental discussion. In agriculture, the equity objective can be used to support international transfers, to legitimize schemes which protect low-income countries, and to distribute adjustment burdens otherwise falling on a small group of nations or a sector within national economies.

It is not surprising that these global goals are, in general, parallel with our national goals of growth, stability, and equity. However, when defined on a global basis they include possible international action to modify what were considered by nations as international constraints. Therefore, the salient feature of these global objectives is that some degree of international action is required for their fulfillment. All international actions, however, are not explained by common objectives. A large part of intergovernmental business is related to the extension onto the international stage of purely (or dominantly) national policy concerns. Expansion of export markets by certain developed countries, for example, may be aimed primarily at increasing domestic farm income and reducing government budget cost for price supports. International discussions and negotiations are aimed at persuading groups of countries to modify their policies to the advantage of others. International growth, stability, and equity objectives may or may not incidentally be furthered by such action. Negotiations to allow developing countries to expand their exports might, however, be deemed to be more directly stimulated by concerns of growth and equity, even though the analysis of such policies may be similar. The fact that it appears to matter to governments, when they convene in the international arena, which countries are helped and which harmed by particular actions is a reminder that objectives over and above the purely national must exist—however imprecisely formulated.

IV   ANALYTICAL APPROACHES IN INTERNATIONAL POLICY EVALUATION

A   "World Welfare" Analysis

The identification of objectives is more in the realm of political than economic science. The economist needs to study the methods of achieving the goals laid out by the political process and devise a calculus for comparing among methods. At the national level the welfare analysis presented in Chapter 5 gives an indication of the tools available. This section is designed to generalize these techniques to the analysis of international problems and policies. To do this we must move beyond the incorporation of openness into national decisions, through the effect of trade possibilities and world market conditions on national policy choice, and beyond the consideration of collusive behavior by groups of countries to further national aims. We must define the conditions under which national actions have implications for other countries which themselves contribute to or detract from desired international objectives.

One approach to the internationalization of national policy analysis is to postulate a world welfare function, as a way of keeping score on the beneficial or deleterious effect of policies. Two different formulations of such a function suggest themselves. First, world welfare (W) can be thought of as the simple sum of national welfare levels (w). Such a measure can be expressed as

$$W = w_1 + w_2 + \cdots + w_n \quad \text{for } n \text{ countries}$$

Under such a formulation, world welfare is increased as each country increases its own welfare. All countries have equal weights. International policy under such circumstances is limited to assisting countries in the pursuit of their own ends. A second alternative is to view world welfare as a weighted sum of national welfare levels:

$$W = \alpha_1 w_1 + \alpha_2 w_2 + \cdots + \alpha_n w_n$$

where α_1 to α_n are the weights assigned to the welfare of each country. Under this specification it is possible to increase world welfare by redistribution of income from those countries with a low α weight to those with a higher value. This view of the world suggests a role for international policy in redistributing income in a way that individual governments would not.

A further distinction can be made between a situation where individual national welfare levels are independent, i.e., the value of one country's welfare is not dependent upon the level of another's, and a case where one country's welfare affects that of others. Thus, if by following policies which increase national welfare a country reduces (or increases) that of another, an externality exists which will show up in the aggregated world welfare function. International policy will therefore be potentially more effective in increasing world welfare if such externalities exist—as they undoubtedly do in a world of interdependent national economies. Combining the case of country welfare weights with externalities suggests that there will be elements of both redistribution and the management of externalities in international policy.

Two problems arise in making operational such a concept of a world welfare function. First, in the absence of a level of effective decision making above that of a nation-state, it is not easy to distinguish between "agreed" distributional weights on the one hand, and the "power" weights of governments in the international political process on the other. Governments meeting together may express support for altruistic distributional objectives but be much less willing to give up their own interests for the sake of others. They may recognize externalities, but be reluctant to act on that knowledge. Thus, in the real world of international politics, the abstraction of a global welfare function may be less helpful than its counterpart at the national level in understanding behavior and evaluating actions. Second, the specification of such a welfare function is inherently more difficult at an international level—though some of its characteristics could be adduced from studying past behavior. Its main virtue is to help distinguish between situations where uncoordinated national policies alone can reach particular goals and where coordinated action can improve conditions in the world *as a whole,* even if such coordination is hindered by the more limited objectives of individual nation-states.

B Global Goods

If the general approach by way of a world welfare function is difficult to operationalize, certain aspects of welfare analysis may have more direct relevance to the study of international policy. One such approach is to generalize the well-known proposition on the provision of public goods. A brief review of those propositions may be useful to set the scene. The ability of the private market to produce and distribute goods and services efficiently relies on two basic characteristics of those products, that consumers will reveal in the marketplace their preferences, and that only those who are willing to pay for the product can enjoy it. In addition, consumers are assumed to have reasonable information on the effects of consumption of the product and be able to choose not to consume it if to do so would cause them displeasure. Many products do not neatly meet these conditions. If, for instance, consumers are asked individually how much they would be willing to pay for a network of roads, or a system of defense, they are probably (and rationally) going to understate the value to them of such services, since they will be able to make use of them even if others pay the bill. This "free-rider" problem implies that it is difficult to use the market to allocate expenditures on such goods and services. Moreover, producers of such goods, in that they cannot charge to individual consumers a price which reflects their (the consumer's) valuation of that good, are unable economically to produce those products to the level collectively desired. Such goods are referred to as "public" or "social" goods. In other cases, consumption levels may be distorted through ignorance on the part of the consumer. The term "merit" goods has been applied to the provision of these products by public authorities. They too will be underproduced by the private sector, and can be thought of as a class of public goods.

One other feature of most public goods is that the consumption or use of them by one person does not reduce the ability of others also to make use of them. There is a zero opportunity cost to consumption (but not production) of those goods by an individual. If the individual were to be charged for its use there would be a distortion in consumption patterns: people who would get genuine benefit from the product will be dissuaded from its use by the charging of any (nonzero) price. Resources to pay for the production of these pure public goods must be financed by other means (such as general taxation) if this distortion is to be avoided. It should be noted that pure public goods in this sense can exist even if producers can charge for the use of the service and consumers can choose not to use it: exclusivity is not essential to the definition of a public good.

The difference between public and private goods can conveniently be illustrated by considering the construction of a demand curve for such goods. In Figure 9-1a, the demand for a private good ($D_{private}$) is shown as the horizontal sum of individual consumers market–expressed demand rela-

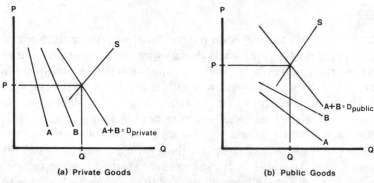

(a) Private Goods   (b) Public Goods

Figures 9-1   Derivation of demand curves for public and private goods.

tionships. The quantity produced Q is distributed to consumers A and B at a price P. By contrast, because both A and B can use the same units of the public good, their individual demand curves must be summed vertically. D_{public}, in Figure 9-1b, represents the demand curve that would exist if both consumers were to reveal their preferences for the public good: the price P will rarely be seen in practice for reasons explained above.

In some cases, consumers can choose not to consume a public good, and hence, avoid some disutility. Households can, for instance, make a decision to buy private educational or health services even when public facilities are available. Other goods are less easy to exclude oneself from: If economic stability is an attribute provided by the state, then the individual will have to live with that stability even if he or she thinks that instability is preferable. Similarly, individuals cannot choose their own level of inflation for the country or its degree of national security. Pollution, if analyzed as a public "bad," i.e., a negatively valued public good, also tends to affect everyone in a certain area, unless they choose to buy some private goods to counteract or avoid their consumption of the public bad.

Producers in the private sector can generally choose whether or not to produce a public good. But if they cannot extract payment from the users, they will presumably choose against production and devote their resources to other activities. Thus, the case for public provision of certain services rests heavily on the failure of the market to generate the revenue necessary for the private sector to be interested. The public good of stability might also provide an example of this: individual producers will underproduce stability if they are not compensated adequately (by individuals or by the government) for their efforts.

These concepts can be related to policy making at the international level by substituting "governments" for "individuals." Countries, even if efficiently producing their own public goods, may still underproduce international public goods (global goods). Similar problems of financing apply, with countries that produce such global goods receiving inadequate payment and those that benefit being unwilling to pay the full cost. Similarly, negative utilities could be created where consumption of global goods cannot be avoided. These extensions of national policy analysis are related to international agricultural policy later in this chapter.

C Externalities and Divergences

A third approach to the issue of international welfare might make use of the notion of externalities and divergences, in both production and consumption. An externality is an effect on an individual or group which is not (adequately) taken into account by the person or persons making an economic decision. Thus, the private cost of producing wheat includes all the items that the farmer has to buy valued at the price he must pay: the social cost includes the inputs and factors valued at their opportunity cost to society and takes into account any spill-over effects on others arising from his production. Similarly, a consumption activity can have both private benefits to the consumer and side effects on others: the social benefit includes these unintended effects. Externalities can be positive or negative, and they can arise from structural characteristics of the product or the market or as a result of policy decisions. The calculus of such effects is simple in concept but tricky in practice: evaluate costs at social prices and benefits at social values.

Gaps between private and social costs (and benefits) arising from market failures and structural problems—the existence of unemployment or monopoly power, for instance—are usually known as *divergences*. Divergences caused by government policy, as would occur if the government set a price for a farm commodity above the social value of that product, are called *distortions*. It follows that a policy which corrects a preexisting structural divergence efficiently does not create a distortion, though an incorrect measure may lead to a "by-product" distortion in some other part of the market even though the target divergence is offset (Corden, 1974).

The concept of externalities can conveniently be related to that of public goods. One can think of the externality as being a public good (or bad) produced jointly with the private good. Figure 9-2a shows the nature of the demand for a joint product. Products C and D are jointly produced (often, but not necessarily, in fixed proportions). The demand for the good can be represented as the vertical sum of the demand for the two individual components. For instance, the demand for soybeans will reflect the demand for both the meal and the oil. In the figure, D_j is the joint demand (as seen by the producer); lines C and D are the components as expressed by (not necessarily the same) consumers. Reference to Figure 9-1b shows that public goods

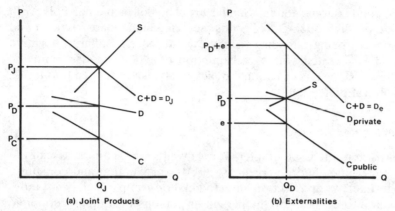

Figure 9-2 Comparison of joint product demand and externalities.

are in fact a special case of joint production. One unit of the public good produces jointly a unit of that good for each consumer. So, by analogy, if product C is a public good (from which the consumer cannot exclude himself)—in this case a positive side benefit from the production of product D—then the social value of D is the sum of the private value (P_D) and the externality e as shown in Figure 9-2b. If the producer cannot capture the reward for producing this benefit then the market price P_D will be below that which is necessary to achieve an equilibrium in social terms. A divergence arising from the externality in production has gone uncorrected. By granting a subsidy to the producer, the market failure can be removed. This example is of an externality in the production process, even though the beneficiary is the consumer. The same diagram could be interpreted as showing a positive *consumption* externality: in that case, the public good is also a joint product with the private good. However, in an open economy it is important to distinguish between cases where the externality is associated with the production or the consumption of the case—for obvious reasons.

The choice of the nation-state as the usual focus for analyzing public goods and externalities is both arbitrary and realistic. It is arbitrary in that the analysis holds for all levels of society above the individual, including the global society. It is realistic in that it reflects the dominance of nation-states as the main social, political, and economic divisions of the modern world. If people identify with a particular country and if that country labels individuals as to whether they are nationals or foreigners, then public goods will tend to be defined at the national level. Taxation, control over foreign trade, monetary arrangements, legal frameworks for commerce and property ownership, electoral practices, and political parties all tend to have the nation-state as their universe. Economic analysis and statistical material reflect and perhaps reinforce this state of affairs. But other levels of decision making, and other groupings of individuals, can be studied with respect to policy decisions, as is attempted in this chapter.

D Some Examples

This brief review of the notions of welfare functions, public goods, externalities, and divergences suggests ways in which to express some of the problems of international agriculture. Imagine, for instance, a class of global goods with characteristics similar to public goods but where the individuals are countries. If such global goods (and their undesirable counterpart, global bads) exist, there is the possibility that the result of individual national decision making underproduces those goods or services. We can apply the same tests as with public goods in national economies. Is there an opportunity cost to consumption, or can an additional country make use of the good without denying others? Several examples spring to mind of joint-consumption products. Information, about agricultural technology, crop conditions, market prices and so on, is generally available to all. Even the existence of a well-organized trading system, with monetary institutions to finance that trade, communications systems to initiate and monitor it, and accepted measures and standards to facilitate trade is in effect a global good. If countries act to injure the system, by unpredictable acts which lessen its value for others, a global bad is created. Since individual countries can choose not to make use of data, technological information, and the trading system no problem of negative utilities (unwilling consumption) should exist. But countries which produce such information, or contribute to the running of the system, are unlikely to be able to restrict its use and thus will not be able to extract adequate payment or rent from those that do.

Other global goods can potentially run afoul of the consumption-exclusion obstacle. It is difficult to exclude one country from the benefits of, say, stability in markets. In this case, no country may wish to be excluded. But if countries have different levels of desire for stability, the provision of a particular level, even by collective decisions involving all affected countries, will leave some overstabilized and others understabilized. Or, alternatively, if global bads are created by individual country action, all countries are affected by those actions even if they would prefer not to "consume" such side effects. Thus, negative marginal utilities can easily arise from the level of production of certain collective goods. Producer-exclusion, the ability of those who produce the public or global goods to restrict their availability, is also possible even in the case where there is no consumer-exclusion. A country could conceivably stabilize world market prices for one group of trading partners and not for another: even though countries cannot opt out of being stabilized, the stabilizing countries can still choose which other countries will benefit.

One interesting example of this might be the collective provision of a public good, such as stability, by a subgroup of trading countries. Thus, in a customs union, a preference area, or a group of countries signing an international commodity agreement, the level of stability may be greater (or less) within the particular group. In effect, a subglobal good has been produced with the property of partial consumer-exclusion (leaving, or not joining the group) and partial producer-exclusion (restricting benefits to members of the group. If the desire for stability were to differ markedly in the world as a whole, production of stability by subgroups could be more efficient. Unfortunately, as seen in Chapter 2, subgroup stability will tend to destabilize the excluded group: the production of a subglobal good is associated with the joint production of a negatively valued good for the countries outside the group.

If the existence of the trading system itself and the stability of this system are collectively consumed goods, can a similar analysis be applied to the benefits from trade? In the normal view of bilateral trade, both the importer and the exporter gain. The benefits from trade are maximized, subject to certain conditions, when each country allows such trade to go unhindered. The exporter gains access to a market which supplements domestic demand allowing greater profits to be made. The importer can tap a cheaper source of supply. After the necessary resource adjustments have been made, each country stands to benefit. This view of bilateral trade as a "positive-sum game" is adequate in a policy-free environment. Another view of trade policy, however, starts from a different perspective, that imports, though of value to consumers, need to be regulated by price or quantitative means as a part of overall economic policy and that exports can be stimulated to benefit employment and income. This view is, on the face of it, mercantilist and, contrary to requirements of efficient resource allocation, is merely an extension of the notion that governments have a responsibility to influence and enhance the income-earning prospects of particular sectors of the economy. The warning of generations of economists that such action is largely self-defeating—that it is better to accept relative cost differences among countries, to exploit them through trade, and to make domestic adjustments as rapidly as possible—has gone unheeded by most nations in the modern world.

In agriculture, in particular, the notion that markets are as much in the power of governments, as up to consumers to create, appears quite common. The notion of the demand facing domestic producers being the central concern of farm policy was discussed in Chapter 5. Control over imports is a key part of controlling that demand. Export policy likewise is aimed at enhancing the size of the market for domestic producers. In this context, trade in a particular sector becomes something granted by the importing country with a measure of reluctance. The government will, under this interpretation, be concerned almost entirely with the *domestic* effects of trade. Under such circumstances it is appropriate to think of changes in trade policy as having external effects not considered explicitly in the domestic decision. The traditional view of trade is as a mutual decision between importer and exporter, both deciding to reap the gains from specialization. This alternative approach suggests that one can view trade as a policy decision, largely by the importer, with incidental external ramifications on the economies of other countries.

It was suggested earlier that an externality can often be thought of as a public good jointly produced with a private good. A negative externality, such as air- or water-pollution arising from a production activity, clearly fits this mold. Similarly, a positive externality, such as the provision of security of supplies, the improvement of health, or the removal of unemployment through a production increase, can be covered in this way. The type of externality arising from trade policy changes is somewhat different. There is a joint product, in the sense of an internal effect and an external effect, but the products themselves can be exclusively consumed and can have a nonzero opportunity cost in use. If a country chooses to allow imports of corn to feed a domestic livestock industry, there will be both a private benefit to livestock farmers and meat consumers and a private gain to the producers of corn in other countries. The benefits will be additive, as necessary for joint products, but will also be granted specifically to particular groups or countries and not consumed at zero cost by all. Thus, there are rents to be had from offers at a trade negotiation to lower trade barriers which accrue to the liberalizing country. In contrast, no such rents are available to the country that holds stocks to stabilize world prices, even though the external benefits may be just as clear.

International agricultural policy can, therefore, be thought of as providing a context in which global goods can be optimally produced, and a market where externalities can be either internalized (in the sense of impinging upon the decision taker) or capitalized (through the reaping of rewards and payments of costs). Clearly, no such policy can deal with all externalities, just as national governments cannot approach truly optimal efficiency policies within their borders. But when externalities are perceived to be large and collective goods highly desirable, the mechanism of collaboration and joint decision making comes into play.

E Efficiency versus Distribution

Just as in national policy considerations one can make a distinction between efficiency and distributional concerns, so international policy can have a dimension outside the role of efficiency per se. In one sense, a distribution, or equity problem can be subsumed under the heading of public (or global) goods. An equitable distribution of assets or income may be a socially desirable objective, and anything which contributes to this is providing a benefit to society. This benefit can be a part of a welfare function in the same way as a more tangible consumption good. But practical welfare analysis suggests a distinction between, on the one hand, efficiency in the use of resources to provide for demand for public and private goods, and on the other, equity in the distribution of income and income-producing assets. Since the latter distribution affects the former demand, the two parts of the welfare problem are imperfectly separable. But one can imagine an iterative policy process which moves forward on both equity and efficiency fronts. So long as the desired income distribution does not totally overturn the efficiency signals this process is likely to work. For example, if the equity objective argues for international assistance for poor countries—apart, let us say, from any "efficiency" benefits which might arise therefrom—then that objective can be pursued in parallel with the improvement of the functioning of markets. Similarly, if efficiency requires the dismantling of protective barriers against low-cost imports of agricultural products into developed countries—quite apart from the "equity" benefits that might accrue to poorer nations—then that can be pursued at the same time as the transfer of technology to developing countries.

One does not have to know the position of the high-level optimum satisfying both distributional and efficiency conditions. Pareto-better moves limited by current income distribution can coexist with attempts to deal more directly with distributional objectives. The practical advice of Pigou might be appropriate for international agricultural policy: a change is for the better if it either increases income while not decreasing the share of the poor, or increases the share of the poor while not decreasing income. The organization of the next two chapters reflects this approach. Chapter 10 looks at ways of improving efficiency in resource use, increasing the provision of collective goods liable to underproduction in a world of individual decision making countries, and allowing for the establishment of mechanisms for the compensation for externalities, at the same time watching for deleterious effects on poor countries. Chapter 11 explores the ways in which countries attempt to make transfers with avowed income distribution aims, through technical assistance, food aid and the like, in ways which at the least do not detract from the efficiency of the use of world resources for the satisfaction of consumers' individual and collective desires.

V INTERNATIONAL INSTITUTIONS

Institutions form a link between the desire for international action and the policies that emerge from international discussion. They not only provide the meeting place and a secretariat to service the meeting, but also play a

role in formulating policy, explaining and convincing individual governments, and forging compromise positions from opposing views. More
broadly, they each have a particular view of world problems, an agenda of
projects which can be produced on demand, a history of proposals and discussions, a clientele and a constitution which gives them certain advantages
and disadvantages. Thus, a discussion of international policy, in all but the
most abstract form, needs to include an understanding of institutions. A
glossary of acronyms is contained in Table 9-1 to guide the reader unfamiliar
with the "alphabet soup" of international organizations.

The key institutions in world agriculture can be grouped as follows:

1 UN—UNGA, ECOSOC, and the coordinating committees. They
make broad policy statements, but are not "operational" in the sense of
implementing any programs. Examples of UN initiatives are the UN Development Decades, the Special Sessions of the General Assembly on Development and on Commodities, the World Conferences on Food, Population,
and the declaration known as the New International Economic Order.
Broad membership and equal votes in the UNGA make it good for airing
grievances but bad for taking action.

**Table 9-1 International Institutions with Particular Relevance to Agricultural
Policy**

UN	United Nations
UNGA	UN General Assembly
ECOSOC	Economic and Social Committee of the UN
FAO	Food and Agriculture Organization
WFC	World Food Council
UNCTAD	United Nations Conference on Trade and Development
UNDP	United Nations Development Programme
WFP	World Food Programme
IFAD	International Fund For Agricultural Development
CGIAR	Consultative Group on International Agricultural Research
ILO	International Labor Office
WHO	World Health Organization
WMO	World Meterological Office
IMF	International Monetary Fund
IBRD	International Bank for Reconstruction and Development*
IDA	International Development Assistance Programme*
GATT	General Agreement on Tariffs and Trade
NGO's	Nongovernmental organizations (e.g., charities)
EC	European Community
CMEA	Council for Mutual Economic Assistance (COMECON)
LAFTA	Latin American Free Trade Area
ASEAN	Association of South East Asian Nations

*Members of the World Bank Group, known commonly as the "World Bank."

2   Specialized agencies of the UN—reporting in general to UNGA through ECOSOC. Most important are FAO, WFC, UNCTAD, UNDP, WFP, IFAD, but others such as ILO, WHO, WMO, etc., have an interest in particular aspects of agriculture. Specialized agencies have specialized secretariats and interests. Influence comes in part from within, through key personnel, and in part from without, through the power of individual countries. They are the natural location for discussion of technical propositions and usually they generate the statistical base for decisions (cf. ministries vis-à-vis legislatures in national government).

3   Parallel agencies, associated with UN system. IMF, IBRD, IDA, GATT, and CGIAR are major examples. All these organizations have a deep interest in agriculture, though many from a generalist rather than specialist viewpoint. They attempt to keep a wider view of economic affairs, either in global terms (IMF, GATT) or in terms of national development (World Bank Group). As such, they try to stay independent of the specialized agencies, with their own experts and their own statistical base. Their voting rights differ from the UN system, and hence are likely to be favored by those with greater voting power.

4   Regional institutions such as the Inter-American, Asian and African Development Banks, as well as other intergovernmental associations (e.g., the EC, CMEA, LAFTA, and ASEAN). Their interest in agriculture is also broadly based, rather than sectoral. Though the programs are typically subglobal in scope, these regional agencies have a potentially significant role in international policy.

5   Commodity groups, such as The International Wheat, Coffee and Cocoa and Sugar Councils. These groups are set up usually to administer commodity agreements and monitor market developments and these agencies become the foci for policy development. The narrower membership helps to get agreement, but limits scope for action.

6   Nongovernmental organizations. They play a peripheral role, as observers and occasionally as lobbyists—but the lobby function in international policy is not well developed. They administer some programs (e.g., the relief work of the World Council of Churches, OXFAM, Red Cross), often with more success than governmental agencies.

These institutions play a role in the shaping of most of the initiatives in the area of international agricultural policy. The next two chapters discuss, from an analytical viewpoint, the policy options open to governments acting cooperatively to achieve international aims.

VI   INTERNATIONAL POLICY INITIATIVES

It may be useful at this point to give an indication of the range of international policies associated with the major institutions. Table 9-2 lists some of these policy initiatives and the institutions most closely associated with them. These are grouped somewhat arbitrarily under the rough headings of trade measures, food security, development assistance, and food aid.

**Table 9-2   Some International Programs in Agriculture Grouped by Major
Policy Issue and Institution**

Category	Institution*	Policy actions
Trade	UNCTAD	Generalized Scheme of Preferences (GSP) Integrated Programme for Commodities (IPC) including the Common Fund for Commodities Commodity Agreements for Coffee, Cocoa, Sugar, Natural Rubber
	GATT	Trade liberalization rounds, e.g., Kennedy Round, MTN. Dairy and Bovine Meat Agreements Code of Conduct for Export Subsidies
	FAO	Fertilizer Supply Scheme
Food security	FAO	Early-Warning System (EWS) International Undertaking on World Food Security (IUWFS)
	IMF	Food Financing Facility (FFF)
	IWC	Wheat Trade Convention of the International Wheat Agreement
	WFC	Food Sector Strategies
Development aid	IDA	Project assistance
	UNDP	Project assistance
	FAO	Investment center
	IFAD	Project assistance
	CGIAR	Research promotion
Food aid	WFP	Food-for-Work, Vulnerable-Group Nutrition, Emergency Relief International Emergency Food Reserve (IEFR)
	FAO	Safeguards against market disruption
	IWC	Food Aid Convention of the International Wheat Agreement
	NGO	Various forms of food aid

*For title of institution, see Table 9-1.

A   Trade Measures

Agricultural trade policy at the international level is a part of broader trade
policy. Among the most relevant trade initiatives for agriculture (excluding
those mentioned under food security) are the Common Fund for Commodities, administered by UNCTAD as a part of the Integrated Programme for
Commodities (IPC), the various arrangements that emerged from the
GATT MTN Round including the export subsidies code and two informal

commodity agreements. Other commodity agreements for coffee, cocoa, sugar, and natural rubber have been set up within the UNCTAD framework. In addition, a Fertilizer Supply Scheme operated by FAO extends international policy into input markets and attempts to offset the negative effect of high world fertilizer prices on developing countries.

B Food Security Policies

These policies attempt to give stability to world grain markets through the encouragement of reserve policies (IUWFS) and an early-warning system (EWS) both under the aegis of the FAO. In addition, developing countries can benefit from the extension of the IMF Compensatory Finance Facility to include food imports (FFF). There is, in addition, a modest international emergency reserve (IEFR), but this is generally considered as a support to multilateral food aid. Lending by donors for the construction of reserve stocks is also a policy response to food security concerns, as is the attempt to develop consistent strategies for the food sector of developing countries.

C Development Aid

Along with food aid the most visible aspects of international policy are the transfer activities which support, in the main, the foreign exchange cost of agricultural and infrastructural investment projects. These are primarily disbursed through the IBRD/IDA, the IFAD, and the UNDP—the latter as a clearinghouse for much of the UN development assistance. In addition, the WFC-sponsored Food Sector Strategies program gets donors and technical agencies together with developing countries to devise strategies including both agricultural production and food distribution. Other development-related policies include the research network administered by the CGIAR and the activities of the FAO Investment Center.

D Food Aid Policies

Much of food aid transactions are bilateral in nature (such as PL480) and hence do not qualify as international policies (see Chapter 11). Multilateral food aid is largely disbursed through the World Food Program, including policies of support for development through food-for-work, and various nutritional and emergency relief functions. Food aid targets are agreed under the Food Aid Convention, which brings together donor countries and attempts to elicit pledges for both bilateral and multilateral food aid. The impact on commercial markets is discussed in an FAO-sponsored committee on safeguards. NGO's, as mentioned, play an important role in the distribution of food aid.

This brief list of policies serves to set the scene for the following chapters. But just as a list of policy measures is not in itself adequate to give a rounded view of national agricultural policy, so the initiatives themselves do not constitute an analysis of international policy. Some are more significant than others, and some are more successful. Rather than go into a detailed examination of each policy individually, it is more interesting to look behind the policy actions to examine the range of approaches to issues, the alternative policy measures that are possible, and the impact of such alternative policies. Existing international policy can then be put in perspective. That is the task of the next two chapters.

REFERENCES

Caves, R. E. 1960. *Trade and Economic Structure; Models and Methods,* Harvard University Press, Cambridge, Mass.

Corden, W. M. 1974. *Trade Policy and Economic Welfare,* Oxford University Press, London.

Shefrin, F. 1980. "The Agriculture Agencies: Objectives and Performance," *Int. J.,* **35.**

UN World Food Conference. 1975. Report of the World Food Conference, E/Conf. 65/20, New York.

Warley, T. K. 1976. "Agriculture in International Relations," *Amer. J. Agr. Econ.,* **58:**820–830.

ADDITIONAL READINGS

Haq, Mahbub ul. 1980. "Negotiating the Future," *Foreign Affairs,* **59:**398–417.

Johnson, D. G. 1978. "World Food Institutions: A 'Liberal' View," *Int'l. Organ.,* **32:**837–854.

Chapter 10

International Action to Improve Efficiency and Stability of World Markets

I INTRODUCTION

In discussing intergovernmental policy actions in agriculture it is useful to make a distinction between those elements that are designed to improve the efficiency of production and consumption and those whose primary aim is to effect redistribution of assets and income. Most policies include both elements: an attempt to improve the efficiency of resource use in developing-country agriculture, for example, may also influence income distribution through a disproportionate benefit to poorer farmers. If the finance comes from international sources then one can also identify the transfer as an international income-distribution policy. Likewise, a policy action to redistribute income among countries, through the granting of preferential or concessional access to grain supplies, will also have an impact on efficiency of resource allocation.

This chapter deals with efficiency criteria and those elements of international policy that impinge upon resource allocation. The next chapter changes the focus to the redistributional aspects of international policy, and concludes with a discussion of the trade-off problem between efficiency and redistribution. Particular international initiatives, as introduced in the previous chapter, are used to illustrate these two aspects of policies.

Efficiency aspects of policy in a global setting can be grouped under three headings:

1 Those that aim at improving the efficiency of production and, hence, lowering the real cost of production of agricultural goods
2 Those that attempt to improve the way in which food, once produced, is distributed among the world's consumers
3 Those that assist in the provision of a stable market environment to the potential benefit of resource use, of consumption levels, and (not incidentally) of policy making

The first category includes policies that direct production to the most appropriate areas, encourage efficient production in those areas, promote the development of technology appropriate to the resource conditions and makes that technology available, and address the underlying problems of the economic environment facing agricultural producers. In the second category would fall actions designed to increase access by consumers to alternative supplies, improve information upon which to base import and consumption decisions, facilitate purchase of food and agricultural goods by countries or individuals through both marketing and financial improvements, and assure a ready supply of foodstuffs to consumers at "reasonable" prices. Other types of policies are focused on both producer- and consumer-related issues—such as those relating to the improvement of the trading system. The third category includes policies which aim to improve stability of prices, revenues, and supplies to participants in the market. These can be oriented specifically to farm income stability, consumer price stability, or to the price levels existing in world markets.

II IMPROVING GLOBAL PRODUCTION EFFICIENCY

A Price Differences among Countries

It is natural for economists to think of improvements in resource use as a fundamental aim of policy. The process of growth is essentially one of making the best use of the resources available to satisfy present and emerging patterns of demand. The small-scale farmer in Africa or Asia tills a limited land area with little in the way of purchased inputs and with skills defined over many decades of experience within the natural environment. The large-scale farmer in a developed country employs sophisticated management techniques to combine purchased inputs with natural resources to produce high-quality crops for distant markets. Despite the dangers of assuming an easy transplantation of "modern" farming methods to "traditional" areas, the underlying objective of agricultural development is to bring the benefits of scientific agriculture and modern management to the mass of farmers apparently trapped in a low-productivity environment. The emphasis might be on the contribution of a growing agricultural sector to the total economy, the enhancement of the income stream in rural areas, the provision of food for urban workers, or the alleviation of poverty-related malnutrition. But the issue is that of improving resource productivity—particularly the labor resource—and, hence, of minimizing the resource cost of providing basic foodstuffs.

Present patterns of agricultural production are undoubtedly inefficient from the point of view of resource use. Political pressures often work against such efficiency—the apparent desire for low food costs for urban workers in many developing countries, and the perceived need to support farm incomes in less-than-efficient sectors of developed-country agriculture are common examples. If governments are determined to pursue these policies then resource-use efficiency is jeopardized. Developing-country governments often pay lip service to the need to improve incentives to domestic agriculture, citing the apparent drain on scarce foreign exchange, the presumed political vulnerability of dependence on imports, and the dangers of instability arising from fluctuating import prices. Large-scale subsidization of agriculture is, however, an expensive business for any country with a large proportion of its labor force on farms. Indeed, agriculture in developing countries is often seen as a source of tax revenue rather than as a sector requiring support (Brown, 1978). Agricultural investment often competes unsuccessfully with other, more modern uses of funds. Moreover, imports of production requisites and investment goods for agriculture can put as much or more strain on the payments position as would importing the foodstuff itself. The balance among these factors determines the extent to which agricultural production objectives are translated into action. The issue for an international policy aiming to improve the efficiency of agricultural production is that of finding the correct level of incentives for developing countries such that their production potential is utilized to the optimum.

Actions of developed countries to support farm income have also tended to distort the ability of the system to generate food at the lowest cost. Frequently, government support tends to gravitate toward those sectors of developed-country agriculture which are uncompetitive. Support prices themselves can get quickly out-of-line with world market conditions, premised as they often are on domestic inflation rates and income trends. This in turn can often be self-perpetuating. The protection of domestic agriculture depresses trade prices and appears to validate the arguments of those who press for cost-based price policies. Farm price supports encourage resources to move into agriculture (or keep them there) and appear to require further support in order to earn adequate incomes. Once again, the issue for international policy is to achieve the right balance of incentives, avoiding overproduction in some areas of high cost which penalizes more efficient farmers (in terms of use of scarce resources) in other areas.

At the risk of oversimplification, one can describe a typical price structure in agriculture among countries as follows: consumers in developed
countries pay relatively high prices for food; producers in those countries receive a price (adjusted for processing and marketing costs) somewhat higher
than that paid by consumers, to the extent that taxpayers contribute to price
support; consumers in developing countries pay lower prices, subsidized by
their governments, and producers in those countries often, unless offset by
domestic taxation, receive prices higher than those paid by consumers but
less than those prevailing on international markets. Central-plan economies,
even those with relatively high incomes, tend to have the low price levels associated with developing nations, with implicit state subsidies to consumers
relative to international prices. Many middle-income countries, on the other
hand, have at least some producer prices which are above world prices. Figure 10-1 illustrates such a price structure. The developing country maintains
a price level of P_p to producers and P_c to consumers, generating a particular
demand for inputs. Similarly, the producer and consumer prices (P'_p and P'_c)
in developed countries determine the quantity of exports available
($Q'_p - Q'_c$) which trade at world price. The differential prices are imposed by
the domestic policies of the countries concerned, and the world market price
(P_w) is determined by the resulting balance of imports and exports.

B Prices for Least-Cost Production

Assuming that this relative price structure is quite common, the question of
international efficiency can be restated. Does the differentiation of producer
prices among these two types of countries imply higher production costs for
the world as a whole? There is a presumption that private resource costs
could be reduced by a shift in the relative producer prices among these two

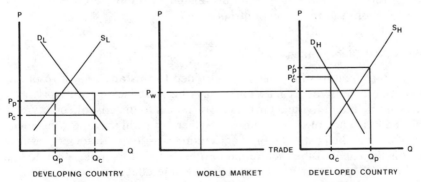

Figure 10-1 Sterotypical price relationship between producer, consumer, and world
price: developing and developed countries.

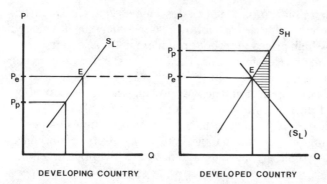

Figure 10-2 Cost savings from equalizing prices among countries.

sets of countries. The simplest way to illustrate this is to abstract the two supply curves from Figure 10-1 and to compare the cost of production of the same quantity of output with different sets of producer prices. This is shown in Figure 10-2.

The additional (private) cost of expanding production in the developing (low-price) country will be approximated by the area under the supply curve—as discussed in Chapter 5—between the old and the new quantities. Similarly, in the high-price country, the resource saving will be indicated by the area under the supply curve bounded by the old and the new production levels. It can be seen from the figure that, so long as prices are different, a cost saving can be obtained by moving towards equal prices. At P_e, the cost of production of a particular quantity of output is minimized. By superimposing the mirror image of the low-price supply curve (S_L) on the diagram for the high-price country, such that points E coincide, the saving can be shown as the shaded area between these two supply curves. The benefit, in terms of lower costs, will be related to the price difference and the price response in the two countries.

C Social-Cost Divergences

One important qualification needs to be added to this analysis of resource use and price incentives. It may not always be the case that the "private" cost, as seen by the individual farmer, corresponds to the cost of society as a whole. The existence of chronic unemployment in rural areas, for instance, would imply that the cost of labor in agriculture was lower to society—since that cost is the value of the production of other goods foregone—than to the farm sector. On the other hand, any negative side effects on soil erosion or environmental pollution that might accompany agricultural production would cause social costs to be higher than those faced by the individual.

Similarly, taxation of inputs would raise the cost as seen by the farmer above the social level, and subsidies would reduce that private cost below the level to society. Under such circumstances, the same price across countries, as shown in Figure 10-2, would minimize private costs for any given output but not lead to a social cost minimization.

Under circumstances of such divergencies (and policy distortions), a rational pricing policy will imply different price levels in different countries. Figure 10-3 illustrates this proposition. Assume, as will often be the case, that the developing country exhibits low social production costs (with few alternative employment possibilities and with high costs of purchased inputs) relative to private costs. On the other hand, the social costs in some developed countries could be above private costs if the full range of negative externalities were taken into account. Under such conditions, the appropriate price level in developing countries would be higher than P_e and that for developed countries would be lower than P_e. These "optimum" prices, P_p^* in the two countries, elicit production at a level where the marginal *social* cost is the same in all locations, even though the private costs diverge.

This argument does not depend on the assumption that *all* developing countries have lower prices than *all* developed countries: clearly, as discussed in Chapter 1, no such generalization is valid. But to the extent that this phenomenon occurs, it illustrates the nature of the issue of international resource allocation and price incentives. From a global viewpoint, there may be significant advantages to the international community in fostering policies which move away from the situation of high-price regimes where they occur in developed countries and from the low-price policies in many developing countries, in terms of lowering the overall cost of producing agricultural commodities. But this example emphasizes that international policy may

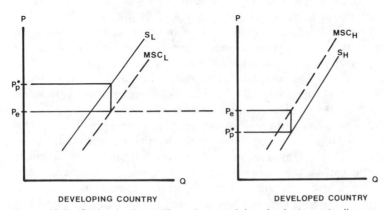

Figure 10-3 Optimal price policy when social and private costs diverge.

have a role in moving even further, in certain cases, towards *higher* prices in developing countries than in developed countries, if in doing so the social cost of food production were further reduced.

D Implications for International Policy

It should be pointed out, if not already obvious, that an international policy for efficient resource allocation which addresses the issue of relative producer prices is in effect pushing individual countries in the direction of appropriate prices from their own national viewpoints. National efficiency pricing would take into account the level of world prices as well as discrepancies between social and private production costs. If international policy did nothing more than encourage such increased national efficiency then it would be useful. But the discussion of the role of such policy in the previous chapter suggests further tasks for international action. One such task would be to modify national government policy when the costs of production look different from an international viewpoint. An obvious example is a production externality, such as river pollution, which impinges upon another country. The domestic cost calculations upon which a pricing decision is taken would normally ignore such an effect. A second task for international policy might be to correct the international income-distributional implications of efficient national policies, or provide finance for such policies in countries that could not otherwise afford them. A further task might be one of providing information upon which to base efficient pricing decisions, particularly when world price levels themselves are often less than reliable—a case which is taken up below.

It would be misleading to suggest that the topic of resource allocation occurs often in this form in international discussions. Nevertheless, a cornerstone of international agricultural policy has been the stimulation of local farm production in developing countries. The implication is that there is currently underinvestment in developing-country agriculture, a contention, in part, supported by the relatively small share of investment funds which are allocated to agriculture in many developing countries, and by the often low prices which farmers in those countries receive. The decisions on investment and prices are not, however, taken internationally, and any form of coercion to modify these domestic decisions—as is sometimes associated with World Bank or IMF lending conditions—is resented.

The related question of optimal investment patterns again tends to be treated on a country basis, spurred on primarily by the agencies with funds to disburse. Wise investment decisions based on national criteria might eventually lead to satisfactory world resource use, but in many cases the result will be to reinforce present distortions in the short run. Moreover, cyclical problems can and do arise when national investment decisions are uncoordinated or based on incomplete information. Since much investment is in the public sector, government-induced production cycles are not uncommon. Allied to this is the issue of resource misallocation as related to the incorrect interpretation of price signals and to the cost of uncertainty generated by government policies and other avoidable actions. In short, the issue of the link between domestic policies, the location of production, and international incentives is one that can be analyzed as an important part of international agricultural policy.

III IMPROVEMENT IN FOOD DISTRIBUTION

A Consumer Price Differences

Just as the interplay of national price policies and the role of world market prices in guiding production decisions can be seen as fundamental to international resource allocation, so those same policies influence the distribution of food to the world's consumers. The food distribution question has a number of facets, ranging from the adequacy of domestic marketing systems to the workings of the international trade system. It is intimately tied up with domestic income distributions and even distribution of available food supplies within the family. There are nutritional aspects, quality and food standard issues and those to do with public and private marketing agencies (Timmer, 1980). But a reasonable place to start the analysis is with the effects on food consumption and distribution of domestic price policies.

B Efficient Consumer Prices

The search for an analytical basis for assessing producer price policy led to a cross-country comparison of farm prices. Figure 10-1 illustrated the stereotypic situation of high consumer prices in developed countries, kept up to generate income transfers to domestic producers, and low consumer prices in developing countries, reflecting low urban wages and the need to match purchasing power with adequate consumption standards. The high-price and low-price situations are reproduced in Figure 10-4, where private and social valuation of food consumption are assumed to be identical. As before, the maximum value in consumption can be extracted by distributing the quantity of food available such that the price level is the same (at P_e) in both countries. The demand curve can be taken as an approximate indication of the value at the margin of food consumption to the consumer (see Chapter 5). The additional value of increasing consumption in high-price countries exceeds the loss in value in low-price countries by the shaded area in the figure. If the high-price countries are developed, the more affluent consumers would gain more than developing-country consumers would lose.

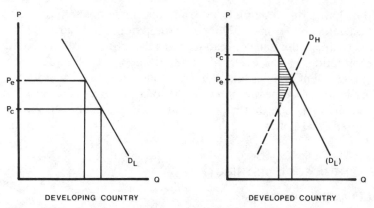

Figure 10-4 Increased consumer value from equalizing prices among countries.

The prospect of a redistribution of consumption benefits (i.e., real income) from poor to rich is unlikely to strike a responsive chord in international circles. If the by-product of removing differential prices among producers, say by removing barriers to trade or by harmonizing producer price levels, is to weaken the position of low-income consumers, then the process of improving agricultural resource allocation comes at a high cost. Just as developing countries acting alone find that the provision of high producer prices conflicts either with the need to keep food prices down or with the requirement to keep financial policy costs low, so at the international level any suggestion of higher prices for food in developing countries is likely to be unwelcome.

C Social-Value Divergences

Is this a case where efficiency at the global level conflicts with equity and humanitarian concerns? Perhaps, but for the economic analyst it suggests a different phenomenon. The need to keep up food consumption in low-income countries has a significance beyond the individual market-based demand relationship expressed by the poor consumer. Within the society plagued by low food consumption levels, the health of the population has a general benefit not captured by the individual's spending pattern. To the international community, in general, adequate consumption of food by poor consumers has a positive value in terms of humanitarian and social stability goals. By contrast, consumption in rich countries may, in many cases, exhibit negative externalities if the health costs of obesity are not fully borne by the individual consumers. Figure 10-5 shows the situation where a positive consumption externality in developing countries is matched by a negative externality in developed countries. The "single-price" solution P_e, efficient in the absence of such externalities, is suboptimal: rather, the price should be set lower in developing countries and higher in developed countries until the marginal social valuation of consumption is equated across countries.

This suggests a major dilemma for global efficiency analogous to that faced by an individual developing country. At the country level the policy problem is to maintain adequate incentives to employ fully and productively the agricultural resources while keeping the price for basic foodstuffs within reach of the low-income family. In international terms, the issue is how to release the considerable potential for low-cost production of agricultural goods in developing countries while not placing consumers in those countries at a disadvantage relative to consumers in the affluent world. Low farm prices in developing countries coupled with high prices in the developed world assists in the attainment of consumption objectives but leads to a high-cost, slow-development bias in the global agricultural economy: high incentives in developing countries and lower prices in developed countries may achieve a reallocation of production and a useful increase in labor productivity in agriculture but violate basic notions of need in consumption. How to square the production incentives with the consumption constraints is a major problem for efficiency policies.

IV INTERNATIONAL PRICES AND EFFICIENCY

The notion that farm-level prices in developing countries should be at, or possibly higher than, the levels found in developed countries, while consumer prices should be, if anything, lower than in those countries, poses the issue of the role of international prices and international trade. In a world free of divergences between private and social costs and between private and social valuations, a regime of unfettered trade would ensure that prices

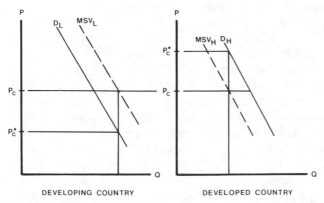

DEVELOPING COUNTRY   DEVELOPED COUNTRY

Figure 10-5 Optimal price policy when social and private values in consumption diverge.

to producers would be similar in various parts of the world (subject to transportation cost gradients and quality differentials), as would prices to consumers. These efficient world prices would ensure that the marginal cost of producing a commodity was everywhere the same, ensuring least-cost production, and that the marginal value to consumers was equalized, giving maximum value in consumption from the available supplies. The world price would settle at a level that would elicit the correct amount of the product and distribute it efficiently.

For few agricultural commodities, if any, can one say with assurance that the world price plays such a function at present. Two opposing views of world prices are apparent. The one holds that since world markets are almost universally influenced by government policies, the world price is distorted and ceases to be a useful price for national decision making. The contrary view holds that whatever the degree of distortion that exists on world markets, a price is a price. The world price for a commodity is the amount of foreign exchange given up or earned by importing or exporting the product. This defines the opportunity cost of domestic production—and consumption. Under this latter view, the world price becomes the appropriate yardstick for the valuation of domestic activities, corrected, of course, for exchange rate distortions and allowing for instability in short-run price levels. The irrelevance of world prices is commonly pushed by those who wish to base domestic policy prices on domestic criteria, i.e., by those who seek to justify protection measures. The dominance of world prices is asserted by those who see many domestic policies as distorting resource allocation by the artificial valuation of goods.

From the viewpoint of international efficiency, the role of world prices is less clear-cut. What is important is the price level (and, hence, marginal value and cost) in the various alternative locations of production and consumption. In one sense, the world price—the price at which export surpluses are bought and sold—is irrelevant providing that *domestic* prices are correctly aligned. The free-trade distribution of production and consumption can be reproduced by the correct set of domestic price levels even if international prices are distorted by (offsetting) trade policies by the importing and exporting countries, though with different implications for income distribution. This does not weaken the case for liberal trade, but merely emphasizes that the key role of the international price in an international efficiency context is one of information. In the absence of distorting trade policies, a country can treat the world price as a proxy for the production cost and consumption value in other parts of the trading system. If price-distorting policies are in evidence, then the world price (as argued by protectionists for different reasons) is not a sound guide to marginal resource costs in other producing countries even though it may still be the best guide to national policies. In this case, an improvement in the pricing policies of one or a few countries may *not* lead towards greater international efficiency (Lipsey and Lancaster, 1956–1957).

The situation becomes more complex if we allow for domestic (and, hence, international) divergences between social and private costs and social and private benefits. In the simplest case, if all countries take steps to correct domestic divergences only by the most efficient means, i.e., by targeted subsidies and taxes, then a free-trade world price (i.e., unhampered by explicit *trade* policies) will again provide an efficient basis for domestic pricing, this time with actual domestic prices modified by optimal taxes and subsidies. But trade policy measures, though they are not efficient for correcting divergences in domestic markets, might still be preferred by some countries. The world price loses its reliability under such circumstances: it becomes the more or less arbitrary outcome of policy choice. To preserve an optimal pricing structure, countries would in effect have to know the nature of prices in other countries to arrive at the true social costs and values and then apply their own domestic corrections to that price level. It can readily be seen that the loss of an appropriate world price benchmark imposes a considerable information cost on decision making.

It may be worth reemphasizing the difference between the global efficiency role of world prices and the role that such prices play in national efficiency calculations. Given a world price, however distorted, it is true that a country should treat that price as the foreign exchange cost of imports or value of exports and price domestic goods accordingly. To do otherwise, tends to lower *national* income. But this does not lead to a globally optimal distribution of production and consumption unless all other countries have either no distorting policies or have domestically corrected policies of their own. If this does not hold, then world prices become a poorer guide to domestic policy from the viewpoint of world efficiency. International policy, if it is to strive for global efficiency, must grapple with this issue of the reliability of world prices and explore the possibility of alternative indicators.

V IMPROVEMENT OF MARKET STABILITY

Stability can be considered, in part, as an adjunct to efficiency in the goal hierarchy and, in part, as a facet of the equity issue. Instability has a cost element, in terms of added uncertainty to producers and inconvenience to consumers, but it also yields potential arbitrage rents to those willing to absorb variations in the marketplace and costs to those who cannot do so. The distributional impacts of instability are discussed in Chapter 11; for present purposes it is enough to assume that there is a global cost to uncertainty which lowers total economic value or raises resource costs relative to a more stable environment. Alternatively, one can fall back on the intuitive notion that people prefer stability, *ceteris paribus,* to instability. Though one could incorporate a discussion of the efficiency-related aspects of stability with resource allocation, it is convenient to accord it a separate place in the exploration of international policy.

Set against the criterion of stability, few would suggest that agricultural markets have performed well. Such markets are notoriously unstable, as was illustrated in Chapter 1. The fundamental policy issue can be simply put. Given that a degree of instability exists in the agricultural system, usually arising from fluctuating output levels, which other variables within the system should be allowed to reflect this instability and which should be stabilized? Experience suggests that countries aim to stabilize domestic prices and consumption patterns at the expense of stock levels, international prices, and foreign exchange costs. This placing of the burden of instability on international markets raises issues different from those of longer-term resource allocation and of equity, though influencing both of these other aspects of market performance. It also suggests that national solutions may not provide the environment of stability desired by all, or most, countries.

Perhaps the most important consequence of instability in international markets lies in the problems that it creates for many governments in interpreting evidence from world markets as a guide to their own domestic farm programs. This represents a resource cost due to uncertainty and to lack of information. In such an atmosphere, rational decisions on long-run resource deployment, both by governments and by individual farmers are difficult to make. Price uncertainty clearly involves a cost to the world as a whole resulting from the confusion as to the interpretation of sudden price changes.

For developing countries the implications of instability of world market prices has another dimension; their own development plans can be disrupted by the variation in their food import costs and export earnings. Although in the past those countries which export agricultural commodities have tended to benefit from price increases in a way that helped to offset higher cereal costs, this coincidence may not be assured in the future. A collapse in tropical beverage prices at a time when wheat and rice were in short supply would highlight this problem. Thus, apart from the uncertainty surrounding the level and trend of world prices, undue fluctuations have a cost which can be measured by the extent to which developing countries have to insure themselves against the variability in their foreign exchange costs of food.

It was suggested in Chapter 1 that world prices are volatile, in part as a result of attempts by governments to avoid the domestic implications of supply variations. The world price under such a system governs international transfers. A steep rise in price for basic foodstuffs tends to transfer income from developing countries as a whole to developed countries, to be restored when prices fall. Three magnitudes—real income, the balance of payments, and the cost of food and farm programs—are destabilized, both in developed and developing countries. Such instability is not only politically embarrassing but also costly in terms of sensible long-run decisions. The instability problem is to find that subset of economic variables where fluctuations are relatively less costly, and to devise policies which channel such instability in their direction. The appeal of reserves as a buffer to supply fluctuation, though not without implications for financial stability, is perhaps understandable in this context.

Uncertainty of a different sort was evident in the decade before the events of the early 1970s. The world prices for many major products had been heavily influenced by the marketing policies of governments, not the least of which are the storage and export subsidy programs pursued by the industrialized exporting countries. While this was in general a period of price stability, uncertainty centered on the concern that the price levels were scarcely enough to cover production costs even in efficient agricul tural areas. Developing countries, whose imports of cereals began to rise rapidly during the 1960s, understood that the attractive terms under which these purchases were made were only possible as a result of considerable subsidies in the form of farm programs and food aid. The price explosion which ended this era seemed to confirm these fears; the same domestic stabilization policies which had generated surpluses began to squeeze world supplies so as to soften the impact of harvest shortfalls on the rate of inflation at home.

VI EFFICIENCY AND STABILITY IN INTERNATIONAL POLICY

A Efficiency and International Institutions

We can now turn from the analytical treatment of efficiency and stability to the role that these objectives appear to play in international policy. Clearly, discussion in most international meetings about agriculture is not explicitly premised on notions of the optimal location of production and consumption. Even in the case of trade discussions, where efficiency seems logically to play a major role, many other issues seem to dominate. In part, this is due to the natural inclination of governments to look at problems from a national viewpoint. But also, it reflects the lack of a clear view as to what can (and cannot) be done to improve efficiency.

Stemming in part from the national viewpoint of individual countries in international meetings on agriculture, the question of national producer and consumer prices is rarely seen as appropriate for discussion. Most countries, as discussed in Chapter 5, view national pricing policies as part of internal equity and income distribution mechanisms, and hence, are unwilling to expose these policies to international scrutiny or influence. In addition, central-plan countries seem not to use price policy in a direct way to influence resource allocation, although even in these economies incentive structures exist which have analogous effects. Under these conditions it would be unlikely that governments would directly negotiate on relative price levels among countries. Relative price levels *within* countries, between products, between agriculture and the rest of the economy, or between producers and consumers are the stuff of domestic policy. To introduce constraints on international relative pricing may seem to overconstrain already difficult decisions.

Trade negotiations in agriculture tend to be seen as an adjunct to domestic policy aims rather than an attempt to improve global efficiency. Concerns are with such issues as export expansion and protection of sensitive import competing sectors. As was suggested in Chapter 9, the mechanism may not exist to allow countries to reap the rewards of improving global efficiency. The General Agreement on Tariffs and Trade (GATT) certainly is premised upon the notion of beneficial specialization in production and expansion of consumer choice. But the treatment of agriculture within the GATT often seems to ignore these principles, allowing national policies to be exceptions to trading rules and ignoring the most significant areas of trade distortion. Developing countries have viewed GATT as mainly dealing with trade improvement among industrial countries, and concentrating on manufactured trade flows and the reduction of tariff barriers. As a consequence, they feel that that institution has little to say on efficient allocation of agricultural resources.

In part, as a consequence of the focus of the GATT in the postwar period, developing countries have associated the United Nations Conference on Trade and Development (UNCTAD) with a closer concern for their trading problems, in particular, the stability and price level in the market for their tropical exports. But the predominant direction of discussions within UNCTAD has been not liberalization of agricultural trade so much as redressing structural "inequities" in markets so as to allow developing countries to be compensated for assumed trading disadvantages. Efficiency enters in a minor way in such discussions which are dominated by the need to improve the terms of trade and gain preferential access into markets in developed countries.

Perhaps the two institutions, in addition to GATT, which seem to have greatest concern for efficiency, as opposed to equity, are the International Monetary Fund (IMF), through its emphasis on improving liquidity and facilitating trade flows, and the World Bank, which allocates its resources in part according to efficiency in domestic resource use. From a global efficiency standpoint, this emphasis may in itself be inadequate, as discussed above; the World Bank is, after all, in the business of helping individual developing countries improve their productivity at *prevailing* world market prices. This need not always be consistent with a broader view of world resource allocation under the circumstances described in this chapter, where world prices themselves may be less than reliable as an indicator of efficient location of production.

B   Stability and International Policy

Stability as an international issue has attracted much more international attention than efficiency per se. In particular, one aspect of stability has taken up considerable time in recent years—that of the optimal level of global stocks of grain. This topic has two elements which can usefully be distinguished. On the one hand, the level of grain stocks held by countries is often regarded as inadequate from a global standpoint regardless of the distributional effects of grain price variations. One can think of this as a global goods issue, as discussed in the previous chapter, amenable to international policy action. Success in negotiating stabilization agreements for grain has, however, been elusive, in large part because of the difficulty in deciding on who should manage (and bear the costs) of such schemes. The second aspect of grain stocks is their significance for developing-country food importers. This "food security" issue has also received considerable attention, and is discussed in the next chapter as an equity or distributional topic.

Stability is perhaps inherently a more amenable topic than efficiency for international discourse. A higher level of stability is generally considered desirable by governments, and the clear international links make it easy to see the advantages of intergovernmental discussion and coordination. At home, both producers and consumers espouse stability as a goal. Governments do not feel that they have to trade-off one domestic interest for another. The rest of this section is taken up with a discussion of stability issues in the international agricultural policy arena.

Three approaches to the stability problem have been discussed in international meetings. The first approach to world market stability involves the strengthening of the link between world and domestic markets, most simply achieved by liberalizing trade. The essence of such an approach is that the less obtrusive is government policy in the decisions relating to production, marketing and distribution of agricultural products, the more the normal market mechanisms will be able to absorb unavoidable changes in supply. The fact that such a solution brings with it the need to reallocate productive resources raises objections by interests adversely affected by such adjustments. To be successful, it requires a positive commitment on the part of governments to allow international price variations to impinge on domestic conditions, not just in normal times, but more particularly when such price movements are most embarrassing. It also requires that governments are sufficiently convinced of the longer-term benefits of trade to resist the temptation to intervene for shorter-run objectives.

The essence of this "freer-trade" solution to instability is greater *consumption* adjustments in developed countries as a direct alternative to the manipulation of stocks to even out production variability. State trading and central-plan countries could likewise adjust their world market purchases to avoid putting strain on available supplies in times of shortage and to increase imports when supplies are more than adequate. Countries which rely more on the price mechanism for controlling imports would be expected to allow price changes to stimulate consumption adjustments directly. The major political problem with this approach is that it clashes with strong stability objectives in these countries not just in terms of the consumer price level but also with respect to the cyclical behavior of the livestock sector. The unwillingness of countries to modify their own stability policies highlights the need for other international measures to stabilize world markets.

The second approach has been to try to regulate world prices directly by means of accords among importers and exporters. Such proposals, often put in the form of international commodity agreements, have long had political appeal. Unfortunately, they are rarely specified in a way that attacks the underlying nature of instability. They tend to confuse symptoms with causes and risk exacerbating the difficulties faced by participating countries.

Price variations are most commonly triggered by changes in market balance arising from fluctuations in supply. Such fluctuations cannot be wished away: they will show up either as variations in consumption or as changes in stock levels. World prices act as one means of determining the international distribution of such stock and consumption adjustments. With unresponsive international prices, stocks would still have to adjust and consumption be reallocated by means of domestic price variations or quantitative controls. Fixed international prices put *more* of a burden on national market management, rather than relieving domestic policies of such a burden.

This is not to imply that international price stability is unattainable. Price stability in international markets can, of course, be achieved—to any degree felt desirable—by mandating variations in domestic consumption and stocks to offset fluctuations in output. In this case, stable international prices would be the outcome of the appropriate use of policy instruments rather than the instruments themselves. In market economies, the appropriate instruments are *domestic* price levels, which regulate both stock levels and use; in central-plan economies, consumption and reserves can be controlled more directly. World market price stability thus requires that consumption and stock levels adjust in all or most trading countries to whatever extent is necessary. The difficulties continually faced by the international community in devising commodity agreements to stabilize world markets indicates the unwillingness of governments to accept the considerable *domestic* discipline and costs which would be associated with successful international price agreements.

The third category of measures that have been much discussed in recent years has to do with the manipulation of reserves of products subject to price variability. At a domestic level, adequate stocks appear to give a degree of autonomy over food supplies which may be missing when resort to world markets must follow poor harvests at home. Even discounting the fact that stocks always seem much more desirable in high-price periods, the interest shown by countries in increasing storage capacity, subsequent to the high prices of the mid-1970s, would indicate that this aspect of marketing may have been neglected. Storage policies can have an important role in some cases of reducing (or capturing for the government) the arbitrage rents of various "middlemen." They can facilitate the development of internal distribution systems and provide more stable seasonal supplies. But holding and managing stocks is expensive, and the profits from stock holding for an individual importing country, in particular if its market is small in size, come basically from speculating successfully on world market price changes, an activity for which many governments may be inadequately prepared. A reserve strategy per se is a sensible addition to a country's food policy, but such a strategy will not always require substantial physical holdings of commodities by the country concerned. A general attempt at the international level to impose an undue burden on developing countries in the form of increased stock holding may be regressive in its effect on income distribution.

International policy may have something to add to purely domestic policy with regard to stocks. Much of the political discussion of reserves has recently revolved around the international coordination of domestic stock policies, on the assumption that such coordination brings benefits over and above those arising from the existence of stocks held under national initiative. Such coordination holds out the hope of additional market stability in exchange for a small loss in autonomy with respect to domestic stocks. Or, to put it another way, one country gains a degree of (collective) control over another's reserves while losing some control over its own. There is an underlying presumption that just as private stocks within a country may be inadequate from a national point of view so national stocks may not be sufficient from an international perspective. Global reserve schemes take this into account by postulating desirable levels of price stability or minimum consumption levels in particular years. This tends to suggest a greater place for reserves than is indicated by examining the economics of stock control from the viewpoint of an individual country.

As indicated above, variations in the level of reserves can achieve substantial increases in price stability. The problems surrounding this conclusion have more to do with the costs of such schemes and the implementational difficulties than with any doubts on its validity. Complete price stability would certainly be costly, and this in itself would encourage governments to find ways of reducing their own commitment: anything less than such an agreement to defend a particular price through stock purchases and sales would require complex management rules binding on individual governments or imposed by an international authority.

C Conclusion

This examination of the role of international policy in the improvement of efficiency and stability has indicated some potential advantages of coordination of national action. The search for efficiency in resource allocation implies national producer incentives and consumer food prices which reflect social opportunity costs. At the international level, such signals may become confused if each country bases pricing decisions on world prices themselves distorted by policies. For international policy to be effective, countries would need a clear indication of their costs relative to others. Under present circumstances, no institution has an overt responsibility to search for such efficiency in world agriculture. Assisting individual countries to improve their own pricing policies is probably about as far as is possible to go in this direction.

International policy has a clearer role in promoting price and market stability, where the benefits from creating stability—or the costs of preventing instability—are not made apparent to each government. Quite apart from the distributional aspects of price stability (discussed below as an aspect of food security) the enhancement of a stable trading environment requires collective action. To date, the various attempts to provide this collective benefit have not been very successful. The temptation to legislate for stability, rather than provide the market conditions under which it will emerge, has been strong. Such stability as exists in international markets is still often the result of national actions taken by major trading countries. Some combination of coordinated reserves on the one hand and domestic policy changes on the other may be needed to improve the stability of markets. This greater degree of stability in turn could prove the most significant contribution to global efficiency, as it would provide a surer footing for national production, consumption, and trade policies.

REFERENCES

Brown, G. T. 1978. "Agricultural Pricing Policies in Developing Countries," in T. W. Schultz (ed.), *Distortions of Agricultural Incentives,* Indiana University Press, Bloomington, pp. 84–113.

Lipsey, R. and Lancaster, K. 1956–1957. "The General Theory of Second Best," *Rev. Econ. Studies,* 24:11–32.

Timmer, C. 1980. "Food Prices and Food Policy Analysis in LDCs," *Food Policy,* 5:188–199.

ADDITIONAL READINGS

Houck, J. P. and Ryan, M. E. 1979. *Economic Research on International Grain Reserves: The State of Knowledge,* Bulletin No. 532, Agricultural Experiment Station, University of Minnesota.

Huddleston, B. 1977. *Commodity Trade Issues in International Negotiations,* Occasional Paper No. 1, IFPRI, Washington, D.C.

Newberry, D. and Stiglitz, J. 1979. "The Theory of Commodity Price Stabilization Rules: Welfare Impacts and Supply Responses," *Econ. J.* **89:**799–817.

Chapter 11

Distribution and Equity in World Markets

I INTRODUCTION

Whereas efficiency and stability are, in principle, measurable, equity—like beauty—is in the eye of the beholder. Nevertheless, one could presumably get consensus on the proposition that an action that materially improved the income of the poor would be equitable and one that worsened the distribution of income by imposing a disproportionate burden on the poor would be inequitable. The structure of the world's food and agricultural system can be examined in this light and the role of international policy in shaping international income distribution can be discussed.

How equitable is the present pattern of production, consumption and trade, and how equitable is the reaction of that system to short- and long-run pressures? At a cursory glance, the present system would seem to have some good and some bad points. The fact that the rich pay more for food, through generally higher prices in developed countries, might almost have been designed by a benevolent world government to offset the underlying disparities in income levels in the world. Governments in industrial countries, through price-support programs for agriculture and through food aid, tend to improve the terms of trade of developing-country food importers; however, those benefits are subsequently distributed. On the other hand, the bulk of the world's stocks of foodstuffs is held in affluent countries, enabling them to enjoy the fruits of arbitrage though also bearing the costs. Greater financial muscle in those countries helps in times of crop shortage, allowing consumption to be maintained through consumer price control, and imports to be purchased on a tight market. Farmers in rich countries receive much more in the way of subventions from governments than do their counterparts in the developing world—if in fact the latter receive any net subsidy at all. On the other hand, support of relatively inefficient developed-country agriculture presumably opens up some opportunities in other sectors for developing countries: the same amount of support going to labor-intensive industries might conceivably have a greater impact on international income distribution than that of the traditional farm programs.

The most serious adjustment problems in the short run to harvest failures are probably borne by the developing countries. The existence of a large grain-consuming livestock sector in the developed world gives a relatively low-cost form of consumption adjustment. Developing countries, constrained by budgetary and foreign exchange considerations, have much less scope for avoiding the implications of either domestic or foreign supply shortfalls; hence, the concern about food supplies commonly known as "food security." In the longer run, the incidence of adjustment costs is less easy to predict. Developed-country farmers have better access to the non-farm employment market and can obtain capital for diversification. If the weight of government support is devoted to ensuring rates of return on investment and labor, as, for instance, in sugar production in developed countries, the burden of longer-run adjustment may well be inequitably placed on developing nations struggling to react to demand and technology changes.

II INTERNATIONAL POLICIES FOR EQUITY

In spite of the difficulties encountered in defining equity, the international community is not void of policies which aim at modest redistributional objectives. Besides international transfers through development assistance and through food aid, the most common type of scheme relies on financial discrimination in favor of developing countries. Support for domestic storage of food crops could also qualify as an equity program under some circumstances. Nutritional programs, where these involve international transfers of resources, could be similarly classified as intercountry income redistribution efforts.

Some might argue that international agricultural and financial markets presently discriminate against developing countries. Under this view, removing such distortions is a way of promoting efficiency rather than redistributing income. For present purposes, it will be assumed that markets currently assess correctly the risks in lending, and that concessional schemes are a form of assistance. In this context they become equity policies insofar as improved access to credit for lower-income countries is achieved at a cost to the richer nations. Food import cost loans, for instance, confer on developing countries some of the benefits presently enjoyed by developed countries of deferred payments, with an additional provision for low interest costs. In addition, the physical underpinning of such schemes must ultimately be the higher level of stocks in developed countries *ceteris paribus*, to allow for greater developing-country variation in import quantities. The aim of such schemes is equity, even if they do not attack the structural problems causing the inequities in the system.

Development assistance for agriculture, whether through bilateral or multilateral channels, is perhaps the most tangible aspect of international policy. At least as far as the donor is concerned, overseas aid raises no particular internal conflicts besides those generally related to finding the funds; the decision to give aid can be reviewed periodically, and there is usually some degree of control over disbursement. In short, it is a relatively easy form of policy to implement at an international level. On the recipient side, aid is useful in swelling the pool of investment resources and technical assistance. Though there may have been a tendency in the past to underestimate the debt burden from a succession of loans, the requests for further assistance continue to grow. Analysis of such transfers has generally and appropriately concentrated on the value of additional resources to recipients, the distribution of aid among recipient countries, and the mechanisms for improving project selection and appraisal. More recently, the internal income distribution implications of particular types of projects and their impact on nutrition have also been studied. Indeed, the major multilateral agencies in the aid field are responsible for stimulating the bulk of analytical work in this area.

Less well researched are those aspects of policy which give balance-of-payments assistance in a more direct way. Although it could be argued on efficiency grounds that the adjudication of risk in the financing of deficits is adequately handled by the market, governments, when meeting together on this subject, usually assume that developing countries require assistance in the form of additional credit lines. IMF lending for general payments problems and specific facilities available to those suffering from fluctuating commodity export earnings are already in place. More recently, a specific facility to help developing-country food importers has been implemented. This food financing facility is appended to the compensatory financing facility already in place within the IMF. In addition, plurilateral schemes such as that covering exports of commodities to the EC—the STABEX plan—exist to help with the payments problems.

The thrust of this type of solution is of a different nature to those involving stock and consumption adjustments. Such plans do not in themselves address the problem of global variability. To the extent that they allow countries to continue and strengthen policies that protect domestic consumption, they increase the need for (and the profitability of holding) stocks. They tend to aggravate the global adjustment problem, and without more flexible stocks or developed-country consumption adjustments would tend, therefore, to destabilize prices. But their intention is to allow more equity by arming developing countries with the financial weapons of the richer nations in the search for food supplies in times of shortage.

Food aid represents a somewhat clearer example of an equity-related policy. Concessional food sales, both bilateral and multilateral, now have a considerable history: indeed, they might be thought of as the traditional approach to the equity issue. Not that food aid has escaped criticism. It has been accused of weakening incentives in recipient countries. Food aid flows have also been too often linked not to need but to product availability and to political expediency. Moreover, the commodity composition of aid is often inappropriate to the dietary pattern within the recipient nations. But a lower import price is tantamount to reducing foreign exchange costs for a particular import volume, the impact of which depends on the way in which the importing government disposes of the food aid on the domestic market. The major difference between this type of policy and that concerned directly with foreign exchange costs is that the granting of a line of credit or the transfer of compensatory finance would be expected to have a more general impact on the economy and on trading patterns as a whole than the concessional sales of commodities.

III SOME ANALYTICAL ISSUES IN EFFECTING TRANSFER

A National and Individual Distribution Criteria

One problem that arises frequently in international discussions of equitable transfers is that of defining the level of aggregation necessary to test for income distribution. Two problems can be separated, one involving intracountry distribution and the other concerning disparate country size. To illustrate the first of these problems, let us assume that a donor country effects an income transfer to a recipient, the former being an affluent industrial democracy and the latter a poor preindustrial society. The transfer, let us suppose, is in the form of a shipment of wheat on concessional terms. The wheat is purchased from the domestic market, using tax receipts, and is sold abroad at a loss to the receiving government agency. That agency then resells the produce on the market at a profit—so as not to disrupt the domestic producer price. As an international transfer, the benefits clearly go from the high-average-income country to the low-average-income nation; in terms of intergovernmental discussions this transfer would undoubtedly be classified as equitable. But it would be naive to believe that there are not people in poor countries who have incomes and assets exceeding those of many developed-country taxpayers and that considerable private wealth is not sometimes associated with the buying and selling of imported commodities in these countires.

Critics of aid policies in general, and food aid in particular, claim this situation is common: supporters of such aid answer that it is rare. The analytical point, in the present context, is that a policy to transfer income from rich individuals to poor individuals, in whatever countries they happen to live, requires instruments for implementation and monitoring beyond that which would be needed for a mere transfer from rich to poor countries. Is the "world welfare function" made up of individuals or countries? If the former, then national income redistribution becomes of international concern: if the latter, then such internal matters are outside the province of intergovernmental discussion. Similarly, the distribution of land ownership within a country—the issue of land reform—is either central to the equity issue or totally outside its scope, depending upon the answer to this dilemma. In practice, it seems that countries prefer to treat *other* country's internal income distribution as fair game for discussion, while avoiding talk of their own income distribution. But the absence of clear resolution to this issue undoubtedly hampers discussion of many questions perceived to be of importance in international agriculture.

The second manifestation of this problem is that of the diversity of size among countries. The UN system is established on the basis of one-country, one-vote. But if, as tends to be the case, the very poor are concentrated in a few large, low-income states, then equitable transfers based on individual merit would allocate aid to those nations proportionate to the size of the problem. Aid flows *per capita* are, however, very uneven: it is "better" to be poor in a small country. Once again it appears that it is country "welfare" indices that are aggregated, rather than those of individuals in the calculus of international transfers. Any economic analysis of such transfers must be sensitive to this issue and be explicit as to which criteria are being used.

B Effecting a Transfer

It should, one would have thought, be easy to transfer resources from one country to another. But action is required by both transferor and transferee. For instance, a country receiving an inflow of foreign exchange must run a deficit on its balance of payments to make room for the transfer: the donor must similarly run a surplus. Preferential access for imports from developing countries assumes that supplies are forthcoming to take advantage of the preference. The element of preference is the addition to price that favored sellers receive relative to nonpreferred sellers. Concessional terms on imports into the recipient country, such as are implied by food aid, depend on such imports being accepted. Low rates of interest on loans is an advantage to the recipient country so long as such loans are actually made, and offers of technical assistance require action by the aided country to be of any effect. This may seem obvious, but it serves to emphasize that transfers depend upon mutual action and cannot be unilaterally imposed.

Even more dependent upon the action by the potential recipient is the targeted aid transfer. The fact that investment flows and budget allocations are fungible, i.e., they can be redirected within the economy by the aided government, means that it is not, in general, possible to specify where a particular transfer will end up. A shipment of cheap grain, for instance, may be sold at normal prices on the domestic market with the profits being used to buy capital equipment for another industry. The domestic aid lobby in the donor country can congratulate itself on providing low-cost food to a poor country with an undernourished population; the actual impact could on occasion be to increase spending on industrial ventures or even armaments. The developing country can justify such switching as part of a general development or other national objective and resent any attempt to monitor or control such fungibility. But, in the context of international agricultural policy, the diversion of aid into other enterprises represents a potential weakness in the system. It is as if a national government in an industrial country paid farm price supports to an independent body that could choose whether to pass the benefits on to farmers or invest the payments in some unrelated activity. The increased emphasis on conditionality in overseas assistance programs, making transfers conditional upon some action by the recipient country, is an attempt to get around the problem. To the receiving country, such conditionality may lessen the attraction of the aid. To the donor, it might be necessary to keep intact the political consensus supporting such transfers. To those concerned with international policy, such restrictions on government action may be the only way to implement agreed policies across countries.

A similar problem of fungibility is apparent on the donor side. Suppose a new scheme is promoted to support food consumption (or production) in low-income countries. Finance for such a scheme presumably has to come from the same donors who are presently supporting other such efforts. How can one tell whether finance for the new scheme is *additional* to that for present programs? If aid flows increase, such additionality may be claimed by the donor. But the donor "pool" of available assistance is undoubtedly limited and not always responsive to new outlets for aid. It is as likely that, if aid is increased, such aid would also have been available in the absence of the new programs. Or, if other transfer schemes are in existence, the "new" aid might be paid for by a reduction in other areas seemingly unrelated in terms of policy. Transfers between governments are dependent upon the way in which the donor government chooses to raise the finance and upon the way the recipient government chooses to use the proceeds. Both may depart from the stated objective of the policy which is being financed.

C   Transfers through the Marketplace

In one sense, transfers are extra market transactions. A pure lump-sum transfer could be devised that had no direct impact on buying and selling decisions in the countries involved—outside of the financial markets, which have to adjust to the monetary value of the transfer. But, just as in domestic policy, international transfers often use the market mechanism, through the alteration of the price of transactions. In such circumstances, the transfer does not have traditional demand and supply elements: the demand for transfer through lower import prices or higher export prices is presumably infinite. The market is thus an administered one, depending upon political decisions in both the transferor and transferee country. This notion can be illustrated by looking at two different types of such transfers—lower import prices through food aid and higher export prices through trade preferences.

At one level, food aid is nothing more (or less) than a concessional (or zero) price on food imports. As such, no separate analysis of such trade seems to be needed. However, the main feature distinguishing food aid from normal trade is its institutional nature. If an exporter were merely to an-nounce a low selling price to developing countries, those countries would be able to make purchase decisions based upon that price in the same way as with commerical or full-price imports. The food aid decision starts, however, with a commitment—often in terms of a monetary amount—to support a food aid program. That level of appropriation for food aid then is translated into a quantity which can be offered to the identified developing countries, based on whatever criterion of need the donor chooses. Some of the food aid may pass through multilateral channels, but there will be a natural tendency for much of the shipments to stay within bilateral programs to gain political advantage and retain some minimal control.

The donor situation in the case of a fixed food aid appropriation is shown in Figure 11-1a, where the lines App1 and App2 are two different levels of appropriations. Depending upon the cost of purchasing and trans-porting the food aid (taking into account any contribution required of the recipient), a particular quantity of food aid can be shipped. At a cost per unit of C_1, Q_{a1} would be available with appropriations at the level of App1, and Q_{a2} would be forthcoming with the higher appropriations level App2. The level of appropriation might be based on the need to move quantities of produce to clear domestic markets. More recently, reacting to the obser-vation that such an appropriations-based transfer system reduces available aid at just the time when it is most needed—when world prices are high—donors have set targets or pledges for food aid quantities. Under such a cir-

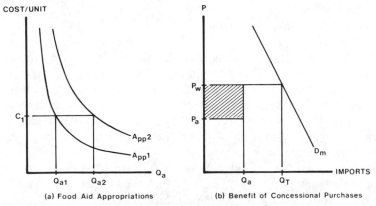

COST/UNIT

C_1

App^2

App^1

Q_a

Q_{a1} Q_{a2}

(a) Food Aid Appropriations

P

P_w

P_a

D_m

Q_a Q_T IMPORTS

(b) Benefit of Concessional Purchases

Figure 11-1   Food aid transfers as seen by donor and recipient.

cumstance, the appropriations needed would vary with world price to keep quantities more predictable. Whatever the mechanism, food aid is essentially supply-determined; one can assume an infinite demand for food aid at any positive level of conditionality.

To the recipient, food aid is rarely the sole source of imports. As a consequence, the import decision is not necessarily based on the price of the concessional trade but on the marginal cost of purchases from the world market. In Figure 11-1b, the total imports of grain are shown as Q_T, based on the world price P_w and the import demand curve D_m. A government-to-government agreement sets the concessional element, $P_w - P_a$, on a quantity of food aid Q_a. The shaded area in the figure is thus the transfer. Should foreign exchange be a constraint, the total level of imports could increase (i.e., D_m could shift to the right), but, in general, one would expect that the main effect is a lower foreign exchange cost by an amount which matches the level of appropriations determined in the donor country. Thus, food aid passes through the market, but the transfers are policy-determined rather than market-determined.

The second example of transfers within the market but not determined by market forces is that of trade preferences. In this case, an importing country decides to allow exports from developing countries to enter free of the duty or tariff imposed on others. The donor country, in terms of the transfer, is the importer; the recipient is an exporter. Once again, the initiation of the program is with the donor, though the constraints might be more in terms of the presumed effect on domestic industires rather than on the cost of foregone duty receipts. If the preferential imports make up less than the total imports from any source of that product, the level of imports will be determined by the marginal (nonpreferential) import cost, inclusive of duty.

The benefit to the preferred country will be the ability to keep the equivalent of the duty which would have been paid.

Figure 11-1b can be reinterpreted to show this case. If the price of imports including duties is P_w, then the market will absorb Q_T. The preferred country will set Q_a (restricted either by supply availability or by tariff/quota) and receive P_w per unit for these sales. The duty $(P_w - P_a)$ is extracted from the market, but not paid to the importing country government. It represents the "transfer" due to the preference. As with the food aid example, the quantity of the transfer inherent in a tariff/quota is determined politically (the degree of preference and the extent of the concession) but is effected through the market. Again, like food aid, the final destination of the transferred income depends upon the policy of the developing country. If exports are controlled by a state agency, a common feature of developing countries, then the benefit can either be passed back to the producers of the commodity in question or absorbed in the government sector; which option is chosen has implications for the real economic benefit of the transfer.

IV TRANSFERS IN INTERNATIONAL AGRICULTURAL POLICY

The place of transfers in international policy is firmly established. Development assistance and food aid are quintessential international policies. Preferential access for developing-country exports has become widely accepted. Relative to policies discussed in the previous chapter aimed at improving the efficiency of the agricultural sector and making more useful the world trading system, transfer policies have significant appeal. In donor countries, the giving of aid appears to avoid the uncertainties of less direct methods of assistance. Food aid seems to meet some of the immediate problems of hunger and malnutrition until such time as domestic agriculture can provide the needed foodstuffs. Project aid and technical assistance seem to offer the hope of increasing the productivity of developing-country agriculture and raising growth rates. Preferential access to markets allows developing countries to expand exports and, hence, generate employment and earn foreign exchange for development. Such transfers have equal appeal for governments. The donor can point to the record (if it is "better" than other developed countries) and can retain some control over which countries benefit. The receiving country government can use transfers to pursue a variety of domestic aims, and can argue for higher levels of aid as necessary to achieve development objectives.

By contrast, transfers do not show up so well in analytical terms, if the underlying objectives are to assist in agricultural development, food security, and equity at the level of the individual. Policies which substitute transfers for, say, trade policy changes, tend to leave the cause of problems unchanged and require continuous renewal. The end result of transfers is essentially outside the control of governments acting collectively. The final destination of funds and commodities transferred is not easily determined, either ex ante or ex post. Fungibility of funds within an economy precludes such a tying of aid to particular types of policy in many cases. Additivity of funds for particular programs is almost impossible to judge. Both the collection and the distribution of transfer funds are essentially national prerogatives. This is not to say that transfers as such as always undesirable, but that their link with equity objectives is sometimes indistinct.

In fact, it is probably useful to make a distinction between transfers which rest for their legitimacy on equity grounds alone and those which are desirable as a way of stimulating desirable change. In the former case, considerations such as the monitoring of the use of funds may be important, but the transfer is an end in itself. Poor countries, and the poor within those countries, get international assistance because they are poor. In such cases, one need not question the use to which such funds are put. In the latter case, transfers are designed to lead to some action on the part of the recipient. International funding is seen as a way of bearing collectively the financial burden and, hence, lubricating the wheels of national policy. In such instances, the lack of control over the use of funds becomes a serious problem. The solution which appears to be emerging is the funding of programs rather than projects, implying ongoing policy change in the recipient country. Food aid tied to a domestic food subsidy scheme, for instance, gets closer to ensuring the desired use of such aid than an unrestricted commodity grant.

The alternative to such links between funding and policies is to make the policies themselves a matter for international action. The CGIAR, in international research, and the WFP, in food and disbursements, are examples of agencies which use international funding to perform certain functions. "Pure" technical assistance, in terms of the provision of skilled personnel, also links the transfer (the salaries of the professionals) to specific actions (the plans or appraisals). Grants of food or foreign exchange, whatever intentions are expressed between donor and recipient, do not have this element of accountability. As such, they would appear to be weaker instruments of international policy, though more acceptable in many instances to national governments.

V EQUITY AND FOOD SECURITY

Instability was discussed in the previous chapter from the viewpoint of market efficiency. The distribution of the burden of instability among countries, however, has a major impact on the issue of equity. The most frequently discussed aspect of equity and stability in international circles has to do with the burden placed on developing countries of world market fluctuations in basic grains. Thus, the issue of food security has come to dominate, along with food aid (treated more fully in Chapter 12), the agenda of international meetings in recent years. Though there are efficiency elements of food security, such as the optimal global level of grain stocks, the particular focus of attention on developing-country problems makes it more appropriate to classify this topic as one of international equity in the face of instability.

The problem of food security has its roots in the uncertainties endemic in the world food system. Chief, but not alone, among these uncertainties is the size of the global and local harvest. Other causes of uncertainty include political events and fluctuations in the nonfood economy. Food security problems are conveniently divided into national (including regional and local) problems and global (including subglobal) problems. The simplest notion of food security is that of stabilizing to a reasonable degree the consumption of foodstuffs by low-income consumers in the face of the uncertainties mentioned above. It is in essence an ex ante concept, dealing with the probability of secure food supplies, with an element of the subjective evaluation of this probability. Analytically, it can be thought of as a public good—inadequately produced by the interplay of private factors because of the difficulty of capturing the rents from its production. It is also a global good—inadequately produced by nations acting alone (for the same reasons) though desired by all. Food security policy can, therefore, be defined as raising the level of food security within a country until the marginal *national* benefits no longer exceed the marginal costs, and then raising it still further until the marginal *global* benefits are equal to the marginal costs.

Food security can be produced in a number of ways, each with a different cost. The distribution of this cost will also be an element in the optimal security policy. The production of food security can use two basic technologies—the removal of the source of the uncertainty and the channeling of the fluctuations into less sensitive variables. Both have a set of costs, and in general, both will need to be used to some extent. Production, stocks, and consumption in the rest of the world determine (for most developing countries) the world market price and the availability of food aid. These elements feed into the domestic system through the import decision. Along with domestic stocks and production, and domestic price policy, this determines consumption levels. The import decision is also dependent upon nonfood export earnings and currency reserves.

Production levels and nonfood markets (coffee prices, oil prices, etc.) are presumably the most unstable elements in the system, though nonfood uses of cereals can also cause instability, as can input supplies into agriculture. The target variables to be stabilized can be thought of as either domestic consumption per se or domestic price levels. These objectives hold in developed as well as developing countries and are unlikely to be relinquished easily. The variables into which instability is most often channeled are stocks (which should, therefore, never be expressed merely as target levels since it is their variability rather than their level which makes them useful) and foreign exchange, which costs less to store. Variable amounts of government finance helps oil the wheels, but cannot in itself change the basic options.

It is convenient to group policies designed to increase the level of security under the headings of stock, production, consumption, trade, and other measures. In each case, one can link the policy measure to the production method and the cost of achieving security. Table 11-1 gives a partial list of solutions to national and global food security problems, i.e., to the underproduction of the food security good. Some solutions are strictly short term—others have a more lasting influence. Omitted are the longer-term "general development" solutions, though clearly over time the vulnerability of a country will be changed much more by structural developments than by specific food security solutions.

Table 11-1   Categorization of Food Security Measures at National and Global Levels

	Local/national	Global
Stock measures	Local stocks Central stocks	Coordinated national stocks Regional stocks Emergency stocks
Production measures	Input availability Water management Disease control Varietal improvement Price policies	Fertilizer supply scheme Research centers Production assistance
Consumption measures	Consumer subsidies Improved distribution State distribution Price policy Waste reduction	Food entitlements Targeted consumption schemes
Trade measures	Bilaterals Futures markets Trade policy Collective buying Foreign exchange reserves	Trade liberalization Concessional sales Commodity agreements Special borrowing facilities

Other measures	Market information
	  and analysis
	Export earnings
	  stability
		Information schemes
		Monetary facilities
		Nonfood trade measures

VI APPROACHES TO FOOD SECURITY

A Stock Measures

The stock options have been fully discussed over the past 10 years. Stocks (or rather their variability) remain crucial to stability though public reserve schemes should not be seen as the only type of food stocks. One additional ton of public stocks of grain can displace up to its own weight in private stocks. Private decisions may underproduce food security, but they do at least produce a large measure of it. It is often unduly costly for the public sector to take over the whole of this burden, in particular, because public stock schemes often do not attempt to recover the rent that the market is prepared to pay. The cost of holding stocks in tropical areas is high, either in terms of losses or of the capital cost of loss-proof facilities. In spite of this there may still be an underinvestment in adequate storage facilities in strategic places in the marketing channels in many developing countries. Government help, together with overseas assistance, could thus be appropriate in providing this investment.

Global stock schemes have been difficult to organize. The central question remains as to whether further initiatives aimed at coordinating national schemes are needed. More price-flexible stocks (or more price flexibility for the same stocks) are still the only feasible way of stabilizing world cereal prices per se. The general move towards nonstock security policies (such as the IMF cereals facility) will certainly put more pressure on world price movements—though that is not a reason to discard such schemes. World stock schemes could even make a "come-back" as a way of containing the cost of nonstock policies. The most constructive approach to global stock policies for food security, as indeed for price stability, may be indirect: create the conditions under which stocks (or stock flexibility) will be adequate, rather than mandating either stock levels or stock triggers. An obvious example of such an indirect approach is to increase the correlation between domestic and world price movements in developed (and CPE) countries—to improve the profitability of private (and public) stockholding.

B Production Measures

Production measures are, in general, examples of the second kind of food security approach mentioned above: stop the instability at its source, rather than channel it ex post into stock variations. The better availability of inputs, and the development of marketing channels which ensure timely and affordable access to such inputs, will often be an effective national policy. Water management, both drainage and irrigation, has also an important role, as does the control of plant disease and the development and adoption of plant varieties which are less subject to yield flucutations. An important aspect of price policies in developing countries is the provision of stable expectations to the farmer as to the market value of his crop.

International policy can contribute to the attempt to stabilize production levels through policies to avoid disruptions in input markets (such as the FAO Fertilizer Supply Scheme), through the transmission of technology aimed at water management and pest control, and more generally through technical assistance at the production level. There have on occasions been fears that new varieties of food crops may have a higher variability in yield than more traditional varieties. Attempts have been made both to breed strains that do not have this characteristic and to preserve a pool of genetic material that will enable plant breeders to retain the advantages of well-adapted local strains. Despite these possibilities, it remains the case that control over production fluctuations is essentially a national concern and one not particularly suited to international action except to the extent that internationally generated technology from a system such as the CGIAR (discussed in Chapter 12) assist national programs to stabilize production.

C Consumption Measures

Measures aimed at consumption stability directly address the issue of food security, though they often fail to recognize that some other part of the system has to absorb the production fluctuations. Many developing countries already have extensive food subsidy systems. These work through fixed consumer prices, state food stores, targeted programs designed to reach vulnerable groups, low prices for staples, or food stamps or other entitlement schemes. These programs require finance, either directly or through the losses of state-marketing agencies; they also test administrative skills and require more knowledge of the level and pattern of local consumption than is usually available.

International assistance can in principle support consumption schemes as well as production policies at the national levels. In addition, international action can attempt to influence developed-country (and CPE) consumption levels so as to make available more grain and other foodstuffs for developing-country consumers. However, these two methods of increasing food security are not often considered—in part, because of a producer bias in both national governments and international organizations. One such policy would be assistance with targeted food subsidy programs. The rationale would be to inject funds into the food system in developing countries at the consumer level, so that families could buy food in the marketplace. This would complement production policies by creating demand for local as well as imported foodstuffs and avoid the dilemma of choosing a domestic price that was at once remunerative to producers and consistent with consumer policy.

Such assistance could be triggered by domestic market conditions, in particular, in developing countries. The country concerned would develop a program that had the aim of protecting vulnerable consumers and that was administratively feasible. The international community would contribute a mixture of cash and food aid to facilitate the operation of the program. This type of scheme is arguably the most direct approach to food security, and could provide a complement to other approaches such as stabilizing world market prices, adding additional borrowing facilities, or setting up more reserves. By contrast, policies which aim directly to influence developed-country consumption patterns in times of food crisis do not seem to have the merit of directness: it might be easier to levy a tax on the developed countries equivalent to the amount necessary to maintain the purchasing power of poor consumers in developing countries.

D Trade Measures

There has been a recognizable trend toward trade policy options as a food security mechanism in the past few years. In part, this reflects the breakdown of the negotiations for a new International Wheat Agreement and the opinion that such global stock management schemes cannot be negotiated. In part, it is a growing recognition that developing countries, perhaps because many are new entrants into temperate-zone food markets, are often their own worst enemies when it comes to buying grain and other products. In terms of national policy, the nonstock options include bilateral trade agreements, the use of the futures markets, the use of trade policies such as variable levies, the use of collective buying agencies, and the provision of foreign exchange reserves specifically for food imports.

The global trade measures mentioned above revolve largely around the level and stability of the price of grain and the cost and availability of foreign exchange. In the international area, there are two basic approaches to the control of grain prices. One is to negotiate an international agreement which mandates particular stabilizing actions and the other is to improve the working of the unregulated market so as to enhance its operation. Both run up against cherished notions of autonomy in the conduct of domestic farm policy in industrial countries. Some of the key actors do not seem to have the ability to build into domestic programs the specific actions required to contribute to grain-price stability, while others feel that to do more unilaterally would impose an inequitable burden on their own economies.

Of the two approaches to this problem, that of improving the functioning of the world market, by reducing the degree of isolation of major sectors of that market, holds out the most promise. At present, it is often confused with the more general issue of trade liberalization. Trade liberalization in agricultural politics is often about export expansion. Developing countries, in general, have been an unintended beneficiary of the resistance of Japan, the EC, and other industrial countries with considerable capacity for farm imports, to see their markets open to aggressive exporting by North America and Australia. The dismal record of trade liberalization talks in agriculture have not hurt those countries that have an interest in low prices. The real issue, if it can be separated, is the response in high-price periods. Thus, "crisis management" may be a more direct way to get at food security issues than trade liberalization per se, though the latter is still relevant to the issue of resource allocation. Mandating particular actions by developed countries at times of high world prices may be much easier than persuading them to open up their markets to more efficient exporters—no matter how desirable on other grounds this latter action would be.

The traditional response to food security needs, and arguably still the best, is the provision of food on concessional terms to needy recipient countries. Food aid has had a bad press in the last decade. It has been (with justification) viewed as a way of getting rid of surplus products in low-price periods, which tends to dry up in times of real need. It is associated with bilateral programs which are guided more by political and strategic than food-policy considerations. And it has been blamed for reducing incentives to local agricultural producers in recipient countries (Maxwell and Singer, 1979). More recently, there have been a number of proposals to revive it in a different form, with the emphasis on the need for assistance by the recipient rather than the availability of grain and/or cash in the exporting country. The problem is that additional funding for food aid may not be available. Hence, the "new" food aid competes with the "old." Moreover, food aid targets, like stock targets, divert attention from the basic need to respond selectively to certain situations.

The frustration over the inability to put together a package which helps to stabilize grain prices was, in part, responsible for the switch of attention to special financial facilities to enable developing countries to borrow in times of high food import cost. The national decision as to whether to use such a facility was mentioned above. From the international viewpoint, the issues are (1) what limits, in terms of countries or commodities, to put on these facilities, and (2) what conditions to put on recipient countries as part of the terms of the loan. On the issue of conditionality, it does seem that the international community might reasonably argue for certain minimum local food security policies as a *quid pro quo* for additional credit lines. This would suggest that particular measures at the individual country level would be implicitly supported by the international community as a contribution to world food security. International policy would be promoting desirable national measures. The distinction between national and international action, already blurred in practice, becomes a nonissue. What starts out as an international measure is in reality a way of achieving change at the national level. Many of the more useful international policies have this same characteristic.

E Nonfood Measures

The last category of measures is a catchall for nonmarket and nonfood policies which nevertheless impinge upon security. These would include actions which improve information and those which, while lying outside the food sector per se, have a bearing on food issues. At the national level, one would conjecture that the ability to collect, interpret, and make use of information on matters relating to food security is largely absent in many developing countries. Data are usually most adequate on commodity flows passing through state marketing channels and crossing national boundaries; data seem generally less adequate on total production (as opposed to marketed surplus), consumption patterns, and price levels. It is not easy to see how the countries themselves can hope to formulate, administer, or evaluate the effectiveness of food security policies in such a data-poor situation. Moreover, the ability of countries to interpret international events must be compromised by lack of knowledge of their own situations. This age-old problem should be recognized as a barrier to effective action.

International action has centered on the distribution of advanced warning of food shortages. This is an essential aspect of food security. Is it possible that this type of activity could be expanded to include other information of relevance to developing countries as they plan their food supplies? One example is the level of stocks. Presently, global stock figures are aggregated from end-of-season national levels—as being the best indication of the carry-over from one "season" to the next. But what is the meaning of a season if harvests are not coincident? The market, and anyone operating in the market, must read to the present (and expected future) stock levels. Obviously, this requires data and/or assumptions on the intra seasonal pattern of consumption. Other examples of such useful information are the level of outstanding commercial contracts, the implicit price expectations of futures traders, and the capacity of transportation channels.

The most significant nonfood measures at the national and international level for assisting food security are in the area of general availability of foreign exchange from export earnings and from lines of credit. (Specific agricultural credit facilities were discussed under agricultural trade measures.) Much remains to be done at the international level to remove trade impediments which hinder export development. Some countries appear to have a limited export capacity and seem unable to earn the foreign exchange to maintain food imports. But all too often such a country is choosing to tax its export (and potential export) sectors and to subsidize food imports through exchange rate policy. So long as the international community is willing to foot the bill, the country may be justified in continuing such policies. But an exchange rate and export policy which make it financially self-reliant (other than the deficit needed to accommodate investment capital inflows) would remove a major case of food insecurity.

VII THE EFFICIENCY-EQUITY TRADE-OFF

A Instruments and Objectives

As in each individual country, the objectives of efficiency and equity at a global level can rarely be attained with a single policy instrument. Some policies move the system towards more efficient use of resources and a more stable environment, while generating a transfer of income that is not necessarily desirable. Other policies concentrate on transferring resources and shielding particular countries from instability, but may have resource costs in terms of a lower total value of world output. The trade-off between these objectives is the essence of international policy making. A balance can be achieved within particular programs or by a mix of different policies. It is useful to conclude by considering some of the aspects of the combination of efficiency and equity involved in international policy.

In terms of the analysis of multiple objectives in Chapter 7, the questions involve the direction in the equity-efficiency objective space in which particular policy instruments operate, the accepted combination of equity and efficiency desired by policy, and the feasible combinations of policies which will move towards that desired position. This simplified view of the central policy issue is illustrated in Figure 11-2. Policy type A improves equity but at the cost of efficiency; instrument B contributes importantly to equity and has some benefit in terms of efficiency, but by itself will not achieve

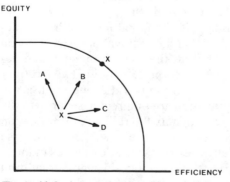

Figure 11-2 International policies and the equity-efficiency trade-off.

the objective pair represented by X; policy C is an efficiency instrument with a positive but "inadequate" element of equity; while policy type D improves efficiency with a negative impact on equity. At least two policy instruments are needed to achieve the dual objective, and they must be combined in appropriate proportions.

Can this issue be related to actual policy questions? It would be misleading to suggest a precise empirical application of the trade-off analysis, if for no reason than that equity is not a simple quantitative variable. But the analysis at least offers an intuitive framework for the consideration of policies. Measures which emphasize equity even at the expense of efficiency (type A, in the figure) might include those that deliberately divert capital to particular forms of agricultural development that would not otherwise be competitive for such funds. IDA and IFAD projects might fall under this heading, unless they are themselves removing a divergence caused by a structural constraint on access to credit. Food aid policies probably also fall under the heading of those that emphasize equity at the expense of efficiency: selling grain at different prices to different countries is not immediately apparent as a device for efficiency in global food distribution. On the other hand, the attempts to remove the foreign exchange constraints which hamper developing-country food imports could be thought of as equity policies which also contribute to efficiency (type B policy). Access to finance for such grain imports may appear to distort the market for such funds, but again may strengthen the role of the trading system to accommodate shortfalls in production.

Policies which stabilize the prices of tropical product exports would seem to assist in improving resource allocation by offsetting the effects of production instability, but they may have equity effects (i.e., type C policy) if the result is the increase in the prices of those products over time and if the production is by low-income farmers or countries. Investment in agricultural research may aid in the search for efficient production opportunities for developing countries and at the same time have beneficial income distributional effects—among countries, if not within those countries. Trade liberalization, however, can have various distributional implications. If developed countries concentrate their efforts on the removal of restrictions on products that they think they can sell abroad, the gains from such international policies may elude the poorer nations (type D policy). Though freer trade may ultimately benefit all participants in the world economy, it is not clear that present modes of trade liberalization are of direct assistance to the poorer countries. And specific measures, such as the rollback of protection of agricultural products in developed countries, could well have adverse consequences for low-income, food-deficit regions. Three examples of international agricultural policy, trade liberalization, food aid, and agricultural research are discussed in the next chapter in the light of this equity-efficiency trade-off and as illustrations of the strengths and weaknesses of cooperation and coordination in the pursuit of common goals. The satisfactory mix of international measures will be as complex as those employed with any particular country.

B   Conclusion

If the notion of common objectives has any relevance, and the idea of common policies among countries to achieve these objectives has any specific manifestation, analysis of these policies and objectives is a priority to ensure intelligent decision making. However, any discussion of international policy must be set in the more general context of a world of largely independent nations. As was indicated in the discussion of efficient pricing from a global perspective, the improvement of domestic policy may be the most important task for intergovernmental discussion, with international policy as such merely supporting and encouraging this improvement. On the other hand, the search for price and market stability, and the generation of transfers which aim to improve income distribution, seem to call for more active international measures. Food security can be attained by either national or collective means, the need for the latter depending largely upon the success of the former.

International policy clearly could be more than the ad hoc resolution of inevitable conflicts of national policies and aspirations that it often appears to be. Provision of global goods, incorporation of externalities into national decisions, and conscious income redistribution are legitimate items for the agenda. Analysis of these problems is a useful exercise, if only to point out the limits of possibilities. But the ultimate direction of such policy lies in the hands of major governments and its effectiveness depends upon their willingness to subject national decisions to collective constraints. For the present, it is probably realistic to think of international policies, as discussed in this section of the book, as of considerable potential benefit particularly for smaller countries but also for the world as a whole. This potential will go unrealized if countries fail to recognize the degree of interdependence among economies and prefer the comfort of domestic politics to the challenge of collective action.

REFERENCES

Konandreas, P., Huddleston, B., and Ramangkura, V. 1978. "Food Security: An Insurance Approach," International Food Policy Research Institute, Research Report No. 4, Washington, D.C.
Maxwell, S. J., and Singer, H. 1979. "Food Aid to Developing Countries: A Survey," *World Development,* 7:225–247.

Chapter 12

International Policies in Action

I INTRODUCTION

As with the other two sections of the book, we conclude this section on international agricultural policies with some more detailed discussion of particular topics, chosen to illustrate the analysis of the previous chapters. The three subjects are (1) trade negotiations in agricultural products, in particular those conducted under the General Agreement on Tariffs and Trade (GATT); (2) food aid for developing countries, including the role of the World Food Programme (WFP) and multilateral food aid; and (3) international research as exemplified by the activities of the Consultative Group on International Agricultural Research (CGIAR) which coordinates a network of research centers in various countries of the world.

Trade negotiations in agriculture are plagued by the high political priorities given by almost all developed-country governments to maintaining the income level of domestic farmers. Yet, the improvement of the trading system for temperate-zone commodities is of fundamental interest both for the developed countries, among whom a large part of the trade takes place, and for developing countries that use such trade as an essential supplement to their own domestic production. Such an improvement can only come through international discussions and agreements. The benefits to all exceed those perceived by each participant individually.

252

Also exemplifying international action is the multilateral organization of food aid. Though linked with the question of trade, in particular in grains, food aid includes issues outside the normal commercial trade problems faced by the major exporters and importers. As a collective policy, multilateral food aid attempts to employ commodities that are in surplus to cover both emergency needs of developing countries and the requirements of low-income consumers through programs of "food for work." The level and the management of such food aid is a key component in the search for equity in international agricultural policy by giving access to food products to those who lack purchasing power.

The CGIAR is premised on the notion that advances in crop breeding and husbandry improvements can be sought with advantage at an international level, with the benefits being distributed to developing countries. As an integral part of the "green revolution" of the past two decades, the international research centers have had technical success. The policy of concentrating international research in certain centers indicates a belief in scale-economies and an acceptance of the notion of a critical mass needed for certain research activities. The justification includes the transferability of the research results to different local environments.

II   TRADE POLICIES AND NEGOTIATIONS IN AGRICULTURE

Governments are ambivalent about trade. Some of their most vocal constituents are against it—or at least that part of trade which appears to constrain their own ability to extract rents. But, in general, governments buy the proposition that obtaining goods from the cheapest source and selling into the most profitable markets makes sense for countries as well as businesses. Agricultural trade is a particularly obvious and profitable form of international division of labor, essential to the reduction of the real cost of providing food. However, the temptation to use trade policy to create rents for domestic interests is as great in agriculture as in other sectors. Those who stand to benefit from such protection can spread fears of undesirable dependence on foreign sources of supply. Export interests can persuade governments to help them find markets abroad for production in excess of domestic requirements. The result is an agricultural trading system riddled with government-imposed distortions but functioning under reluctant acquiescence with the underlying logic of trade.

This section of the chapter outlines the changing nature of agricultural trade relationships, in particular between the western industrial democracies. One part of the problem lies with the development of farm policy in the various countries, but other factors interact with these policy developments, in particular macroeconomic forces and changes in nonfarm trade policy. The role of the GATT in agricultural trade negotiations is discussed, both in terms of past activities and present issues. This section ends with a commentary on the role of agricultural trade relationships in the search for efficiency in international resource allocation.

A   The Agricultural Trade Problem among Industrialized Countries

The underlying problem bedevilling agricultural trade relationships among countries at a similar level of development can be traced to the heavy involvement of governments in their domestic agricultural sectors. Though this problem is not unique to agriculture (the steel and textile industries provide other examples of a similar conflict), it has perhaps reached its peak in this sector. Ironically, the agricultural industry in most industrial countries is one of the most competitive. Despite some growth in corporate enterprises, the sector is characterized by small independent units making individual decisions based on local conditions. The government stands back from the production process but takes charge of market conditions, at least for the major crops and livestock products, thereby hoping to create a favorable environment in which the farmer can make a respectable living.

The size of this market can be manipulated with a variety of instruments including state purchasing, the discouragement of overseas supplies, the subsidization of exports, and the granting of aids for domestic use. The role of the government in such activities immediately conflicts with the interests of other governments similarly engaged. State buying, if not simply for intraseasonal supply smoothing, leads to disposal on other markets. Import restrictions are seen by foreign governments as hindering their own market objectives. Consumer subsidies usually involve trade restrictions if domestic farmers are to gain. In short, unless by chance the favored commodities differ by country, domestic policies geared to enhancing income opportunities for domestic farmers immediately run contrary to those of other countries. In spite of this seeming incompatibility between trade and domestic policy, a large volume of trade in farm products exists among industrial countries.

The situation can be made worse by nonagricultural events, particularly those that influence macroeconomic variables. Imagine a situation where the exporting countries face problems in their overseas markets caused by slow income growth, historically high exchange rates vis-à-vis the importers' currencies, and high support prices in those importing countries. Add to that a weak domestic off-farm employment situation (and perhaps some pressure from forthcoming elections) and one has a recipe for heightened agricultural trade problems as seen by the exporter. This will translate into additional pressures by exporting countries for increased access to import markets. If the importing countries in turn have, as a result of low farm incomes, been trying to expand the markets for their own producers, this additional external pressure will trigger a defensive reaction which could lead to further limitations of market access—as described in Chapter 7. The revival of economic growth, at home and abroad, may remove some of the problems for the exporter; the importer may find it more difficult to reverse the rhetoric and reduce protection for the domestic agricultural industry.

B   The Issues in Agricultural Trade Negotiations

The discussion in Chapter 9 defined the broad trade problem for the world agricultural economy as one of location of production (and distribution of consumption). The specific manifestations of the problem, as seen by the developed countries, may look far removed from concerns of global efficiency. In fact, several different trade issues can be identified which are likely to form the backdrop to any international discussions on agricultural trade over the next few years.

Developed-country exporters face serious conflicts regarding export subsidies and export credits in the markets for such products as wheat and dairy products. These issues involve developing-country exporters, in such products as beef and sugar. The use of aggressive export aids (including liberal export credits) to expand markets and dispose of surpluses is a major distinguishing feature of agricultural trade. In no other major sector is so much production put into world markets at less than domestic production cost. If one country engages in such practices, other exporters have to follow the lead or lose markets. The risk of allowing these practices to continue unabated is that they tend to sour trade relations in other fields. In addition, the instability in agricultural markets gives confused signals to other producers, including developing countries, as discussed in Chapter 10.

A more traditional trade problem of access to markets raises the most political problems at a time of high domestic unemployment and relatively low farm incomes. Negotiations on this issue involve developing-country exporters as well as developed-country suppliers. The products involved include cereals, oilseeds, dairy products, meats, sugar, and fruits and vegetables. Protectionism is now generally recognized as significantly greater in agricultural than in manufactured trade. The degree of protection afforded to developed-country agriculture tends to rise and fall with world market prices—being higher when prices are low. However, the reduction in trade barriers in manufacturing has left agriculture out on a limb. The heart of the matter has always been the unwillingness to force painful adjustments onto the domestic farm sector. There is no reason why this will change, at least until consumer opinion is mobilized to object to the hidden taxes which they pay to protect weak sectors, and until the rest of the economy grows fast enough to offer genuine alternatives to rural people who might be displaced.

Some of the more recent problems of agricultural trade have to do with the emergence of trading arrangements not adequately covered in the GATT. These include the problems arising from state trading, the proliferation in certain markets of bilateral agreements, the negotiation of "orderly marketing" arrangements and other voluntary export restraints, and the use of a variety of other "nontariff" barriers to trade. The first includes the issue of trade relations with central-plan economies, for which trade is an adjunct of policy rather than a result of private decisions within a policy-determined framework. Bilateral trade agreements have emerged in large part as a response to this problem. Trade works best with a free flow of information: predatory behavior by those with a monopoly on certain types of information is disruptive. Such bilaterals seem to offer information on future import intentions on the part of the central-plan countries, and at the same time fit in with the predilection for quantitative advance planning by those countries themselves. As indicative statements of intent, rather than commercial contracts, bilaterals pose less problem for trade structures than is often feared. They do not in themselves destabilize markets, though they may often be tied to domestic policies which have that effect. Voluntary export restraints, on the other hand, serve as an alternative protectionist device to import quotas and pose analogous problems for agricultural trade.

A further set of trade issues have to do with the granting of preferences for developing countries, the emergence of trade groupings and customs unions, and other departures from unconditional most-favored-nation tariff schedules. Export preferences, such as food aid, fall either under this category or under export competition—depending on the generality of the schemes in question. Trade preferences in agriculture have not been a marked feature of trade. Sugar and beef provide the main examples of preferential access to markets though food aid, and could be classed as a bilateral preference system for access to supplies.

Suggestions have been made to expand preferences, such as through the Generalized System of Preferences (GSP), to agricultural products from developing countries. EC policy towards the Mediterranean basin countries includes an element of such preferences. The problem once again, as with nonpreferential access, is basically one of competition with domestic suppliers. The favorable treatment for tropical products already exists—they enter industrial-country markets on much better terms than do temperate-zone products. Preferences for competitive products are essentially income transfer mechanisms. As such, they compete with other uses for aid funds, and the distributional implications may not be ideal, favoring a few developing countries who have agricultural export potential in these products.

The issue of market stability is closely linked with other trade issues, but may be conveniently separated. Commodity markets where instability problems are serious include cereals, oilseeds, sugar, and the tropical products. The problem of price instability is of broad concern to all trading countries. However, its manifestation is different in different situations. Developed-country importers and CPEs have devised effective ways to shelter their economies from the direct effects of international market instability in temperate-zone commodities through border mechanisms which neutralize world price movements or through state trading which has the same effect. Exporting countries either employ stock policies or marketing agencies which can again neutralize variability. The problems that this unwillingness to allow consumption adjustments to dampen price shocks creates for international markets has been discussed at length in Chapter 2.

C The GATT and Agricultural Trade

The institution most concerned with the conditions under which goods are traded internationally is the General Agreement on Tariffs and Trade. Set up after World War II, the GATT provides a set of rules which the "contracting parties" agree to observe, and acts as a forum for the negotiation of changes in trade barriers. The basic propositions embodied in the GATT were a part of the Havana Charter, negotiated and agreed on in 1947, which represented a comprehensive treaty covering a wide range of trade issues including the role of developing countries and the market for primary products. The charter was to set up an International Trade Organization (ITO), intended as a counterpart to the IMF which covered international monetary matters, and the IBRD which dealt with investment assistance to developing countries, both of which had emerged from the Bretton-Woods Conference in 1944. The U.S. Congress, however, was unable to ratify the setting up of the ITO, and the GATT emerged as that part of the Charter that could be implemented without congressional approval. On such shaky ground grew the postwar trade system for industrial countries (Ryan and Tontz, 1978).

The GATT is plainly liberal in intention, emphasizing the mutual benefits of freer trade, outlawing export subsidies and quota restrictions, and encouraging mutual reductions in consolidated tariffs. It preaches nondiscrimination among member states, through the extension to all other contracting parties of the market access granted to the most-favored nation—subject to defined exceptions for customs unions. It allows for conflict resolution and for trade sanctions against violations of the agreement. Though originally oriented largely toward industrialized countries of the Organization for Economic Cooperation and Development (OECD) bloc, its membership has now expanded to include many developing countries and some central-plan economies. Seven rounds of multilateral trade negotiations have been successfully completed since the inception of the GATT, which have led effectively to a low-tariff system for manufactured products in developed-country markets.

Agriculture from the start proved a problem area for the GATT system of more liberal trade. Agricultural policies were largely excluded from the agreement's strictures against quantitative import restrictions on trade (Article XI) as a response to the feeling, particularly in the United States, that domestic policy measures should not be subject to international limitations (McCalla, 1969; Warley, 1976). Although other parts of the agreement do require that governments manage their domestic agricultural policies so as not to harm the legitimate interests of others, and oblige governments to consult on agricultural trade problems, these provisions have rarely been applied. Waivers were frequently sought to exempt particular policy actions from the GATT code. Most notable among these derogations was the waiver granted to the United States in 1954 which effectively removed the major elements of U.S. agricultural policy from international scrutiny. More recently, the tacit acceptance by most countries of the Common Agricultural Policy of the European Community has reinforced the notion of the primacy of domestic policy in international trade discussions.

The relative ineffectiveness of the GATT to deal with illiberal elements in national policy has not prevented the incorporation of agricultural discussions in the various GATT rounds of trade negotiations. Though many of the important agricultural trade issues were not on the agenda, a modest degree of liberalization has been achieved through the reduction of tariffs and the establishment of tariff-free quotas for certain products. A number of tariffs on (at the time) minor traded goods were "bound" in the Dillon Round of trade talks in the early 1960s, when the newly formed European Community negotiated the necessary changes in member state duties on imports from third countries. Many of these commodities, such as soybeans, protein meals and cassava, later became big-ticket items in international trade—to the discomfort of EC policy makers.

In the Kennedy Round, later in the 1960s, a major divergence of views emerged about the nature of agricultural trade policy, with the United States arguing for a return to the GATT notion of a market-oriented trading system, and the European Community generally favoring managed markets through commodity agreements (McCalla and Learn, 1967). The EC proposed a temporary binding of support levels (relative to negotiated reference prices), but this was rejected by the United States as perpetuating protectionist policies in importing countries. Finally, an "agricultural component" of the Kennedy Round was agreed, which included in particular an International Grains Arrangement (IGA) (1967), a modified version of earlier International Wheat Agreements. The stabilization provisions of the IGA had a short life, as surplus grain production pushed prices below the established minimum and countries proved unwilling to hold domestic output in check.

In the most recent round of talks, the Multilateral Trade Negotiations

(MTN)—also known as the Tokyo Round—concluded in 1979, agriculture was again on the agenda. The underlying issue was again the extent to which agricultural trade was to be subject to the same rules as trade in manufactured goods. Should markets be free or managed? Should domestic policies be the subject for negotiations? Should export subsidies be banned or otherwise controlled? Should quantitative trade barriers be phased out? And should importers be able to shield their markets from disruption? Disagreements on these fundamental issues persisted through the MTN and prevented any substantial progress towards liberalization. Some quantitative restrictions were relaxed, two commodity agreements were concluded (for dairy products and for bovine meat), neither endowed with the instruments to stabilize markets, and an attempt was made to incorporate a code of conduct for export subsidies (Houck, 1979).

This last development, the attempt to bring agriculture within a set of rules governing export subsidies and countervailing duties, held out the most promise for liberalization. The code reinforced the obligation of countries to avoid export subsidies which lead to a "more than equitable" share in world markets or which undercut prices. However, the implementation of the code, through the repeated challenge within the GATT of certain practices (such as the EC's export refunds), has not been as successful as might have been wished. Interpretation of such concepts as an equitable market share leads inevitably to conflicts and can render meaningless the spirit of the original agreement.

D Trade Relationships and Global Efficiency

The inherent conflict of interest among countries in agricultural markets is likely to continue as long as governments are directly involved in managing the markets for domestic producers. At one level, these issues can be dealt with in traditional trade policy terms. Liberalization of import regimes, for instance, would doubtless help the efficiency of agricultural policy, as well as the pocketbooks of consumers. But negotiable deals on access to markets have proved difficult to conclude, and in any case, may not get to the heart of the domestic policy clash. Such an approach is only one aspect of the reconciliation of domestic policies with the role of the international trading system to provide for efficient allocation of global resources.

The present trading system is inefficient for reasons discussed in Chapter 10. Similar goods are produced at vastly different prices in different parts of the world. Consumers, likewise, face very different price levels for the same commodity. Price differences would exist even in a freer market as a result of transport costs and quality variations. If optimal subsidy and tax policies were applied to correct for divergences between social and private costs (and valuations), producer and consumer prices could be even more diverse. But the present pattern of prices does not seem to reflect even these social efficiency criteria. The GATT, and other international organizations, have clearly not been able to move world agriculture significantly in the direction of efficiency.

Although trade liberalization has always been considered as a *sine qua non* for efficient resource allocation, experience in agricultural trade suggests that there may be merit in downplaying this particular route to efficiency. Trade talks polarize the participants into mercantilist exporters, seeking to expand their markets, and protectionist importers clinging to their self-sufficiency. The world market becomes the battleground for this conflict. Two countries, both with similar domestic price levels but one an exporter and the other an importer, meet on this battlefield to berate each other's policies. The exporter demands better access, and the importer accuses the exporter of dumping produce on the world markets. Looked at from a global viewpoint, they are both providing output at a cost which may be higher (or lower) than in other parts of the world. This issue is not, in these terms, directly a question of trade policy—though trade instruments may be supporting the domestic prices. *Both* countries should be under the same pressure to reduce (or increase) price levels to improve world resource allocation. Whether trade between them increases or decreases as a result of their contribution to global efficiency is of secondary importance. To concentrate upon trade flows rather than upon domestic policy prices is to risk unproductive or counterproductive conflicts.

The improvement of global resource allocation is itself dependent upon the willingness of governments to override their domestic interests, including those of the agricultural ministries, for the sake of contributing to the development of the agricultural system as a whole. Just as developed-country domestic farm policies represent the major resource transfers in international agriculture, dwarfing the amount of development assistance going abroad, so the same policies dictate trade patterns and influence world prices. The extent to which these policies can be made more responsive, and responsible, in international terms is of interest to all countries.

The solution often put forward is to engage in direct negotiations on national farm policies. Certainly some discussion in international meetings could clarify issues and suggest solutions. But the analysis of externalities and the provision of global goods stressed in this section of the book suggests that mere "encounter sessions" on domestic policies are not enough. The task for international agricultural policy is to devise mechanisms for offsetting the impact of national policies on world markets where such impacts are negative, and of encouraging the development of policies which have positive benefits to other countries.

Though easier said than done, the task is within the scope of international organizations. A clear analysis of the options is presumably a first stage in this process. The formulation of clear goals for the development of the trading system, the provision of food security, the location of production, and the other international objectives discussed in this book would provide a basis for such an analysis. The instrumentalities to achieve such goals need to be defined and the implications for national policy need to be made clear. The scope for international policy may be limited in this area, by particularly strong domestic constraints, but some progress is needed as an adjunct to other aspects of international agricultural development.

III FOOD AID AND INTERNATIONAL EQUITY

Food aid has played, over the past 30 years, a significant role in providing food supplies to low-income countries. It has also been criticized for being arbitrary, erratic, and even deleterious to the recipient. This part of the chapter examines the role of food aid as a deliberate attempt to transfer income or purchasing power to poor countries and poor consumers. First, the development of food aid in recent years is reviewed in order to give an idea of the magnitude of these programs. Then the policies which have shaped the flow of food aid are discussed, in particular, the multilateral policies such as the creation of the World Food Programme and the negotiation of the Food Aid Convention. Although an evaluation of food aid per se is not attempted, since the uses to which aid is put vary so widely, an evaluation of such aid policies as a way of transferring income is offered at the end of the section.

A Developments in Food Aid

The large-scale movement of food on a continuing basis between countries as a gift or on soft terms, whether for humanitarian or political reasons, seems to be a phenomenon of the past 30 years. It is also a phenomenon largely associated in its early years with the United States, and is therefore, explicable more in terms of U.S. economic and political conditions than those of intergovernmental policy (Libbin, 1980). In the aftermath of World War I, the United States had granted food aid to Germany and to Russia to prevent starvation and incidentally relieve excess supplies at home. After World War II, the concept was widened to include aid to Yugoslavia, to foster its independence, and then to countries such as Pakistan, Egypt, South Korea, Israel, Turkey, Poland, Brazil, Indonesia, Portugal, South Vietnam, and Cambodia to support their development plans and secure their allegiance. As noted by both supporters and critics of food aid programs, many of these countries are now large commercial importers of U.S. grains.

United States food aid gained rapid acceptance in large part because it combined several motives including those of foreign policy, surplus disposal, market development, and development support. The same multiobjective nature of food aid led to criticism: it was undoubtedly less than optimal in each of these areas. The internationalization of food aid, starting in the early 1960s, was, in part, a response to this same phenomenon. Bilateral food aid was seen as overtly political, the destination of such aid changed rapidly with the emergence of new tensions, the volume of aid varied with the size of the agricultural surplus, and the need for aid did not always correspond to the willingness of the U.S. Congress to supply concessional imports. As a result, the pattern of food aid changed to include other donors, including some countries that were not grain exporters, and other programs that were less tied to political motives. In 1965, 94 percent of food aid came from the United States; by 1975 the share of the United States in food aid was down to 58 percent, and has stayed at roughly that level since that time. Multilateral aid has risen from zero in the early 1960s to account for about 20 percent in recent years.

The sources of cereal food aid are shown in Table 12-1, along with the totals, for the last decade. Besides the dominance of the United States in such aid, and the change in the U.S. share, the variability in the level of food aid is significant, from the high point in 1971–1972 of 12.5 million tons to a low of 5.8 million tons 2 years later. This fall is generally attributed to the practice of defining food aid contributions, by the donor, in value terms—a budget appropriation which buys less when world prices are high. The level of cereal aid increased again to over 9 million tons in 1976–1977 and has stayed at roughly that level into the early 1980s. Food aid by the European Community collectively and by member states individually is now the second biggest source, displacing Canadian aid from that spot. The growth of EC aid is undoubtedly related to, amongst other things, the accumulation of surplus grain in recent years: unlike that of other donors, EC food aid rose during the period 1972–1973 and 1974–1975 despite the high world prices. The total of cereal food aid can also be compared with the target level agreed at the World Food Conference, in 1974, of 10 million tons: by the standards of such international agreements, the proximity to the target can be viewed as a success.

The distribution of food aid between bilateral and multilateral programs is shown in Table 12-2, which expresses such aid flows in monetary values. The value of food aid (in current dollars) rose from $1.1 billion in 1971 to almost $3 billion in 1981. The share of multilateral aid is 21 percent of the total, at $630 million in 1981. The value of food aid shows less of a decline in the mid-1970s, indicating that transfers themselves continued over the high-price period, though representing less grain. Clearly, the need for grain by developing countries is likely to be greater in periods of high world price, but seen as an income transfer the continuity of appropriations over a period of years is not without importance.

Food aid in total is only a small and declining share in total world cereal trade. But food-deficit developing countries still rely on such aid for about

Table 12-1 Total Cereals Food Aid (Bilateral and Multilateral) by Donors, 1970–1971 to 1981–1982 (thousand tons)

	1970–1971	1971–1972	1972–1973	1973–1974	1974–1975	1975–1976	1976–1977	1977–1978	1978–1979	1979–1980	1980–1981	1981–1982
United States	9,039.1	9,219.6	6,948.3	3,186.4	4,721.5	4,273.0	6,068.1	5,992.1	6,237.6	5,339.4	5,212.4	5,341.3
Canada	1,318.0	1,093.0	808.0	663.6	612.0	1,034.0	1,176.0	884.0	735.0	729.8	600.1	600.0
Australia	230.2	215.1	258.8	222.2	329.6	261.2	230.0	251.8	328.9	314.9	370.3	485.2
France	243.8	142.7	209.6	197.5	113.0	180.5	133.5	188.5	126.3	167.3	143.8	197.8
Italy	184.9	95.0	36.0	10.3	74.4	67.8	57.4	37.9	29.9	99.4	51.7	104.7
W. Germany	108.5	261.7	206.1	226.0	140.0	159.0	165.2	149.6	140.7	141.5	178.6	197.4
EC*	105.4	195.7	320.5	603.4	871.2	297.0	555.2	709.1	611.7	597.0	714.0	846.6
Japan	753.0	731.0	528.0	349.9	182.2	33.1	46.5	135.4	352.0	688.0	913.6	507.1
Total Above	11,982.9	11,953.8	9,315.3	5,459.3	7,043.9	6,305.6	8,431.9	8,348.4	8,562.1	8,077.3	8,184.5	8,280.1
Total	12,357.3	12,512.8	9,964.1	5,818.7	8,399.4	6,847.0	9,022.4	9,215.5	9,499.7	8,887.0	8,941.6	9,140.2

*Community aid over and above national aid given by individual countries.
Source: FAO/UN, Food Aid Bulletin, FAO Commodities and Trade Division, Rome, 1984.

Table 12-2　Multilateral and Bilateral Food Aid, 1971 to 1981 (million U.S. $)

	Multilateral	Bilateral	Total	Multilateral (as % of total)
1971	47	1,085	1,132	4.2
1972	250	1,027	1,277	19.6
1973	185	947	1,132	16.3
1974	242	1,280	1,522	15.9
1975	357	1,773	2,130	16.8
1976	273	1,524	1,797	15.2
1977	369	1,543	1,913	19.3
1978	424	1,624	2,048	20.7
1979	482	1,810	2,292	21.0
1980	649	1,970	2,619	24.8
1981	629	2,306	2,935	21.4

Source: FAO/UN, Food Aid Bulletin, FAO Commodities and Trade Division, Rome, 1984.

one-sixth of their total grain imports—down from 37 percent in 1971. For some countries the dependence upon food aid is much higher than this average. Table 12-3 shows the top 20 food aid recipients in recent years—the list changes somewhat with the political winds—together with their population, income level, and total cereal imports. It is clear from the table that food aid is not in direct proportion either to population or to income level. In part, this reflects the political selectivity of national bilateral programs. In part, it results from the different needs of different countries for food imports. But it also illustrates the country-weights, rather than people-weights, inherent in international policy (as discussed in Chapter 11): small countries tend to do better per head of population than large countries in most international programs.

　　The bulk of food aid is shipped as cereals. Other foodstuffs, such as vegetable oil and dried skim milk, move, also, into food aid channels, and the significance of these other products has increased somewhat in recent years. As with cereals, the availability of noncereal food aid is often tied to the level of surpluses in donor countries. Vegetable oil aid dropped from 396 thousand tons in 1971 to 86 thousand tons in 1975, as commercial markets were in short supply, but rebounded to 285 thousand tons by 1978. Dried skim milk shipments have also varied between 71 thousand tons and 333 thousand tons over this period. Discontinuities in supply make difficult the incorporation of these products into long-term nutritional programs supported by food aid.

　　One important feature of food aid is the terms under which it is granted. All multilateral programs and most non-U.S. bilateral programs are in essence gifts, with no repayment on the part of the recipient. Much of U.S. bilateral food aid is on concessional terms, such as local currency sales and long-term credit sales with low interest rates, though there has been a tendency to spend the local currency and the debt interest on further projects within the country. The share of grants within total food aid is now about two-thirds, up from one-half in 1970. This compares well with financial aid, where the grant component has often been less, and is particularly important in view of present debt burdens.

B Food Aid Programs in International Policy

The increase in multilateral aid programs and the improvement in the stability of food aid have been featured over the past few years. Prior to the early 1970s, there had been three major initiatives in the area of food

Table 12-3 Food Aid, Population, Income, and Cereal Imports, Major Recipient Countries, 1977–1978 to 1981–1982

	Food aid in cereals, avg. 1977–1978 to 1981–1982, (thousand tons)	Mid-1981 population (millions)	GNP per capita (dollars 1981)	Total cereal imports 1981 (thousand tons)	Aid as a % of total imports
Afghanistan	75	16.3	190	97	77.32
Bangladesh	737	90.7	140	1,079	68.30
Egypt	1,865	43.3	650	7,287	25.59
Ethiopia	228	32.0	140	207	110.14
India	435	690.2	260	1,523	28.56
Indonesia	382	149.5	530	1,979	19.30
Mozambique	155	12.5	380	369	42.00
Pakistan	277	84.5	350	305	90.82
Senegal	153	5.9	430	458	33.41
Somalia	330	4.4	280	432	76.39
Sri Lanka	226	15.0	300	667	33.88
Sudan	195	19.2	380	305	63.93
Tanzania	237	19.1	280	265	89.43
Vietnam	142	55.7	280	1,150	12.35
Jordan	84	3.4	1,620	619	13.57
Korea, Republic of	678	38.9	1,700	7,687	8.82
Morocco	120	20.9	860	2,758	4.35
Peru	116	17.0	1,170	1,245	9.32
Portugal	255	9.8	2,520	3,942	6.47
Tunisia	99	6.5	1,420	960	10.31

Source: IBRD, *World Development Report 1983*, The World Bank, Washington, D.C., 1983.

aid. In 1954, at the start of the substantial U.S. bilateral programs under the Agricultural Trade Development and Assistance Act of 1954 (PL480), countries had agreed on a set of Principles of Surplus Disposal, within the FAO Committee on Commodity Problems. This code of conduct specified that donors were to take steps to avoid the disruption of commercial channels—a major concern of other exporters at a time when the United States was seeking relief from surplus production. In 1970, this code was strengthened by the definition of "usual market requirements" by developing-country importers, which were to be respected in formulating food aid policies. The monitoring of food aid flows continues to the present, though the notion that food aid should be additional to commercial sales is difficult to sustain in practice and lessens the potential value of such aid to the recipient.

The second initiative had been the establishment of the World Food Programme (WFP) in 1962, arising out of the FAO Freedom from Hunger Campaign. The WFP was set up as a specialized agency of the UN under the joint direction of the FAO and the United Nations Development Programme (UNDP), the body which handles the bulk of UN technical assistance. The WFP was designed to elicit pledges of cash, commodities, or shipping services from donor countries and to use these for the provision of emergency relief and developmental food aid to developing countries. The Programme received a boost from the change in the U.S. PL480 in 1966, which designated more funds for multilateral programs (Title II); disbursements grew from 57 thousand tons in 1963 to 545 thousand tons by 1970. The growth of the WFP is shown in Table 12-4, together with the amounts controlled by WFP arising from a share in the contributions to the Food Aid Convention (FAC) and the International Emergency Food Reserve (IEFR).

The third initiative on food aid arose from the negotiation of an International Grains Arrangement in 1967, which comprised a Wheat Trade Convention for stabilizing world wheat prices and a FAC which established targets for (bilateral and multilateral) food aid flows. Though the stabilization provisions were stillborn, the FAC was successfully implemented and has been renewed periodically since its inception. The first contributions were agreed at 4.5 million tons per year, and have more recently risen to 7.6 million tons of cereal equivalent food aid. As these commitments are below actual food aid flows, the FAC can be seen as putting a floor under such aid quantities rather than increasing them per se. In addition to this floor, the FAC encouraged nonexporters of cereals among the developed countries to participate in the program—a trend started with the WFP—and attempted to share the burden of food aid more evenly among the exporters themselves. The FAC also embraced the notion of "triangular" food aid, the purchase of developing-country cereal exports by developed-country donors for use as aid to other developing countries.

Food aid, as with other forms of international agricultural policy, came

**Table 12-4   Total Cereals Food Aid
Shipments by WFP, 1963 to 1982**
(thousand tons)

	Regular WFP	Additional contributions		Total
		FAC	IEFR	
1963	57.1			57.1
1964	62.5			62.5
1965	118.1			118.1
1966	236.9			236.9
1967	257.8			257.8
1968	204.4			204.4
1969	279.8	166.0		445.8
1970	545.1	171.0		716.1
1971	449.9	181.0		630.9
1972	313.1	137.4		450.6
1973	302.4	97.3		399.7
1974	334.5	169.5		504.1
1975	562.5	188.5		751.0
1976	340.6	163.2	19.0	522.8
1977	672.4	148.9	97.5	918.8
1978	594.7	149.4	196.8	940.9
1979	527.5	202.4	207.1	937.0
1980	534.0	187.0	269.1	990.2
1981	359.2	221.4	370.4	951.0
1982	527.4	304.9	451.7	1,284.1

Source: FAO/UN, *Food Aid Bulletin*, FAO Commodities and Trade Division, Rome, 1984.

under scrutiny at the 1974 World Food Conference, a high-level meeting on agriculture which attempted to set the agenda for international organizations. The conference proposed a number of modifications to food aid programs, including a 10 million ton target for annual aid flows, an increase in multilateral aid, better terms (i.e., more grants) for bilateral aid, more continuity to allow for forward planning of aid flows, a greater degree of coordination of food aid, more triangular aid, and the establishment of an International Emergency Food Reserve (IEFR) of one-half million tons. Some progress can be detected on most of these fronts. Food aid, as mentioned previously, has approached, if not reached, the volume target; the share of food aid passing through the WFP, the main multilateral channel, has increased somewhat; the grant component has risen; the FAC (which predated the conference) has satisfied at least some of the need for forward planning; and the IEFR has approached its target level albeit with some reluctance on the part of major governments. Coordination of food aid is now handled through the Committee on Food Aid Policies and Problems (CFA), a new body set up by the World Food Conference.

C An Evaluation of Food Aid Policies

Food aid has had a significant impact on the ability of low-income countries to obtain food from abroad. On the other hand, it is not always clear that such aid has been an effective way of either promoting development or stimulating consumption. Critics have stressed the inferiority of food aid relative to direct cash transfers or to development assistance aimed at productive investment; the possible disincentives to local producers if domestic prices are depressed; the arbitrariness of much of the bilateral aid flows when viewed in terms of need; and the implicit support that aid gives to urban-biased policies of low food prices. Supporters have countered by arguing that food aid has often been used effectively by recipient governments to boost food supplies, save foreign exchange, underpin reserve policies, and run nutritional programs. Moreover, if the food aid is consistent with the needs of donors to dispose of surpluses then such aid will not necessarily compete with financial aid within the donor countries. Presumably, the reconciliation of these views is that food aid can either be positive or negative in its effect on recipients depending upon the circumstances of its use.

More relevant to the present discussion is whether food aid is a good example of international policies to effect transfer among countries. At one level, the experience seems to have been favorable. A conscious attempt in recent years to establish a set of policies for food aid has led to improvements in the operation of these programs. The WFP has continued to provide a mix of emergency relief, supported by various nongovernmental organizations, and development assistance through food-for-work schemes emphasizing public investment. Relative to many of the initiatives which emerged from the World Food Conference, the food aid policies have been quite successful.

In spite of these successes, food aid also demonstrates the difficulties of international transfer programs. The distribution of food aid among countries does not conform to any clear criterion of absolute need by poor families. National programs in donor countries have begun to introduce income-level criteria for disbursement of aid, but the donor has little control over the distribution of the benefits within the recipient country. WFP food aid is more clearly targeted, though at a narrow range of development projects which may not always represent the best use of international assistance. The commodity composition of aid seems still to be unrelated to the specific needs of recipients. Whether even such a program as food aid can ever be adapted to transfer income effectively is a moot point, but in a world where few programs work as envisaged, the record does not seem all that bad.

IV TECHNOLOGY TRANSFER AND THE CGIAR

A Introduction

The preceding two examples of international policy at work have involved formal international institutions—the General Agreement on Tariffs and Trade and the food aid agencies of the UN—both organized to accomplish international tasks which could not be done by individual nation-states. In this section, the discussion focuses on an informal mechanism established in an ad hoc fashion to support a process of technology generation and transfer to developing countries, financed by developed-country donors. The Consultative Group on International Agricultural Research (CGIAR) was established in 1971 to provide a vehicle by which independent donors could fund a growing family of independently organized International Agricultural Research Centers (IARCs).

The discussion of the CGIAR proceeds as follows. First, there is a brief discussion of conceptual issues in international transfers of technology. Next, a description of the origins and current status of the CGIAR is presented. This is followed by a discussion of the impacts of the CGIAR. The section concludes with an evaluation of this particular type of international policy.

B Conceptual Issues in Technology Transfer

Both developing and developed countries have a national and an international interest in improving the capacity of developing countries to increase indigenous food production capacity. The motivation for developing countries revolves around their own income growth and food security. For the developed countries, the objective of assisting LDCs to increase food production may be motivated by concerns about mass starvation and political instability and by notions of global equity. Developed countries have an objective of assisting low-income food deficit developing countries to improve their food production by improving the technology of production.

Given this goal, there are several alternatives open to developed countries in their quest to increase production efficiency through technology transfer. These include the direct transfer of developed-country technology to developing countries via technical assistance, either bilaterally or multilaterally; financial and technical transfer to developing-country national research programs, again bilaterally or multilaterally; support of the development of human capital through training programs and other educational activities; and encouragement of developed-country scientists to apply their expertise to tropical and subtropical agricultural problems. But all these approaches are essentially between a donor agency and a single developing country. Thus success in one country is less likely to reach others. Further, such approaches imply that every country must develop a research program immediately capable of at least adopting available technology to local conditions. Bilateral approaches also raise the specter of undue political influence.

An alternative is to argue that technology appropriate for improving production capacity in poor countries is a public good of the sort described in Chapter 9. Public investment in applied agricultural research and technology development in developed countries has been justified as a public good. The absence of public sector involvement, it is argued, results in social underproduction of research and technology by the private sector. Though the proportion of agricultural research expenditures made by the private sector is rising in developed countries, such as the United States, there still remains a large public sector investment. In a broader sense it can be argued that certain kinds of applied research have applications that transcend national boundaries which give them the character of an international public good. This would suggest that nations individually will underproduce this global good. These research activities include germ plasm collection, evaluation, manipulation and rapid testing against diverse environments; development of systems of pest management and disease control; and developing international research and training networks. Thus, on a conceptual basis alone there is a case to be made for international policy on technology development and transfer. If developing-country budget constraints, both in terms of fiscal and human resources, are added, it is highly likely that developing countries will significantly underinvest in research. Evidence now suggests that investment in agricultural research has extremely high payoffs (Evenson, 1981). Thus financial aid for such activities may have a high rate of return, at least in the longer run.

C The Origins and Current Status of the CGIAR

The CGIAR is an informal association of some 39 national governments, international and regional organizations, and private foundations who provide support to 13 independent International Agricultural Research Centers (IARCs) (CGIAR, 1980). The current constellation of centers is described in Table 12-5. However, some of the centers themselves predate the CGIAR. The Rockefeller Foundation established a joint research effort with the Mexican government on wheat in 1941. From this beginning grew the International Wheat and Maize Research Institute (CIMMYT) which was formally constituted in 1966. Rockefeller also established programs on tropical crops (Colombia) and on potatoes (Mexico-Peru) in the years preceding 1960. These programs eventually were incorporated as CIAT (1967) and CIP (1971). In 1959, the Rockefeller and Ford Foundations began a formal collaboration to establish international research institutes with sharply focused research mandates to increase yields of food crops of primary importance to developing countries. The institutes were to devote exclusive attention to applied research and technology development. They were to work through and strengthen national research programs, and the ultimate test was that their research should "increase yields in farmers' fields." Associated with the research programs were to be applied training programs and the development of international networks for germ plasm collection and maintenance and exchange of materials, research results, and information.

The first center formally established in 1961 was the International Rice Research Institute (IRRI) with headquarters in Los Banos in the Philippines. It had a single-commodity focus and a worldwide or global mandate to work on rice. IRRI focused at the outset on irrigated rice and, building on previous research done in national programs particularly in Japan, China and the United States, produced a dwarf, high-yielding, fertilizer-responsive rice (IR-8) which was quickly and widely adopted. The second center to be formally established in 1966 was the Centro Internacional de Mejoramiento de Maíz y Trigo (CIMMYT) headquartered in Mexico. Drawing on earlier Rockefeller Foundation work and on previous work in the United States, Canada and Europe, CIMMYT released dwarf wheats to other countries which had already been successfully introduced into Mexico. These two developments of dwarf varieties led to the term the "Green Revolution" which was used to describe the rapid adoption of the new wheat and rice varieties.

The two foundations next established two regional-ecological zone and systems-oriented centers—CIAT in 1967 and IITA in 1968. CIAT was originally charged to work on tropical lowland farming systems with emphasis on Latin America and IITA was charged to work on tropical agriculture in the humid and subhumid tropics of Africa. Finally, the foundations intended to formalize the potato program which became CIP in 1971.

By 1969, it had become clear that the needs and demands for additional international research activities were growing and that the foundations no longer wished to bear the financial burdens of the existing centers, let alone the building of future centers.

Four meetings were held during 1969 and 1970 where the leaders of the major national and international funding agencies reviewed the opportunities for cooperation in increasing food production in developing countries. In October 1969, the president of the World Bank proposed to the United Nations Development Programme and the Food and Agriculture Organization that the three institutions jointly organize long-term support for an expanded international agricultural research system.

The result was the establishment in 1971 of the CGIAR, under the joint sponsorship of the World Bank, the UNDP, and the FAO. The bank provides the CGIAR with its chairperson and secretariat, while the FAO provides a separate secretariat for the group's Technical Advisory Committee (TAC). The TAC is made up of 13 agricultural and social scientists,

Table 12-5   International Centers Supported by CGIAR

		Center	Location of headquarters
1	CIAT	Centro Internacional de Agricultura Tropical	Cali, Colombia
2	CIMMYT	Centro Internacional de Mejoramiento de Maiz y Trigo	Los Banos, Mexico
3	CIP	Centro Internacional de la Papa	Lima, Peru
4	IBPGR	International Board for Plant Genetic Resources	Rome (FAO)
5	ICARDA	International Center for Agricultural Research in the Dry Areas	Aleppo, Syria
6	ICRISAT	International Crops Research Institute for the Semi-Arid Tropics	Hyderabad, India
7	IFPRI	International Food Policy Research Institute	Washington, D.C., U.S.A.
8	IITA	International Institute of Tropical Agriculture	Ibadan, Nigeria
9	ILCA	International Livestock Center for Africa	Addis Ababa, Ethiopia
10	ILRAD	International Laboratory for Research on Animal Diseases	Nairobi, Kenya
11	IRRI	International Rice Research Institute	Los Banos, Philippines
12	ISNAR	International Service for National Agricultural Research	The Hague, Netherlands
13	WARDA	West Africa Rice Development Association	Monrovia, Liberia

Source: Herdt, R. W., 1984, The Role of International Centers in the Emerging Agriculture Research System, Paper presented at the University of Minnesota Agricultural Research Policy Seminar, April 1984.

Date of establishment	Research mandate and geographic emphasis	Budget 1983 ($US million)
1967	Dry beans—World Cassava—World Tropical pastures—Latin America Rice—Latin America	22.5
1966	Wheats—World Maize—World Triticale—World Barley—World	19.4
1971	Potatoes—World	11.2
1974	Plant genetic resources—World	4.1
1976	Barley Lentils Broad beans } Dry areas of No. Africa and West Asia Wheat, Chick pea Forage crops Farming systems	20.0
1972	Sorghum, millet, pigeonpea, chick pea, ground nut—World Farming systems—Semi-arid tropics	23.2
1975 (1979-CG)	Policy research—Production } World Nutrition, trends, trade	3.8
1968	Rice, maize, cassava sweet potato, cocoyam, soybeans—Africa Yam, cowpea—World Farming systems—Humid and subhumid tropics of Arica	22.3
1974	Livestock production systems— Tropical Africa	11.8
1973	African livestock diseases— theileriosis and trypanosomiasis	9.5
1960	Rice—World Rice cropping systems—Asia	22.5
1980	Strengthening national research programs—World	3.5
1971 (1974-CG)	Rice—West Africa	2.8

nominated by the three co-sponsors and approved by the CGIAR members, and drawn approximately equally from the developed and the developing countries. The TAC regularly reviews the scientific and technical aspects of all center programs and advises the Consultative Group on emergent needs, priorities, and opportunities for research.

Like the international centers, the Consultative Group is an unconventional institution. It operates without any legal charter, written rules, protocols, or bylaws, entirely by the common consent, shared interest, and goodwill of its members. Meetings, held once or twice yearly, to consider program and budget proposals, policy issues, and other matters from the centers, are informal and collegial. Decisions are reached by consensus; donations are on a voluntary, bilateral basis between individual members and centers. The CGIAR, while it is active in coordinating and stimulating financial support for the system, does not itself actually grant funds.

Subsequent to the formation of the CGIAR, nine new centers (activities) have been added (see Table 12-5). The first budget of the CGIAR in 1972 was $(U.S.)20 million. Estimated expenditures in 1984 were $(U.S.)177 million and requests for 1985 approached $190 million. The centers employ 750 Ph.D. level senior scientists and more than 6,000 support personnel (Herdt, 1984). In sum, the system has grown explosively from 4 to 13 centers and 20 to 190 million dollars (U.S.) in 13 years. The number of donors has increased from the original 15 to nearly 40 in the same period. However, the majority of the support for the CGIAR has from the beginning, come from a few major donors—United States (25 percent), World Bank (10 to 15 percent), Canada, Japan, West Germany, the United Kingdom, and the Inter-American Development Bank (IDB). While the founding foundations accounted for nearly half of the budget in 1972, they accounted for less than 1 percent of the funding in 1983.

D   International Impacts and Consequences of CGIAR Activities

Some of the research supported by the CGIAR has had very high payoffs for developing countries. Indian wheat supplies tripled between 1961 and 1980, largely as a result of yield increases associated with the new varieties. Wheat production increased from 11.4 million metric tons in 1967 to 26.4 million metric tons in 1972 and reached 34.7 million metric tons in 1979. India is virtually self-sufficient in food grains, a far cry from 1965–1966 when emergency imports of 10 million tons were necessary to provide minimum food supplies. There has also been a widespread adoption of new rice varieties in Colombia, Philippines, and Bangladesh, rapid increases in wheat production in Mexico and Pakistan, and in maize production in Mexico and Kenya (Plucknett and Smith, 1982). It has been estimated that the value of increased supplies of rice generated by high-yielding varieties based on IRRI germ plasm exceeds \$2.5 billion (Plucknett and Smith, 1982, p. 219).

All these examples, of course, relate to three major commodities—wheat, rice, and maize—which had received considerable research attention from developed countries prior to the establishment of CIMMYT and IRRI. However, the adoption of these commodities to tropical conditions is a major contribution. Other work being undertaken by the centers is necessarily longer term. For example, important subsistence crops, such as cassava, various beans and lentils, millet, sorghum, sweet potatoes and yams, had had little previous attention from research organizations in developed or developing countries. Therefore, a backlog of basic information on genetic structure, physiological characteristics, and nutritional needs was unavailable. Good progress seems to be being made on many of these crops but startling breakthroughs such as occurred in wheat and rice have not yet emerged.

Further, much subsistence agriculture, particularly in Sub-Saharan Africa, is conducted by small farmers using complex farming systems often involving both plant and animal production. Basic understandings of traditional farming systems are required before technical improvements consistent with the farming systems are possible. These kinds of activities are necessarily both longer term and more location-specific. Thus, the payoff from most of the newer ecological zone systems centers is yet to emerge. However, evaluations of research approaches and research quality undertaken by TAC have been positive.

In addition to explicit research and technology developments, which have direct application in production systems, the centers have fostered an international network of scientists in national programs and the IARCs. This network provides for training, exchanges of material, research results and information. Thus, the contribution of the CGIAR to strengthening national programs is considerable, though difficult to quantify. Clearly, the CGIAR is viewed by developing countries as an apolitical organization of high quality and great usefulness. This result comes through very clearly in the reports of developing-country user seminars appended to *The Second Review of the CGIAR* (1981).

E   Evaluation of the CGIAR as an Example of International Policy

The CGIAR is an atypical international organization. It has no constitution, legal status, or well-defined mechanism for collective decision making. It does, however, provide a desirable global public good and appears to have been successful in a number of commodities and has considerable potential for further advances. How then should the CGIAR be evaluated as an example of international agricultural policy?

First, in terms of the global goals outlined in Chapter 9, it potentially can make a contribution to growth, stability, and equity. The development of improved production technology allows developing countries to utilize limited land resources more efficiently. Thus, it improves the efficiency of global resource use, provided that developing countries pursue the necessary complementary policies to encourage farmer innovation. Given the dual objectives of most CGIAR centers of improving yield stability as well as increasing yields, successful adoption of CGIAR technology should contribute to stability of domestic food supplies and, therefore, reduce instability in either net import demands or net export supplies which should in turn contribute to stability in world markets. Finally, it presumably contributes to increased equity in three ways. First, if the technology is scale neutral (i.e., is equally useable by small as well as large farmers), it should improve the income position of farmers. Second, it has the potential of reducing food costs to consumers, which will confer relatively greater benefits to low-income consumers who spend higher proportions of their income on food. Third, since the costs of the research are borne in the main by developed countries, the CGIAR is an indirect means of income transfer to developing countries. Thus, potentially, at least, the CGIAR can make a significant contribution to lessening income disparities within and between countries.

The positive characteristics of this international policy approach appear to be the following:

1 There are clear-cut and sharply defined specific objectives. The organization functions with clear notions of exploiting the comparative advantage of an international research network.

2 The informal association of independent actors and the resulting lack of a large international bureaucracy seem to contribute to a considerably lower use of international resources to support administrative and bureaucratic pursuits.

3 The informal and collegial nature of the group characterized by the lack of a legal structure or clearly defined voting rights has kept larger geopolitcal issues from intruding heavily into the affairs of the CGIAR. This basically apolitical character distinguishes the CGIAR clearly from bilateral aid.

4 The independence of donors and centers coupled with informality lends to the CGIAR degrees of flexibility not common in more entrenched international organizations.

5 It is still small in relative terms and therefore is not as vulnerable to changes in donor policy as a more expensive agency might be.

The limitations of the CGIAR are, in a number of cases, the other side of some of the advantages just cited.

1   The CGIAR lacks a mechanism of formal decision making. Processes of discussion and consensus become increasingly difficult as numbers of donors and centers increase. This is particularly acute if the sum of donor contributions, independently allocated to individual centers, does not meet some or all of the center's budgetary needs. Currently, TAC is involved in this process but its capacity to make comprehensive programmatic decisions is limited by its transitory and part-time nature.

2   The independence of donors and centers could lend instability to the system. Donors individually make annual decisions about contributions to individual centers. Thus, potentially the level of support to particular centers could be highly unstable from year to year. While there now exists a small stabilization mechanism, the potential for funding instability could be seriously debilitating to long-term research enterprises. Center independence means that particular centers can pursue programmatic changes which may not be consistent with overall group priorities. Further, they may take on competitive research projects or become competitive in relations with national programs. The number of conflicts between centers over commodity and geographic mandates has risen significantly in recent years.

3   Despite the fact that the objectives of the CGIAR are to assist developing countries, there are limited opportunities for users to participate in decision making. Representatives of developing countries are nominally members of the group (selected in various FAO regions). However, the absence of voting procedures and collective decision making makes their role very limited.

4   The ad hoc nature of the group makes long-term planning for coherent programs difficult.

5   The group has been criticized in the past on the basis that the Green Revolution technology was more useable by larger farmers and more favored regions thus worsening between farmer and within country income distribution. More recent evidence has blunted, but not eliminated this charge.

6   Finally, the greatest potential constraint to large global impacts for the CGIAR is the fact that it depends, for its ultimate success, on complementary actions by developing countries. This is so because successful use of CGIAR technology requires the existence of effective national research and extension programs to get the technology to farmers *and* the pursuit by national governments of appropriate price, trade, input, macroeconomic, and investment policies. Thus, unlike direct technical assistance projects, usually carried out by national and multilateral aid agencies, the CGIAR must participate in institution building, which, if unsuccessful, dooms the research activities of the centers to ineffectiveness.

F   Concluding Comments

The CGIAR is a relatively young, small and narrowly focused experiment in international policy. To date it seems to be quite successful at least in comparison to other international efforts to develop and transfer technology. It has maintained a delicate balance between donor and center independence and the needs for allocative decision making and program coordination. This balance is, however, fragile and will be made more so by either further expansion or severe budget constraints. Despite these potential difficulties, it represents an ad hoc, nonbureaucratic, apolitical and flexible approach to international policy where shared goals by developed and developing countries seem to be coming to fruition.

REFERENCES

CGIAR. 1980. *Consultative Group on International Agricultural Research,* CGIAR Secretariat, World Bank, Washington, D.C.

———. 1981. *The Second Review of the CGIAR,* Consultative Group on International Agricultural Research, Executive Secretariat, World Bank, Washington, D.C., November 1981.

Evenson, R. E. 1981. "Benefits and Obstacles to Appropriate Agricultural Technology," *Annals of the American Academy of Political and Social Science,* **458**:54–64.

FAO/UN. 1984. *Food Aid Bulletin,* FAO Commodities and Trade Division, Rome.

Herdt, R. W. 1984. "The Role of International Centers in Emerging Global Agricultural Research System," paper presented at the University of Minnesota, Agricultural Research Policy Seminar, April 1984.

Houck, J. P. 1979. "Agricultural Trade: Protectionism, Policy, and the Tokyo/Geneva Negotiating Round," *Amer. J. Agr. Econ.,* **61**:860–873.

IBRD. 1983. *World Development Report 1983,* The World Bank, Washington, D.C.

Libbin, S. 1980. "Twenty-Five Year Review of Public Law 480 and other U.S. Food Aid Programs, Fiscal Years 1955-1979," IED/ESS/USDA, Washington, D.C., ESS Staff Report.

McCalla, A. 1969. "Protectionism in International Agricultural Trade, 1850–1968," *Agricultural History,* **43**:329–343.

———, and Learn, E. W. 1967. "Nonequilibrium Fixed-Price Schemes in Agricultural Trade," *Agr. Econ. Res.,* **19**:111–116.

Plucknett, D. L., and Smith, N.S.H. 1982. "Agricultural Research and Third World Food Production," *Science,* **217**:215–220.

Ryan, M. E., and Tontz, R. L. 1978. "A Historical Review of World Trade Polcies and Institutions," in *Speaking of Trade: Its Effect on Agriculture,* Agricultural Extension Service, University of Minnesota, Special Report No. 72, pp. 5–19.

Warley, T. K. 1976. "Western Trade in Agricultural Products," in A. Schonfield, (ed.), *International Economic Relations in the Western World 1959–1971,* Oxford University Press, London.

Index